Esquire

The Meaning

WISDOM, HUMOR, AND DAMN GOOD ADVICE
FROM 64 EXTRAORDINARY LIVES

# of Life

Esquire

The Meaning

WISDOM, HUMOR, AND DAMN GOOD ADVICE
FROM 64 EXTRAORDINARY LIVES

# of Life

Edited by Ryan D'Agostino
Introduction by David Granger

HEARST BOOKS
A division of Sterling Publishing Co., Inc.

New York / London
www.sterlingpublishing.com

{ CONTENTS }

A dozen years ago,

a writer (Mike Sager) sat down with an actor (Rod Steiger), and a routine magazine interview turned into something else, something timeless. The actor shared what he had learned over a remarkable lifetime, and his wisdom, boiled down to its essence, ran in *Esquire* under the headline "What I've Learned." That headline has run in every issue since—634 people have sat down with us since Steiger—and "What I've Learned" has become the most enduringly popular element of *Esquire* magazine.

These distillations of wisdom gathered over a lifetime are nearly perfect distillations of what it is that *Esquire* aspires to be: They are useful, as in: "Okra is the secret to good gumbo." —Michael DeBakey, pioneering heart surgeon. They are profound: "Vision is something that you have in your mind." —Ray Charles. They are encouraging—most of these people have been through crises that make you wonder how they're still here: "I can't always control my body the way I want to, and I can't control when I feel good or when I don't. I can control how clear my mind is." —Michael J. Fox. They are almost always funny: "He who laughs last didn't get the joke in the first place." —Rodney Dangerfield. And they always reinforce the notion that life is a fascinating, irresistible gift that needs to be, first, enjoyed and then savored.

After a few years of publishing a "What I've Learned" in every monthly issue of Esquire, we began devoting our January issue to a broader quest for the knowledge that resides in people who have lived compelling lives. After September 11, 2001, it became clear that people all over our country were hungry for perspective and advice on life in a world that seemed suddenly hostile and confusing. In 2002, we began turning over our entire January issue to "What I've Learned's." We called the issue The Meaning of Life. Every year, it has become an indispensable tool for navigating the new world we find ourselves inhabiting.

For something so brief, the work involved in each of these interviews is intense. Our writers first immerse themselves in the life of their subject—read his or her books, watch his or her movies, review the history of their tenure as a head of state or leader of industry. Any scrap of detail can launch the conversation in some unexpected direction, and that's when you get the best stuff. The interview itself is surprisingly creative, sneakily subversive. A frontal assault is almost never the way to tease out wisdom that people don't even know they possess. Neil Young described the "What I've Learned" process as "spiritual," and that is an apt descriptor.

We engage these people on topics they have never discussed before—especially with a stranger—and try to keep them slightly off balance by mixing inquiries into the profundities of love, work, and life with the banalities of daily living. I think my favorite question of all time was one that Cal Fussman asked John Kenneth Galbraith. After discussing marriage, friendship, arrogance, John F. Kennedy, Winston Churchill, religion, and many other topics, Cal tossed in this question: "How much is too much to pay for a pair of socks?" To which Dr. Galbraith answered: "A good rule of conversation is never answer a foolish question."

What we are offering here, with this new edition of *The Meaning of Life*, is a distillation of that distillation. We've chosen our 64 favorite "What I've Learned's" and offer them to you (and, once more, to ourselves) as both entertainment and illumination. As we confront the challenges and the opportunities the 21st century lays before us, the perspective afforded by the wisdom in these pages can illuminate where we've been and shine a light on the path ahead.

David Granger, Editor in Chief

April 1, 2009

Muhammad Ali { CHAMPION—BERRIEN SPRINGS, MICHIGAN }

GOD WILL NOT place a burden on a man's shoulders knowing that he cannot carry it.

PARKINSON'S IS MY toughest fight. No, it doesn't hurt. It's hard to explain. I'm being tested to see if I'll keep praying, to see if I'll keep my faith. All great people are tested by God.

THE SUN is always shining someplace.

I CAME BACK TO LOUISVILLE after the Olympics with my shiny gold medal. Went into a luncheonette where black folks couldn't eat. Thought I'd put them on the spot. I sat down and asked for a meal. The Olympic champion wearing his gold medal. They said, "We don't serve niggers here." I said, "That's OK, I don't eat 'em." But they put me out in the street. So I went down to the river, the Ohio River, and threw my gold medal in it.

SINCE that day, things in America have changed 100 percent.

WHEN YOU'RE RIGHT, nobody remembers. When you're wrong, nobody forgets.

SILENCE is golden when you can't think of a good answer.

"WE HAVE ONE LIFE / It soon will be past / What we do for God / Is all that will last."

GOODNESS? My mother.

WHEN YOUR MOTHER dies, it really hurts. But with time, you get used to it. That's nature's way.

MY definition of evil is unfriendliness.

THE BEST WAY to make your dreams come true is to wake up.

COMEDY is a funny way of being serious. My way of joking is to tell the truth. That's the funniest joke in the world.

IT'S POSSIBLE FOR the heavyweight champion of the world to be with one woman.

LOVE IS A NET that catches hearts like fish.

RUBBLE is trouble.

THE MORE WE HELP others, the more we help ourselves.

I LIKE Joe.

WATCHING GEORGE come back to win the title got me all excited. Made me want to come back. But then the next morning came, and it was time to start running. I lay back in bed and said, "That's OK, I'm still the Greatest."

IF I could meet anybody? The prophet Muhammad.

WHAT YOU ARE thinking about, you are becoming.

I'M MOST proud of my family.

ENJOY YOUR CHILDREN, even when they don't act the way you want them to.

LIGHTING THAT TORCH in Atlanta didn't make me nervous. Standing up to the government—*that* made me nervous.

WISDOM is knowing when you can't be wise.

THE ONE THING I don't understand is war.

BROODING over blunders is the biggest blunder.

I'D LIKE TO LIVE to a hundred.

I JUST WISH people would love everybody else the way that they love me. It would be a better world.

Interviewed by Cal Fussman | Photograph by Neil Leifer

BORN LOUISVILLE, KENTUCKY—01.17.42

> HEAVYWEIGHT PRIZEFIGHTER, ANTIWAR PROTESTER, AND INTERNATIONAL AMBASSADOR OF GOODWILL. ALI'S EXTROVERTED, COLORFUL STYLE, BOTH IN AND OUT OF THE RING, HERALDED A NEW TYPE OF MEDIA-CONSCIOUS CELEBRITY ATHLETE.

> AT THE HEIGHT OF HIS FAME, HE WAS DESCRIBED AS "THE MOST RECOGNIZABLE HUMAN BEING ON EARTH."

Robert Altman { DIRECTOR—NEW YORK CITY }

> **I NEVER KNEW** what I wanted, except that it was something I hadn't seen before.

WORDS don't tell you what people are thinking. Rarely do we use words to really tell. We use words to sell people or to convince people or to make them admire us. It's all disguise. It's all hidden—a secret language.

WISDOM AND LOVE have nothing to do with each other. Wisdom is staying alive, survival. You're wise if you don't stick your finger in the light plug. Love—you'll stick your finger in anything.

I LOVE FISHING. You put that line in the water, and you don't know what's on the other end. Your imagination is under there.

WHETHER IT'S A BAD NOVEL being translated to the screen or a good novel being butchered or how to keep the restroom clean in a filling station, it's all the same thing: you gotta entertain people.

THE WORST TRAP you can fall in is to start imitating yourself.

THE ONLY place there's a lotta room is at the top, because nobody really wants to be there.

YOU CAN'T KNOW it all. You don't have the time.

I DON'T KNOW WHAT self-doubt is. But when I don't know what I'm doing, it shows in the work.

THERE'S been a few times when I just realized, "God, I don't think there's any real way out of this other than just to finish and see if we can slip it by."

I LOVED RADIO DRAMA. Each audience member had his own picture. When you heard the creaking door, everybody had his own door.

I WAS GOING to Santa Fe one time, and somebody said, "It's great down there, you know—it's a real artists' colony." I remember saying, "I didn't know they colonized." Of course, they don't. That's the one thing artists *don't* do.

WHEN PEOPLE ask for advice, what they're really asking for is help.

I'LL GIVE YOU the same advice I give my children: never take advice from anybody.

I'M NOT VERY SMART about money. I don't know much about it. I certainly don't collect it or save it or store it. And I might regret it one day. But I don't think so. I've always felt that I could survive some way.

I DIDN'T MIND military school; I kind of liked it. I thought it was a nice little adventure.

I WAS A PILOT. I flew a B-24 in the South Pacific. I did forty-six missions, something like that. We got shot at a lot. It was pretty scary, but you're so young; it's a different thing. I was nineteen, twenty. It was all about girls.

MR. AND MRS. SMITH get married, they have problems, they get back together, and they live happily ever after. End of the movie. Two weeks later, he kills her; grinds her body up; feeds it to his girlfriend, who dies of ptomaine poisoning; and her husband is prosecuted and sent to the electric chair for it. But here's our little story with a happy ending. What is an ending? There's no such thing. Death is the only ending.

JAZZ HAS ENDURED because it doesn't have a beginning or an ending. It's a moment.

I WAS A PRETTY GOOD GOLFER, and it got so that it obsessed me. And I was just *pretty* good. And then when I'd get a job, I couldn't play every day; I could play only on the weekends. About four strokes sneak back into your game. And finally I thought, "I'm just not having any fun with it. I'm tortured by this. I hate it." And I just quit.

EVERY AD for every film is exactly the same.

WE MAKE TOO MUCH of the good and too much of the bad.

I LOVE gallery openings where everybody runs around drinkin' that crappy goat-piss white wine and you can't see the work at all. And you realize that the artists—and them people all *think* they're artists—they can't like anybody else's art. They can admire it if it still leaves them in the same place—if it isn't direct competition to them—and they can say, "Oh, well, of course I'm a great admirer of that." It's very safe.

I KNEW SAM Peckinpah slightly. We shared the same editor for a long time. But we were jealous of one another. We were all jealous of anybody who was succeeding. I've always been more openly expressive in my admiration for European and Asian directors, and I think maybe it's because they're not a threat to me. They're in a different cubbyhole.

HOT AIR just came in from the window. Hot air comin' that way, and hot air comin' this way.

I'VE ALWAYS had the final cut.

Interviewed by Scott Raab | Photograph by Neil Drabble

BORN KANSAS CITY, MISSOURI—02.20.25

DIED LOS ANGELES, CALIFORNIA—11.20.06

> A FIVE-TIME ACADEMY AWARD NOMINEE FOR BEST DIRECTOR—FOR *M*A*S*H* (1970), *NASHVILLE* (1975), *THE PLAYER* (1992), *SHORT CUTS* (1993), AND *GOSFORD PARK* (2001)—ALTMAN NEVER WON. NO OTHER DIRECTOR GARNERED MORE NOMINATIONS WITHOUT A WIN.

Bryan Anderson { SOLDIER—ROLLING MEADOWS, ILLINOIS }

THIS IS THE GRIPPER. It's like a robot hand, a stronger tool. There's a sensor on the inner and outer parts of my forearm. All I do is pretend my hand is still there and open and close it.

WHEN I DON'T HAVE HELP, it'll take me ten minutes to put my legs on. The first time I ever did it, it took me an hour.

FIVE, TEN, FIFTEEN years from now, can you imagine the prosthetics they're going to have? They're going to have *Terminator* shit, stuff that's not going to come off. It's just going to be your limb. That's what I'm hoping for anyway. I'm doing fine right now. I can wait. I've always been taught in the Army: expect the worst, hope for the best.

I USED TO BE a gymnast. I started my freshman year and went to State all three years. Parallel bars, floor, rings, vault, then pommel horse. I hated the pommel horse. I may not be able to do gymnastics like I used to, but I still do little stuff. When I fall out of my chair, I do a handstand to get back in. I lift up my body, push off, and snap up.

I WANT TO BE A STUNTMAN. I could be on prosthetics, and they could blow my legs off. They have a harness attached to me, they pull me back, there's blasting caps on my legs, and boom! My legs are gone.

THE DOCTORS SAY some people have phantom feelings, like your legs and hands are still there. They wake up and they can feel their feet. They try to stand up and then they fall. Not me. I have pain, and the feeling sometimes, but not that much. Every once in a while, I'll have an itch on my knee. Mostly it's a tingling in my feet. It sucks.

YOU HAVE two options once this happens: roll over and die or move on. I chose to move on. I'm still me. I'm just 75 percent off. "Get a great deal on Bryan Andersons this week." You know who actually told me that the first time? My mom. We were in Vegas, talking about T-shirts we should make, and she said, "75 percent off." She said, "You should get a shirt showing off your personality."

SMOKING SAVED my right hand. I'd be a quadruple amputee if I wasn't smoking. I'd normally have my hands on the steering wheel, but I was smoking, so I had just my left hand on the steering wheel. My hand still got messed up, but if I had my hand down there, I would have been done.

WE WERE LAUGHING, and then *boom!*

I WAS GOING REALLY SLOW at the time. Whoever it was looking out, who armed it, waited for all the civilian traffic to go by. They were aiming for the third truck, so when my front tires rolled over the infrared laser, it exploded. They built it into the cement and painted it to look like the curb and sidewalk. It took most of my front end off instead of going into the cab. But I still had a little extra come at me. My gunner had some shrapnel in his ass. My team leader had shrapnel in his hip and his wrist. I didn't hear the blast. I saw the smoke and the fire come through the door, but I didn't hear it.

THEY THOUGHT I was going to die, saying, "Hang on, hang on." In my head, I didn't ever have that feeling that I was going to die. And just in case, I kept telling myself, Keep breathing, do the motion, stay awake. It was when I got on the bird that I felt safe to pass out. I woke up at Walter Reed.

BUT I ACTUALLY FORGOT that I'd lost my left hand, because when I woke up in D.C., I went to scratch my face with my left hand. I looked up at the ceiling. "You couldn't have given me a break?"

MY MOM SAID nobody's allowed to cry in front of me, and they didn't.

ONE DAY I was in the shower looking at myself, and I kind of lost it a little bit. That's when my self-consciousness really shot up. Dude, nobody wants me like this. It went bad from there. I couldn't sleep. My chest was getting tight, like I was going to have a panic attack. I didn't think I was thinking about it. I just started freaking. I didn't want to be inside. I didn't want to be outside. I didn't want to be anywhere. I didn't want to kill myself, but I just felt like I didn't want to be anywhere. I didn't want anybody to be around me.

I THINK IT WILL BE GOOD for my kid to see someone like me, so when they grow up and they see someone like me, they won't make a quick judgment on them.

EVERYTHING that has happened to me since I've been hurt has happened to me because I've been hurt. I got to go to the Pentagon. There's this quarter-mile-long hallway that is just filled with people, and I mean filled with people. There's a little space to go through and everyone is clapping and crying and coming up and hugging you. OK, that's great. But what about all the people who did the same exact thing that I did that didn't get hurt? They should get the same recognition we do. We all did the same thing. Some people just got the shit end of the stick, that's all. It's all luck.

I DON'T REGRET anything.

Interviewed by Brian Mockenhaupt | Photo by Christopher Griffith

BORN ARLINGTON HEIGHTS, ILLINOIS—04.09.81

> ON OCTOBER 23, 2005, IN BAGHDAD, IRAQ, A ROADSIDE BOMB DESTROYED THE HUMVEE ANDERSON WAS DRIVING. THE EXPLOSION SEVERED BOTH OF HIS LEGS AND HIS LEFT FOREARM.

> ANDERSON HAD SIGNED UP FOR THE ARMY IN THE SPRING OF 2001. HIS SCHEDULED REPORT-FOR-DUTY DATE: SEPTEMBER 11.

> A STANDOUT GYMNAST IN HIGH SCHOOL, HE PLANNED TO BECOME A STUNTMAN AFTER LEAVING THE ARMY. THAT HASN'T CHANGED.

Alan Arkin { ACTOR—SANTA FE }

THINGS ARE NEVER going to turn out the way you think they will.

IMPROVISATION has been crucial to my whole life; it's what we're doing all the time.

WHAT I'VE LEARNED about teaching is to refer back to the root of that word, which is *educo*, which means "to pull from." Education does not mean jamming information into somebody's head. Rather, it's that ancient idea that all knowledge is within us; to teach is to help somebody pull it out of themselves.

DURING THE McCARTHY ERA, there was a huge dichotomy in the country. Elvis was the big thing. It was just kind of mindless euphoria on the one hand, and on the other hand, people were living in fear for their lives—in fear of total annihilation. It was very schizophrenic.

TODAY there's still a great element of fear, but I don't think anybody's having a very good time.

I'M NOT A POLITICAL ANALYST, but what I see is a sort of worldwide paranoia. Everybody knows: The. Jig. Is. Up. Nature is pissed off and everybody's waiting with bated breath for the other shoe to drop. Everybody knows it. Nobody's free from that fear.

NO MATTER WHAT you do or where you are, you're going to be missing out on something.

HOLLYWOOD is a strange place. The class structure here is more rigid than almost anyplace I've ever experienced. It's made more difficult by the fact that it's constantly changing. You never know what class you belong to unless you're one of the two or three people that have been in the same echelon for a long, long time.

IF YOU'RE LOOKING outside yourself for substantiation of your own happiness, you're going to fail.

MARRIAGE requires searing honesty at all costs. I learned that from my third wife.

CHILDREN LEARN from what you are rather than what you tell them. What you try to jam into their heads isn't going to be worth beans if the way you're living your life doesn't look like that.

I USED TO HAVE a lot of philosophies of acting; they all fell apart over the years.

ANYTHING you're rigid about, sooner or later, the rug is going to get pulled out from under you.

WE DON'T HAVE A LOT OF RULES in our house, but I do have one: I'm good for one minute of hair talk. When she asks me, "How does my hair look?" the timer goes on.

ACTORS are not as interesting as I used to think they were.

THERE HAVE BEEN TIMES I wished that I had goals that didn't require other people giving me stuff.

I DON'T KNOW if acting was a calling for me. I feel like it came out of a lot of emotional needs—the same old actor bullshit: I need attention. I need love. Blah, blah, blah. And the truth is, being an actor doesn't help with that at all. The approval's not really the kind of approval you need, anyway. What someone like that needs is one-on-one, personal caring. The anonymity of show business caring doesn't help. Like my manager tells me all the time, "They love you." Finally I said, "I don't want to hear that word anymore. They don't love me. Maybe they like my work a little bit. But they don't love me. They don't even know me. If they never saw me again, it wouldn't make any difference. If we were both drowning, they would shove me under to get on the raft."

It took a long conversation to convince the people that I was right for *Little Miss Sunshine*. They were thinking of somebody, I think, about ten or fifteen years older than I was. They thought I was a little virile. Well, "virile" was the word they used.

I READ SOMEWHERE that some people believe that the entire universe is a matrix of living thought. And I said, "Man, if that's not a definition of God, I don't know what is."

TRUTH IS ALWAYS unfolding. It's not an absolute.

MEDICINE? Oh, Jesus. Can we not talk about that?

AS YOU GET OLDER, you have to change your view of what your life is. Your physiology is going to demand certain things of you, and you either have to pay attention to it or die. I'm on regimens now—there are things I have to do. If you surrender to it, there's a certain peace you can achieve, rather than saying, "I gotta be the way I was."

I RECITE the Robert Browning poem to myself all the time. You know the quote? "Grow old along with me! / The best is yet to be, / The last of life, for which the first was made." I'm praying it's going to be true.

Interviewed by Mike Sager | Photograph by Emily Shur

BORN BROOKLYN, NEW YORK—
03.26.34

> ARKIN'S ACADEMY AWARD FOR BEST SUPPORTING ACTOR IN 2006, FOR *LITTLE MISS SUNSHINE*, CAME TWENTY-EIGHT YEARS AFTER HIS LAST NOMINATION—FOR BEST ACTOR IN *THE HEART IS A LONELY HUNTER* (1968).

> HE WAS AN ORIGINAL MEMBER OF CHICAGO'S SECOND CITY COMEDY TROUPE IN THE 1960s.

> HE COWROTE THE HIT "THE BANANA BOAT SONG."

Jeff Bezos { FOUNDER AND CEO OF AMAZON.COM—SEATTLE }

THE LANDSCAPE is littered with the corpses of people who have made predictions, so I won't try to predict what America will look like a hundred years from now. Nobody remembers what you said anyway, unless you're Nostradamus.

MY GRANDFATHER TAUGHT ME that it is harder to be kind than it is to be clever. That has always stuck with me.

PEOPLE THINK OF liberty or freedom as being happiness, but it's not. Those very smart people who wrote "Life, liberty, and the pursuit of happiness" had it right.

MORALE comes not from things that you layer on to make people happy. It comes from being able to build. People like to build. The question is, could it be done? The answer is, absolutely.

GO TO BED EARLY and wake up early. The morning hours are good.

LOVE and sex? People will die for love.

IT'S IMPOSSIBLE to interact with an eighteen-month-old child and not come away with the impression that people are fundamentally good.

WHEN YOU'RE A LITTLE KID, you have no idea how much your parents love you.

A THIRD WORLD jail would not have a chance against my wife.

I'M CERTAINLY the kind of person that has to grow on a woman. It takes repeated exposure to wear down her defenses.

I WEAR THE SAME THING every weekday, and I have for ten years. I don't like to think about what I want to wear in the morning. You should definitely stay away from asking me fashion questions.

WHAT CHARACTERISTICS do I look for when hiring somebody? That's one of the questions I ask when interviewing. I want to know what kind of people *they* would hire.

IT SEEMS fundamentally unfair to me that there is this physical speed limit in the universe—the speed of light—and you can't go faster than that. To have this huge universe out there and to not be able to get on a faster-than-light-speed ship and go explore the galaxy . . . I really think very, very deep in the human psyche there is this need to explore. The pre-Einstein people didn't know that there were any limits to speed. And one of the things that comes out of Einstein's theory is that the speed of light is an absolute limit, that you can't go faster than that. And that seems unfair to me.

EVERYONE ALWAYS SAYS that parenting is not a popularity contest. I think that grandparenting is.

DEBT IS A USEFUL INVENTION. It's why people can afford houses before they reach seventy. They can actually have the house while they need it and then work and pay for it. That's very, very useful.

WHAT I WOULD REALLY LIKE people to say about Amazon is that we raised the bar on customer experience for every industry all over the world. Some companies have missions that are even bigger than the company; an example of that would be Sony. Sony, coming out of World War II, said that their mission was "We are going to make Japan known for quality." They had a mission that was bigger than Sony. It was a mission for Japan. And we have a similar mission.

SOMETIMES I THINK the *Time* Person of the Year is chosen for the man, and I think sometimes they are chosen as a symbol of something, and my selection was clearly that. They weren't choosing Jeff Bezos so much as they were choosing me as a symbol for the Internet. Yeah, my parents were very proud. I mean, they are parents. They are not objective.

WHEN YOU'RE YOUNG, deferring gratification is not a honed skill. As you get older, you get better at the marathon mentality.

PEOPLE need to think of themselves as fortunate.

AT THE END OF THE DAY, when you're eighty years old and looking back on your life, you want to have minimized the number of regrets you have. That's what should drive people—not how much money they have. It's regrets that I think haunt people at the end of their life.

Interviewed by Cal Fussman | Photograph by Larry Sultan

BORN ALBUQUERQUE, NEW MEXICO—01.12.64

> BEZOS WROTE THE BUSINESS PLAN FOR AMAZON.COM DURING A CROSS-COUNTRY MOVE TO SEATTLE WHILE HIS WIFE DROVE. THE COMPANY LAUNCHED IN 1994.

> IN 2000, HE BEGAN WORK ON BLUE ORIGIN, A SMALL COMPANY DEVOTED TO SUBORBITAL SPACE FLIGHT AND SPACE TOURISM. THE COMPANY'S MOTTO IS *GRADATIM FEROCITER*, WHICH TRANSLATES TO "STEP BY STEP, FEROCIOUSLY."

Christie Brinkley { SUPERMODEL—NEW YORK CITY }

OH, YEAH, I know all the blonde jokes. There's a blonde walking along the side of the river. All of a sudden she sees a blonde on the other side and she calls out, "Hey, do you know how to get to the other side?" And the second blonde says, "You *are* on the other side." I can laugh.

CATTLE CUTTING is the most fun you can have on a horse.

I PHOTOGRAPHED THE REMATCH between Sugar Ray Leonard and Roberto Duran—the "no mas" fight. I was the first one to notice that Duran had a stomachache. I photographed them putting an ice pack on his stomach between rounds, and editors later called me for that shot. I'd watched the whole thing unfold. I was at the eight o'clock weigh-in that morning, and Duran didn't make it. I had pictures of the twelve o'clock weigh-in, when he did make it. And I knew what he was doing during those four hours: laxatives, steam room, all that stuff in order to make the weight. And, you know, those laxatives don't stop working just because the fight's on. Here you've got a macho man in the ring . . . and that's what happened. *No mas! Get me to the bathroom!*

ONE OF MY mom's big expressions was "Honey, live each day like it's your last." This has led to a very interesting life. There aren't many corners of this world that I haven't adventured in. Then again, there aren't many bones I haven't broken.

THE BEST BEAUTY SECRET is sunblock.

OPPENHEIMER, what were you *thinking*? Nuclear energy should have been our scientists' deepest, darkest secret, to be taken to the grave.

ART is what makes us human.

WHEN I WAS PHOTOGRAPHED editorially, I felt as if I was part of the process. I was constantly trying to visualize the page. If they said they wanted a horizontal double-page spread, I was constantly trying to give the photographer new ways of seeing me horizontal.

I AM TOO BUSY to be held back by stereotypes.

IT'S A FUNNY THING with models. Say you're going to be posing in a skimpy bikini. You go to the location with your bikini on under your clothes. When it's time to pose, a lot of girls will look for a place to take their clothes off where people aren't looking. Then they'll reappear in something much skimpier than the act of taking the clothes off.

THE WAY PEOPLE RESPOND TO ME has evolved. When I was doing the *Sports Illustrated* work, it was loud. Woooowww! I actually had to move because we were living on the water and the boaters would pull up and start singing, "Uptown Girl! C'mon out! *Woo-hoo!* Show us your bathing suit!" The sound effects became just too much. Then all of a sudden, I was past the whoop-and-holler phase, and women I'd never met were coming up to me and telling me the most intimate details of their pregnancies.

I KNOW Disney World like the back of my hand.

LOVE IS SACRED, profound, joyous, and all of that. Sex is . . . fun. When the two come together, *then the two come together.*

WHEN YOU'RE FAMOUS, being married to someone who's famous is difficult—because if people think it's you but they're not sure, they may walk by. But if they think it's you and they see your partner, it confirms it. Being married to Billy was like a confirmation factor.

I'VE CRASHED in a helicopter. I've had emergency airplane landings, engines blown out, hydraulics fail. I've had it with flying.

HILLARY CLINTON is a really good mom.

I COULDN'T COUNT THE HOURS I spent by my stereo deciphering Joni Mitchell's lyrics and adding them to my life's meaning. When I got the chance to meet her, there were so many things I wanted to say, and I was so overwhelmed that I couldn't talk. She said, "You know how many times people ask me if I'm your mom?" I tried to speak again, but nothing came out.

ONE MODEL I'd really like to meet is Carolyn Murphy.

CHILDREN ARE MAGICIANS who make adults smile.

Interviewed by Cal Fussman | Photograph by Stephen Danelian

BORN MONROE, MICHIGAN—02.02.54

> BRINKLEY WAS THE FIRST MODEL TO APPEAR ON THE COVER OF *SPORTS ILLUSTRATED'S* SWIMSUIT ISSUE FOR THREE CONSECUTIVE YEARS.

> SHE PAINTED THE COVER OF THEN-HUSBAND BILLY JOEL'S 1993 ALBUM *RIVER OF DREAMS*.

> BRINKLEY'S ONLY TWO MAJOR FILM ROLES WERE AS RED FERRARI GIRL IN *VACATION* (1983) AND WOMAN IN FERRARI IN *VEGAS VACATION* (1997).

George Carlin { COMEDIAN—VENICE, CALIFORNIA }

I WAS IN MY MOTHER'S BELLY as she sat in the waiting room of the abortionist's office. Dr. Sunshine was his code name. I was fifty feet from the drainpipe, and she saw a painting on the wall that reminded her of her mother, who had recently died. She took that as a sign to have the baby. That's what I call luck.

MY FATHER DRANK and was a bully. For the first five years of my brother's life, my father beat him with a leather-heeled slipper. Had I been subjected to that kind of treatment, all bets are off. His absence saved my life.

MY MOTHER had great executive-secretarial jobs in the advertising business and raised two boys during the Second World War. She used to say, "I make a man's salary." That's heroism.

I'M SURE HITLER was great with his family.

I USED TO COLLECT the most colorful curses I heard and write them down. I actually carried in my wallet things like "kraut cunt" and "burly loudmouth cocksucker" and "longhair fucking music prick," which was a thing Mikey Flynn yelled at a Juilliard student that he was kicking in the head.

I DON'T LIKE authority and regulation, and I do my best to disrespect it, but I do that for myself. It's self-expression only.

SEX without love has its place, and it's pretty cool, but when you have it hand in hand with deep commitment and respect and caring, it's nine thousand times better.

IF IT'S MORALLY WRONG to kill anyone, then it's morally wrong to kill anyone. Period.

IT'S AMAZING to me that literacy isn't considered a right.

I WAS ARRESTED for possession and cultivation of marijuana in the early '70s, and it was thrown out. The judge asked me how I felt about it, and I said, "I understand the law, and I want you to know I'll pay the fine, but I cannot guarantee I will not break this law again." He really chewed me out for that.

CENSORSHIP that comes from the outside assumes about people an inability to make reasoned choices.

THE FIRST THING THEY TEACH kids is that there's a God—an invisible man in the sky who is watching what they do and who is displeased with some of it. There's no mystery why they start that with kids, because if you can get someone to believe that, you can add on anything you want.

I WOULD DIE for the safety of the people I love.

I WISH that we could measure how much the potential of the mind to expand has been stunted by television.

BECAUSE OF MY ABUSE OF DRUGS, I neglected my business affairs and had large arrears with the IRS, and that took me eighteen to twenty years to dig out of. I did it honorably, and I don't begrudge them. I don't hate paying taxes, and I'm not angry at anyone, because I was complicit in it. But I'll tell you what it did for me: it made me a way better comedian—because I had to stay out on the road and I couldn't pursue that movie career, which would have gone nowhere, and I became a really good comic and a really good writer.

I STOPPED VOTING when I stopped taking drugs. I believe both of those acts are closely related to delusional behavior.

THERE'S NO morality in business. It doesn't have a conscience. It has only the cash register. They'll sell you crappy things that you don't need, that don't work, that they won't stand behind. It's a glorified legal form of criminal behavior.

IF EVERYBODY KNEW the truth about everybody else's thoughts, there would be way more murders.

THERE'S NOTHING WRONG with high taxes on high income.

LENNY BRUCE opened all the doors, and people like Richard Pryor and I were able to walk through them.

GIVEN THE RIGHT REASONS and the right two people, marriage is a wonderful way of experiencing your life.

I THINK that the assassinations of the Kennedys and Martin Luther King showed that all of the wishing and hoping and holding hands and humming and signing petitions and licking envelopes is a bit futile.

BLACKS are deliberately kept down. Poor communities are deliberately underfunded.

I DON'T THINK PEOPLE SHOULD get credit for being honest and brave. I think there's a lot of genetic shit going on there.

SOMEDAY they'll find a gene for putting on your overcoat.

THERE'S A PULSE IN NEW YORK, even on the quietest street, on the quietest day. It's full of potential.

IF THERE'S EVER A GOLDEN AGE of mankind, it will not include men over two hundred pounds beating children who are less than one hundred pounds and it will not include the deliberate killing of people in a formal setting.

I DID SOMETHING in a previous life that must have been spectacularly good, because I'm getting paid in this life just magnificently, more than one would dare imagine or hope for.

Interviewed by Larry Getlen | Photograph by Peggy Sirota

BORN BRONX, NEW YORK—05.12.37
DIED LOS ANGELES, CALIFORNIA—06.22.08

> IN THE LATE 1960S, CARLIN'S LANDMARK ROUTINE, "SEVEN WORDS YOU CAN NEVER SAY ON TELEVISION," EXPLORED THE LIMITS OF FREE SPEECH AND GOOD TASTE.

> CARLIN'S EIGHTEEN COMEDY ALBUMS EARNED NUMEROUS GRAMMY NOMINATIONS AND AWARDS. HE ALSO EARNED FIVE EMMY NOMINATIONS.

Ray Charles { MUSICIAN—LOS ANGELES }

> **MUSIC** is about the only thing left that people don't fight over.

PEOPLE COULDN'T UNDERSTAND why my mama would have this blind kid out doing things like cutting wood for the fire. But her thing was, "He may be blind, but he ain't stupid."

I AM my own engineer.

I REMEMBER ONE NIGHT we did a thing with Duke Ellington. He was on an oxygen tank until they called him to come out onstage. But he went out there, and you'd never have known there was anything wrong with the man. That's what music can do. If you're sad, you can go home and play some records and make yourself feel better. If you're in the hospital and you're sick, music can be soothing. I know I'm gonna get shot down for this, but I think music is the greatest art form ever, bar none. I know that people who are into movies or into sculpture or writing or whatever are gonna say, "Ray, you must done lost your brain." And they're probably right. But I still think that music is the greatest art form ever.

THEY SAY WAR has a purpose, but I'm not sure I agree.

I'VE ALWAYS THOUGHT that people want you to be one of two things: they either want you to be a clone—meaning just like them—or they want you to be their footstool, so they can control you and tell you what to do.

SIGHTED PEOPLE sometimes forget that blind people have a mind.

I DON'T ANALYZE myself. I just do what I do.

YOU BETTER LIVE EVERY DAY like it's your last day, 'cause one day you're gonna be right.

I'M A FIRM BELIEVER in God himself, but that's as far as I can go. I'm not any denomination. I'm not Catholic or Presbyterian or Baptist or Methodist or Jewish or Muslim. I'm none of those things. And I'm sure that's just fine with God.

I DID DRUGS because it was my pleasure.

NOWADAYS THEY SAY you need to get a special chip to put in the TV so the kids can't watch this and that. In my day, we didn't need that. My mom was the chip. End of story.

THE PIANO is the foundation, and that's it.

ALL MY KIDS know me.

ADDICTION can be very, very bad. But addiction in itself isn't bad; it's a question of what you're addicted to. That's where the chickens come home to roost. You can be addicted to good habits, you know what I mean? You can be addicted to your woman. Addiction in itself is kind of like money. It ain't bad or good. It's what you do with it.

WHEN YOU WRITE A GOOD SONG, it will be good even if it's sung by somebody with a bad voice.

WE ALWAYS gonna have racism.

WITH SINGING, the name of the game is to make yourself believable. When somebody hears you sing a song and they say, "Oh, that must have happened to him," that's when you know you're transmitting. It's like being a good actor. You make people feel things, emotions and whatnot. But you gotta start with yourself. You got to feel it yourself. If you don't feel it, how do you expect someone else to?

I DON'T REMEMBER MUCH about what it was like to see. The main thing I remember is my mom, how she looked. And I remember colors.

I'VE ALWAYS BEEN the kind of person who, if there's anything that can kill me, I want to know something about it.

PEOPLE SAY, "Ray, you a genius; Ray, you a cornerstone; Ray, you this and you that." Those are nice accolades, and I certainly appreciate it when people think well of my music and what I've tried to do with it. But in my heart, I mean . . . I don't kid myself. I know I'm not a genius. A genius is somebody like Art Tatum or Charlie Parker. I don't come close to those guys. I just happen to be a guy that can do a lot of little things and do 'em well.

IT WOULD BE a real bitch if I ever lost my hearing. I know I couldn't be no Helen Keller. That would be worse than death.

VISION is something that you have in your mind.

THIS IS a girl's bike, man. Why would I be riding a girl's bike? You didn't think I was gonna notice that, right? You guys are trying to sucker a blind man!

Interviewed by Mike Sager | Photograph by Gregg Segal

BORN ALBANY, GEORGIA—09.23.30

DIED BEVERLY HILLS, CALIFORNIA—06.10.04

> ALTHOUGH HE WAS BLINDED BY GLAUCOMA AT THE AGE OF SIX, CHARLES LEARNED TO READ AND WRITE MUSIC AND COULD PLAY SEVERAL MUSICAL INSTRUMENTS BY THE TIME HE LEFT SCHOOL.

> HE WON TWELVE GRAMMYS AND WAS INDUCTED INTO THE ROCK AND ROLL HALL OF FAME IN 1986.

BORN LEXINGTON, KENTUCKY—
05.06.61

George Clooney

{ ACTOR—LOS ANGELES }

> **MY FIRST MEMORY** is when I was four years old: a family reunion at my uncle George's farmhouse. Uncle George was one of those great guys, a true character who claimed to have been a World War II bomber pilot and dated Miss America, one of those guys who walked into the room and lit it up. You remember how Al Pacino talked in *Scent of a Woman?* "*Hooo-waaaaaaah!*" Uncle George talked exactly like that. Complete conviction. He'd say something like, "Don't eat that mustard! Mustard will give you a heart attack!" He'd just make it up. But to this day, I'll be putting mustard on my hamburger and wondering . . .

Uncle Chick was there, too. Greatest con artist in the world. He'd gotten meningitis when he was a kid, lost his eye, and had a glass one inserted. He worked in an office during World War II, but he'd go into taverns, put his glass eye on the bar, and say, "Would you buy a drink for an Army man who lost his eye?"

I remember us kids sitting around at this reunion and Uncle George telling stories: "Chick, take off your finger for George Timothy and Ada Frances." Uncle Chick had this fake finger, and he'd do one of these moves and put the finger on the table. "Now, Chick, take out your teeth." And Chick took his dentures out and laid them on the table. "Now, take out your eye and put it on the table so the young ones may gaaaaaaaze upon it." Chick took out his glass eye and stuck it on the table. And Uncle George said, "Now, Chick, unscrew your head." And all of us kids took off running, because when you're four years old, you believe anything is possible.

At a very early age, I learned how to tell a story.

THE BEST LESSON my mom taught me was how to be scrappy. She was a beauty queen and had her own television show. But for her birthday, she'd buy herself a table saw. She put a roof on our house. My father—great as he is—couldn't pick up a hammer. It was my mom who was up there pounding the shingles in. But more than that, she taught me how to be realistic and survive in weird situations.

I have this buddy, Giovanni, in Italy. Over the summer, we're out riding motorcycles in the middle of nowhere. I go through this intersection, there's nobody around. Giovanni comes through, and, out of nowhere, this lady in a car comes racing across and crushes Giovanni's leg. I get back to him, and it's a mess. Blood and bone everywhere. No ambulance for a hundred miles. People start coming over. I don't speak the language, but somehow I'm making them understand: "From you, I need this.

>>

> CLOONEY HAS BEEN NOMINATED FOR FOUR OSCARS, SEVEN GOLDEN GLOBE AWARDS, AND TWO EMMYS.
> IN 2005, HE WON THE OSCAR FOR BEST SUPPORTING ACTOR FOR HIS ROLE IN *SYRIANA*.
> HE RECEIVED THE 2007 PEACE SUMMIT AWARD FROM THE NOBEL PEACE PRIZE LAUREATES FOR HIS HUMANITARIAN WORK.

From you, I need that." We get towels, we use bungee cords to make a splint, we get a car.

Keep your cool, get the job done—that's what I got from my mother.

You know, after all these years, it's still hard to explain my father. But the best way I can tell you about him is this: There are people in life who you wish you could be at a certain moment in time. Something happens, and the moment calls for you to say just the right thing—and most of us don't say it. The right words come to you later, in the car when you're driving home. "That sonuvabitch, you know what I should have told him?. . ." My dad was the guy who always had the perfect comeback at the moment it needed to be said. You'd watch and go, "Wow!" He was an idealist, too, and it's easier to be the friend of an idealist than the child of an idealist— because the idealist will make his child an example.

At a very **early age,** I learned how to **tell a story.**

WHEN BOBBY KENNEDY WAS KILLED, my dad was a journalist doing a TV show in Columbus, Ohio. It's right on the heels of Martin Luther King's death, a really frustrating time. My dad comes into my room, and I can tell that something's up. He says, "Give me your toy guns. Give them all to me." So I give him all my toy guns—plastic squirt guns, whatever I have. He puts them in a bag, and then he goes on his show and says, "My son gave me these. He said, 'I don't want to play with them anymore.'" Now, he did it to make a point, and it was a great moment in television. My dad understood that the message would be more important coming from a seven-year-old. But it's different when you're the kid. You're like, "Whoa, that was my favorite toy gun!"

LOOK AT AMERICAN HISTORY. Start with the Salem witch hunt. The conservative view was, "Well, they're all witches, and they should be burned at the stake." But the liberal view was, "Maybe there aren't any such things as witches." Liberals thought that women should be allowed to vote. We thought it'd be OK for blacks to sit at any lunch counter they wanted. We've always been on the right side of history eventually. So I don't understand how you lose the moral argument. We don't have to put the word "compassionate" in front of "liberal" the way conservatives do to prove that we give a shit about people. I think we should change what we call ourselves. I think we should be ruthless liberals. We need to show that we're tough, that we really give a shit about people.

I REMEMBER when I was a kid, going out to eat with my family and other families. Going out to dinner was a very big thing in Kentucky back then. We weren't wealthy at all, and shrimp cocktail was something you really looked forward to. And just as the waiter put the shrimp cocktail in front of you, the man from the other family would say something like, "What's the problem with those people?" And my mom would immediately be telling us, "Eat fast! Eat fast!" Because we all knew *those people* meant *black people*, and my father was going to make a scene, and we'd all have to leave the restaurant. At the time, I was thinking, "Can't you just shut up and let it go so we can all eat our shrimp cocktails?" But he never did let it go. And I'm really proud of that. But now, years later, I had to watch him say, "I'm fiscally somewhat liberal and morally somewhat liberal, but no, I'm not a liberal."

Are you kidding me? We should be embracing the word!

AND LET'S NOT FORGET gay marriage. Now, what's the big argument about? Who really thinks the sanctity of marriage works? What is there, a 50 percent divorce rate? So the argument about gay marriage becomes "What's next? Can you marry a goat?" And you come back with "Okay, let's make marrying a goat legal. Let's make it legal! If you're some backward jackass who wants to marry a goat, go right ahead!" It's illegal to jump off a building. But you get these people saying, "This is destroying our morals." What? Because two people love each other and want to express it?

The gay-marriage argument is ridiculous. Eventually it's going to happen, and everyone who stood against it is going to look like George Wallace on the steps of the schoolhouse trying to keep black kids from entering white schools, and we're going to have to explain why these people acted like dumbasses and how they were actually not such bad people after all.

IF I WERE PRESIDENT? Well, I'd do a few things . . .

You realize that in order to be elected, I'd have to run on the "Yep, I did it" ticket. "Is it true that you did drugs?" Yep, I did it. "Did you sleep with . . .?" Yep, I did it. And if I was somehow elected after all that, then I'd be shot, because the first thing I'd try to do is take oil off the table. But let's say I tried to do it. Remember when Kennedy got the space program going in 1961, saying in ten years we'd put a guy on the moon? At that point, rockets were falling off launch pads and monkeys were getting killed and there were people who said, "This guy is out of his mind." But we did land on the moon in 1969. And new technologies came out of that experience.

SO IF I'M PRESIDENT, I say, "We're at war? Really?" Because it doesn't seem like it. Usually when you're at war, people sacrifice. Let's face it, Rosie the Riveter ain't exactly out there. The only sacrifice I see is coming from the 150,000 kids who enlisted and had the war dropped in their laps.

I KNOW, IT'S A DRAG. Do I love the sound of a '57 Chevy? Yeah, I do. But the world is different, and at some point we're going to have to deal with it when the oil runs out.

IF WE TAKE OIL OFF THE TABLE NOW, suddenly all of those little countries that really didn't come into power until the thirties—and did so only because there was oil under their sands—don't get to control our economy. We take away the thing that makes them so powerful, and we create a new technology along the way. It's a new day.

MY AUNT ROSEMARY TAUGHT ME a lot without ever saying a word. She taught me how to handle success—not by handling it well, but by handling it badly. In 1951, she was on top of the world, on the cover of every magazine. She went on the road for five years, came back, and rock 'n' roll had come in. Elvis was king, and rock was male driven. The rules changed. And she was devastated. She started to believe that she'd lost her talent. She had nervous breakdowns, got screwed up on drugs, had a bad manager who made bad investments, blew a lot of money, and then got hit by the IRS. Luckily, she had the staying power to reinvent herself and come back. But she was knocked down for about twenty years. So what you learn from that—the really good lesson—is you're never as good as they say you are and you're never as bad as they say you are.

ONE THING YOU LEARN selling women's shoes is that all women lie about their shoe size. All women. And I mean all women. What is this horribly screwed-up thing that women have been taught that large feet are not attractive? A lady would come in with a 9½ wide and say, "I'm an 8." I'm looking at her, knowing she's a 9½ wide, and I'll say, "Eights are going to hurt." But she'll jam her foot into an 8 and say, "I'll take them!"

TO ME, Al Cowlings is the best example of a friend. I embrace Al Cowlings for being the guy O. J. called up and said, "Dude, they're framing my ass. Start up the car. Get me twenty thousand dollars and a passport. Let's get on the road." It's very easy to be a friend when the pressure's not on. I embrace the man who can get in a car and drive his buddy in the blindness of all reality and truth—which is his buddy just murdered two people. I'd like to have friends like that. I'd like to think I'm that friend. However, the bigger truth is that you're on the run with a guy who just murdered two people. Once your eyes are opened, what do you do?

I DIDN'T LEARN MUCH from marriage because I didn't let it be much of a learning experience. That's not to say I didn't love and adore the woman I married. But what I wasn't really prepared for was the idea that, if things start going really badly, you actually need to work them out. I was twenty-eight years old. I wasn't as tolerant as I should have been.

You're never as good as they say you are and you're never as bad as they say you are.

DIVORCE WAS INTERESTING for me because divorce meant failure. Not that my parents scolded me for it or anything like that; they've always been very supportive. But in general, they don't fail. They muscled through tough times in their marriage, because they weren't about to not be married. It was a different time.

UNCLE GEORGE WAS SITTING in his bed—sixty-eight years old. He looked at me and said, "What a waste . . ." To this day, I don't know if he was talking about the smoking that destroyed his lungs and barely let him breathe at the end or the drinking or if he was talking about his life in general, that he hadn't become the man that all that promise asked him to be.

But I came to the conclusion that I was not going to wake up one day at sixty-five and say, "What a waste." At the very least I was going to grab as much out of this life as I could.

The idea is to keep opening up, to keep going. My inclination would be to put a wall up and protect all of the things that I own, that I've created and feel comfortable with. I gotta keep shoving that wall down and say, "OK, let's go to places I don't understand completely or don't feel completely comfortable in." You hope you can do it. I don't know if you do it all the time. You try. That's the secret.

Interviewed by Cal Fussman | Photograph by Sam Jones

Katie Couric { NETWORK NEWS ANCHOR—NEW YORK CITY }

> IT'S A LITTLE HARDER than I thought it would be.

I FELT A LOT OF PRESSURE on election night. Some people out there are rooting for me to fail. But going in, I thought, "I can do this," and when I finished, I thought, "You know, I was right."

IT'S A JOB. It's an important job, but it's a job. And I try to keep it in its proper place. Other days, I feel like it's consuming me and kind of taking over my very being.

I DIDN'T DRESS UP in a blazer and sit at a desk when I was a little girl and read the news, so my life has unfolded in a way that I haven't really had that much control over.

I NEVER WENT SEARCHING for the *Today* show opportunity—I never saw myself in that role. I never really saw myself in this role. Timing has been everything for me in my life. It's been interesting so far. It's been challenging.

BEING THE YOUNGEST OF FOUR, I developed a certain amount of wily charm that got me through when maybe my brains weren't sufficient.

ANYBODY who worries all day about North Korean nukes is just going to fret their lives away—and get very bored.

MY HUMANITY is authentic—there's a lot of feigned humanity on television, a lot of cloying, unctuous humanity.

I TRY TO BE DIRECT. That's sometimes one of the hardest things to do. I suffer from the syndrome that many women do: they don't want to be called a bitch. With women there's very little leeway for that kind of expression, which is healthy.

I HAD SORT OF A PERFECT LIFE until I was forty. Jay used to say I was born on a sunny day—everything just sort of went right for me. Everything changed when I turned forty.

AFTER JAY DIED, I addressed people who are in that parallel universe, because it's so isolating and I wanted them to know that I understood that they were almost in this surreal, dreamlike state of fear and anxiety and frustration and powerlessness.

I HATE WHEN PEOPLE SAY, "He lived a good long life." My husband died when he was forty-two. He got ripped off.

WHAT IS LOVE? That is risky business. I'm definitely open to it. It's much more complicated when you're forty-nine with an almost-teenager and a teenager and you have a very public life. It's hard to make the pieces fit together.

IF YOU'RE NOT WILLING to lose, then you'll do whatever it takes to win, and you become someone you're not.

CELEBRITY. I hate that word.

I HATE the word "panties." It's a cheesy word for underpants.

I PLAY THE PIANO. When I'm sad and depressed, I play. It makes me cry, and it makes me feel better. Is that weird? Oh my God, I'm so boring.

WHEN YOU'RE RAISED PRESBYTERIAN, you're supposed to become a member of the church in seventh grade. I had a tough time when our minister showed me a diagram of Jesus on a throne surrounded by my family. I had a tough time with the idea that Jesus was more important than them. I didn't become a member.

I FEEL SOMETIMES like I am the personification of a Rorschach test and that people pin their own hopes and dreams or disappointments and frustrations and displace those things sometimes.

I'M IN A BIT of a box.

YOU HAVE TO BE UNWAVERING in your convictions that you're doing something good, because there are a lot of circling vultures that will eat you alive.

MY YOUNGER DAUGHTER READ SOMETHING on some AOL blog, and it really bothered her. I said, "When people say something like that, they're not talking about me as a person, they're talking about me as a commodity." I said, "Please, don't take it personally for me."

YOU GUYS even take a shot at me. You have something in the November issue, something about how since I've become an anchor, you don't know me anymore. You don't know me anymore? Bite me.

I TRY TO HAVE DINNER with my kids every night.

THEY SEE ME taking chances with this job and trying my best.

EVEN IF THE PERSON doesn't go off-message, sometimes events do.

SOMETIMES I THINK I WANT TO WRITE A BOOK, and sometimes I think, "How can I remember everything that's happened to me?" I can barely remember to put on deodorant. But I'd like to. I've certainly had a different life than the life I imagined I'd have.

GOD? I hope so.

Interviewed by Tom Junod | Photograph by Michael Edwards

BORN ARLINGTON, VIRGINIA—01.07.57

> COURIC, WHO BEGAN HER CAREER AS A DESK ASSISTANT AT ABC NEWS IN 1979, COANCHORED NBC'S *TODAY* FOR FIFTEEN YEARS.

> SHE BECAME THE ANCHOR OF THE *CBS EVENING NEWS* ON SEPTEMBER 5, 2006, MAKING HER THE FIRST SOLO FEMALE ANCHOR OF A NETWORK EVENING NEWS PROGRAM.

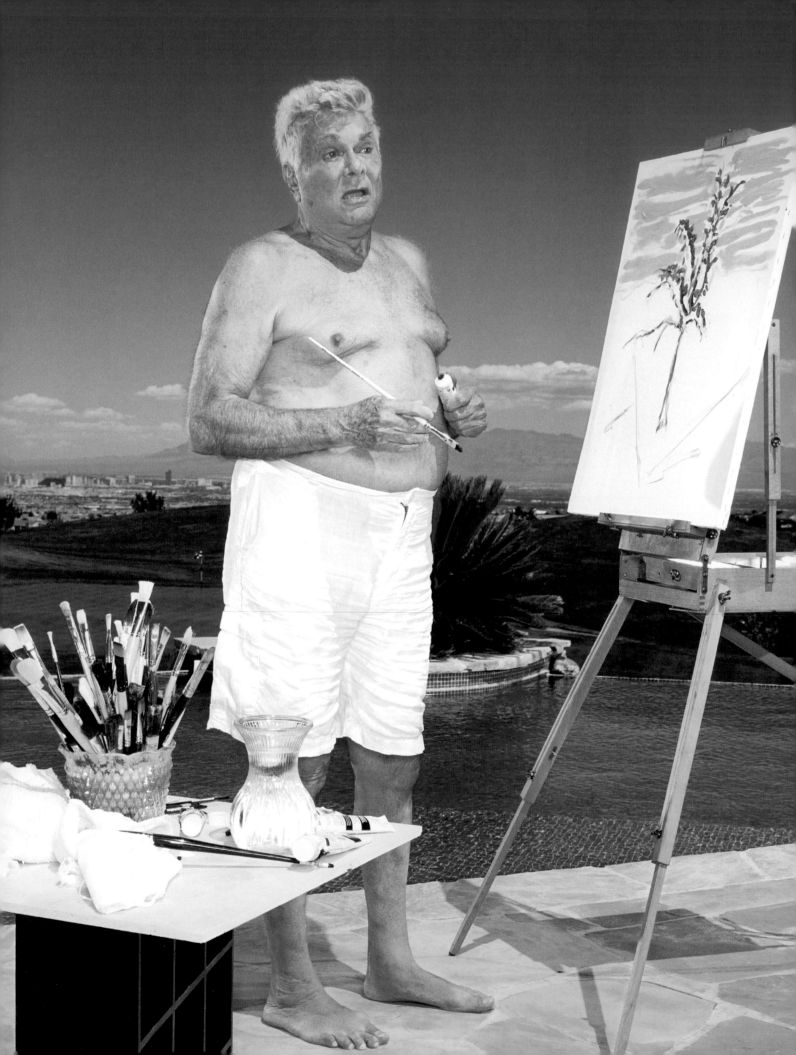

Tony Curtis { ECCENTRIC—LAS VEGAS }

> **HOW MANY PEOPLE** on this planet are van Goghs? Imagine an abstract painter who's fucking nuts, who cuts off his ear, who lives with potato eaters when he could live better. Sells one painting his whole life. Imagine finding a nut like him in the Bronx. Wouldn't be hard.

AS A KID, I never felt that I had anything or I was anybody. That was my ignorance. I never felt gifted. I paid no attention in high school. Once, I got every word wrong on a spelling test. The teacher gave me a minus zero because I even misspelled my name. I forgot to put the t in *Schwartz*.

IF YOU DON'T KNOW your gift, you've got no lift.

IT'S BEEN SAID that you can't understand anybody unless you understand their sexual life. A lot of people are frightened by that. Not me.

IT'S NOT HARD TO UNDERSTAND America's fascination with Marilyn Monroe. She was the first girl to wear see-through blouses. I met her in '49 at Universal. I was already under contract. She was looking for a contract. I must've been twenty-three or twenty-four. We met at the studio and started to go out. We were together for six or seven months. Steady. Fucked our heads off— you'll excuse the expression. At the time, nobody knew how big she'd become. I never felt her figure was so proper; I thought it was a little lumpy in places. She was a redhead back then, and at the time she seemed no different from all the other young women with nice knockers trying to get into movies. But then she developed that stupid-woman—no, I don't want to call it that—it was more like a naive, little-girl quality. In movies, she started to talk slowly, as if she was thinking of the words she was going to say, and that became her magic. That and the see-through blouse fit together perfectly.

SEX is something you can become good at, like fencing. You can learn how to fence. You can learn how to fuck.

WHEN I LEFT THE NAVY, I used the G.I. Bill to get into the Dramatic Workshop, which was located at the President Theatre on Forty-eighth Street. Walter Matthau and Harry Belafonte were students there, too. We were all just trying to make it. Later on, I went out to California, and good things started happening for me. When I came back to New York to do a promotion for *City Across the River,* they gave me a suite at the Sherry-Netherland and a huge black limo. I took it around to show my buddies in the Bronx and then went by the Dramatic Workshop. It was a terrible, rainy afternoon, and who do I see out in front? Walter Matthau. He's got a long, heavy coat on with a *Racing Form* sticking out of the pocket, and he's looking down at the gutter. Here I am in this nice, warm limo. And there he is, this grumpy guy surrounded by a cold, miserable world. The look on his face says, "What's ever going to happen for me? Nothin'!" So I tell the driver to pull alongside him and stop. Now Walter's watching the limo. I roll the window down, look at him, and say, "I fucked Yvonne De Carlo!" Then I roll the window back up in a hurry and tell the driver to get the hell out of there.

NO, NO, NO, HE WASN'T MAD! For years, Walter loved to tell that story at parties. He'd make it last twenty minutes.

I WAS IN PALM BEACH with Joe Kennedy just before the inauguration. I don't know why, but the old man loved me. He must've got a kick out of my movies. We were sitting in this study having a drink when the phone rings. He picks it up, and it's his son. He's listening for a while, and then he gestures for me to come over and sit next to him. He held the phone so I could hear. Jack is reading the inaugural address he's working on over the phone: "Ask not what your country can do for you. Ask what you can do for your country." I didn't realize the importance of those words at the time. But wasn't that neat? I heard that! Heard that before anyone else. I love having had those experiences.

SOMETIMES I WALK AROUND like Jesus. I go to a party— nobody knows I am, but I'm Jesus. That was an acting-class experience, you know. They'd send you out of the room, and the instructor would say, "When he comes back, he's Jesus Christ. Treat him as such." So I'd walk in the room and everybody would stop, look, and part for me. And I'd say to myself, "What the fuck is this? Whoever I am, I like it."

MY FIRST FOUR MARRIAGES taught me how to do the fifth. Look how lucky I am. I've got a wife in her thirties. She's sweet, and we have a wonderful relationship—and still I look at girls. I've gotta be careful.

I WAS NEVER AROUND when my kids were growing up. I was divorced from their mothers, so I didn't get to know them very well. I'm sorry—well, I'm not sorry. I just didn't. A few of my children I like very much. A couple I have no relationship with. I'm having a good time with the grandchildren. They come in and draw and make boxes with me and do the stuff that all kids love to do.

WANNA HEAR SOME POETRY? Here's one I wrote: "You cannot ask a fish not to swim / It's the only thing that makes him him."

I'M EIGHTY YEARS OLD. Eighty fucking years old. I don't feel any different now than I did when I was thirty. And here I am, sitting next to you now, with all my faculties. Some areas, I'm not what I used to be. My feet hurt. I don't pee on time. My eyes are going. My hearing's going. So I've gotta take care of those things. But I'm lucky. I have no disease that's going to kill me—not yet. Dying—I just don't feel like it.

I COULD BE a handsome man at ninety.

Interviewed by Cal Fussman | Photograph by Jeff Minton

BORN NEW YORK, NEW YORK—06.03.25

> CURTIS'S MOST FAMOUS ROLE WAS AS JOE/JOSEPHINE IN BILLY WILDER'S *SOME LIKE IT HOT* (1959). HIS COSTAR WAS JACK LEMMON, BUT IT WAS VERY CLOSE TO BEING JERRY LEWIS (SEE PAGE 88).

> CURTIS BECAME AN AVID PAINTER IN HIS EIGHTIES. IN 2007, HIS WORK *THE RED TABLE* WAS DISPLAYED AT THE METROPOLITAN MUSEUM OF ART IN NEW YORK CITY.

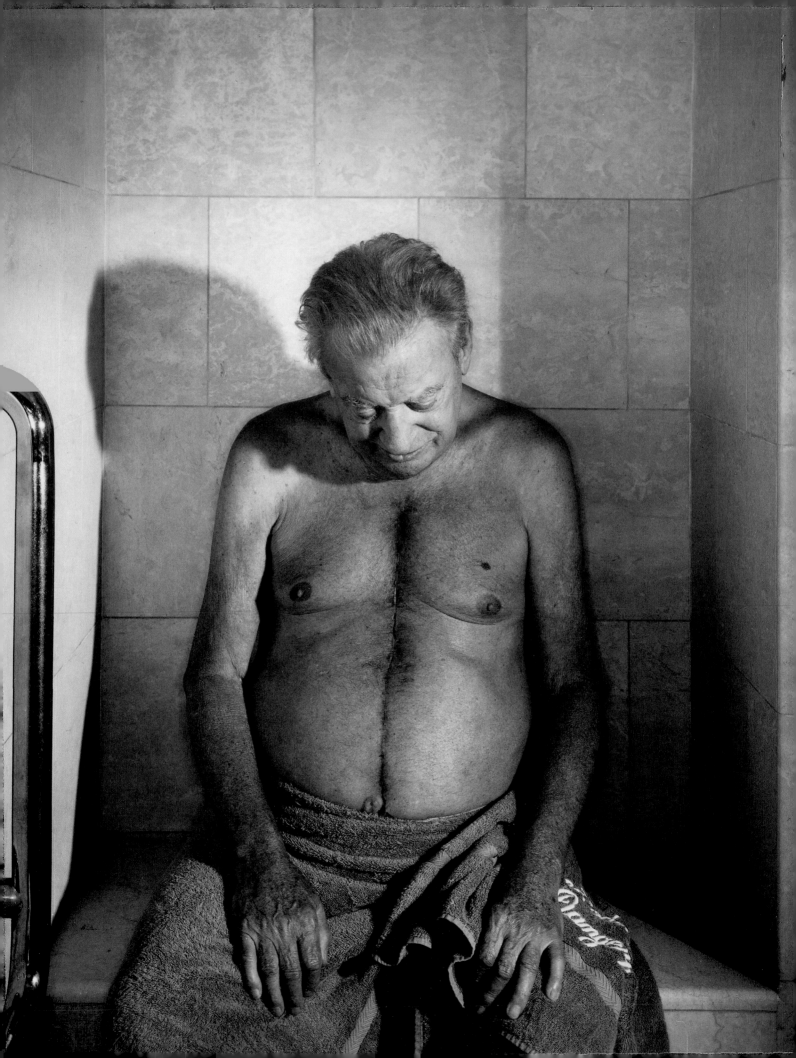

Rodney Dangerfield { COMEDIAN—LOS ANGELES }

 WHAT GOOD IS BEING THE BEST if it brings out the worst in you?

YOU KNOW YOU'RE UGLY when you go to the proctologist and he sticks his finger in your mouth.

I WANT a girl just like the girl that Dad kept on the side.

MY CHILDHOOD WAS BAD. No father. Mother was greedy and brought me up awful—never made me breakfast once. I don't want to get started. One story is worse than another.

THE ONLY NORMAL PEOPLE are the ones you don't know too well.

WE LIVED in a neighborhood that was too rich for us. When I was young, I had to deliver groceries to the homes of the kids I went to school with. I had to go to the back doors to make the deliveries. It was embarrassing. That was one thing out of a hundred.

PEOPLE seldom live up to their baby pictures.

I'VE BEEN WRITING JOKES since I'm fifteen. Not out of happiness, but to go to a different place, because reality wasn't good to me.

A SENSE OF HUMOR is rare. It isn't telling a joke about how there are three ways to get to heaven. It's being in a restaurant and hearing someone say, "Everyone's got their tale of woe," and then turning around and saying, "Unfortunately, in life, there's more woe than tail."

I GOT MY FIRST BREAK and became a singing waiter at eighteen or nineteen. I couldn't make a living at it. I quit. Then I got married and sold aluminum siding. My wife had problems physically. It was not good.

NEVER TELL your wife she's lousy in bed. She'll go out and get a second opinion.

YOU'LL FIND OUT it's lonely at the top when there's no one on the bottom.

WHEN I WAS FORTY, I was getting divorced, living in a low-class, dirty hotel in New York. My mother was dying of cancer. I owed twenty thousand dollars. That was about the lowest. I came back to show business, and I couldn't get a job. I was turned down by every small-time agent in New York.

I STARTED OVER AGAIN with an image: "Nothing goes right." Then when *The Godfather* came out, all I heard was "Show respect. With me, you show respect." So I changed the image to "I don't get no respect." I tried it out in Greenwich Village. I remember the first joke I told: "Even as a kid, I'd play hide and seek and the other kids wouldn't even look for me." The people laughed. After the show, they started saying to me, "Me, too—I don't get no respect." I figured, let's try it again.

WHEN YOU WALK up five flights of stairs at four in the morning, there's definitely a hooker involved.

I CAN'T figure women out. They put on makeup for three hours. They wear things that make them smaller. Things that make them bigger. Then they meet a man and they want truth.

IT WOULD BE GREAT if people never got angry at someone for doing something they've done themselves.

IF sex is a pain in the ass, then you're doing it wrong.

I INTRODUCED fifteen or twenty new comedians who made it big. Jerry Seinfeld, Jim Carrey, Tim Allen, Roseanne, Dice. That makes me feel good.

AFTER I GOT DIVORCED, I said to myself, "I will never, ever get married again." It was in cement. I went through a really rough twenty-five years, but it happened again. I fell in love. I told her, "Baby, I don't want a prenuptial agreement. This is it." Everyone told me I was nuts. Well, my new wife and I are married six years, and we get along great. You can make anything work if you're both givers.

IF EVERY MAN was as true to his country as he was to his wife, we'd be in a lot of trouble.

TIME AND TIDE and hookers wait for no man.

I RECENTLY had double-bypass surgery. As they wheel you in, the doctor always gives you a last look. You know that look. That look of confidence to make you feel good. I always say to every doctor, "If I don't make it, I'll never know it."

IT'S GREAT to have gray hair. Ask anyone who's bald.

I'VE LEARNED TO CONTROL everything. I don't get angry at anything. Somebody can do me wrong. That's life. What good is it to get angry?

MAN, who don't like spaghetti?

I AM THE WORLD'S oldest teenager. I've never lost my youthful attitude.

IF I COULD HAVE DINNER with anyone who lived in the history of the world, who would it be? That depends on the restaurant.

I'M A DOWNER. I've been depressed my whole life. Figure it out.

HE WHO LAUGHS LAST didn't get it in the first place.

Interviewed by Cal Fussman | Photograph by Dan Winters

BORN BABYLON, NEW YORK—11.22.21
DIED LOS ANGELES, CALIFORNIA—10.05.04

> DANGERFIELD GOT AN AUDITION TO BE ON *THE ED SULLIVAN SHOW* BY SNEAKING INTO A DRESS REHEARSAL; THE APPEARANCE WAS HIS BIG BREAK.
> HE OPENED THE FAMED MANHATTAN COMEDY CLUB DANGERFIELD'S IN 1969; THE CLUB HELPED LAUNCH THE CAREERS OF TIM ALLEN, ROSEANNE, JERRY SEINFELD, AND LOUIE ANDERSON, AMONG OTHERS.

Michael DeBakey { HEART SURGEON—HOUSTON }

> **ONE OF THE RAREST THINGS** that we do is think. I don't know why people don't do it more often. It doesn't cost anything. Think about that.

THERE ARE QUESTIONS that I'd like answered. But there aren't any answers to those questions.

IF WORLD LEADERS WERE DOCTORS, I think they would be more concerned with the welfare of people. There would be less poverty. There would be medical care for everybody, no matter whether people paid for it or not.

IN ANY GOOD SOCIETY, every member should be interested in the health of every other member—because if any member is unhealthy, it's a burden on the society.

WHAT ADVICE would I give a doctor preparing for surgery? First and foremost, walk into the right operating room. After you've got the right room, make sure you've got the right patient.

I'VE DONE MORE than sixty thousand heart operations. I used to start operating at six in the morning. Sometimes I wouldn't finish until ten or eleven at night. I've been fortunate in that I need very little sleep. I can get along well on four or five hours.

OKRA is the key to good gumbo.

I'M NOT SURE I CAN ANSWER that question specifically. But the operation I did in '53 for aneurysm of the thoracic aorta gave me great satisfaction. It had never been done successfully before, and lots of doctors took the position that you shouldn't try it. You've got to push ahead in spite of them. I learned that lesson early.

I DON'T THINK the difference between ninety-nine and a hundred is important.

I SCHEDULED MY LAST OPERATION when I was ninety. I just felt that I'd done enough and should turn it over to my colleagues.

IF YOU HAD A HEART PROBLEM right now and needed an operation and I was the only doctor around, sure, I'd do it.

THE BEST LESSON my mother taught me involves an orphanage we had in town. Every Sunday after church we would get in the car and drive to the orphanage. Mother would bake bread and cookies, and she would go through our clothes and give the items we'd outgrown to the children at this orphanage. One Sunday, she was putting clothes in the basket, and I noticed she had put one of my favorite caps inside. I immediately protested, but she reminded me that I had a new cap. "The child that's going to get this cap doesn't have a parent to give him a new cap," she said, "and you do." She told me I ought to be glad that I could give up the cap. I never forgot that.

BEING COMPASSIONATE, being concerned for your fellow man, doing everything you can to help people—that's the kind of religion I have, and it's a comforting religion. I don't get involved in discussions of intelligent design. You can't answer those questions, so why fool with them?

IT'S IMPORTANT for a patient to go into an operation with confidence. The functions of the heart will be abnormal if they go in scared to death.

THE WORST THING, of course—and you're never quite prepared for it—is when the patient dies during the operation. You die a little every time that happens.

THERE WAS A HISTORIAN in the fourteenth century who wrote a book about what he knew of the world, and, for that time, it was pretty good. One of the interesting observations he made is that all the tribes that have difficulty feeding themselves are lean and healthy and those that have plenty of food are fat, lazy, and unhealthy.

PEOPLE OFTEN USE WORDS in a loose way that covers over what they're talking about. I like to choose words that get to the basics.

THE DOCTOR WHO OPERATED ON ME only a few years ago was one that I trained. I was lucky to have somebody like that.

NEVER HAD A SYMPTOM. The pain came like a bullet out of the blue. I was alone when it started. My wife and my daughter had gone out. The pain is often described as the worst pain you can have. The pain was so severe that I would have welcomed anything to relieve it—including death. I wasn't going to fight it. I look upon death as a part of living, just as some trees lose all their leaves in the winter and have them replaced in the spring. But at the same time, part of me was thinking, "What caused this pain?" Part of me was doing a diagnosis on myself—which, as it turned out, was correct. Aortic dissection. I'd written more articles about the condition than anybody in the world, and I resigned myself to having a heart stoppage. The pain didn't teach me anything about the heart. It simply emphasized what I had already learned.

I WAS A LITTLE SURPRISED to find myself recovering after the surgery—then gratified to have been given a second life.

DURING MY RECOVERY, I played possum. I pretended to be sleeping and listened to what the doctors standing over my bed were saying about my condition. Then I'd argue with them about the therapy. I'd make them prove that I needed it.

I GUESS it's hard to be my doctor.

Interviewed by Cal Fussman | Photograph by Darren Brown

BORN LAKE CHARLES, LOUISIANA—09.07.1908
DIED HOUSTON, TEXAS—07.11.2008

> DeBAKEY PIONEERED NUMEROUS CARDIOVASCULAR PROCEDURES, INCLUDING THE CORONARY BYPASS AND THE ARTIFICIAL-HEART TRANSPLANT.
> IN 1954, HE DEVISED A TECHNIQUE TO REPAIR ARTERIES USING A DACRON TUBE HE MADE ON HIS WIFE'S SEWING MACHINE.
> IN 2006, HE BECAME THE OLDEST SURVIVOR OF THE PROCEDURE HE INVENTED.

Robert De Niro { ACTOR—NEW YORK CITY }

> **I LIKE IT** when interviews are brief. Are we done yet?

WHEN I WAS A TEENAGER, I went to the Dramatic Workshop at the New School. The school had a lot of actors under the G.I. Bill—Rod Steiger, Harry Belafonte, the generation ahead of me. I went in there, and the director said to me, "Vy do you vant to be an acteh?" I didn't know how to answer, so I didn't say anything. And he said, "To express yourself!" And I said, "Yeah, yeah, that's it. That's right."

WE USED TO roller-skate. Not like these souped-up Rollerblades they have today. Roller skates with ball bearings. We'd hang on to the back of a truck and go for a ride for a couple of blocks until the streetlight turned red and the truck stopped. Then one day they changed the lights to a stagger system. Only we didn't know. All the lights changed up an avenue at intervals so you could go twenty or thirty blocks without stopping. Suddenly, I'm stuck on the back of one of these trucks, and after four blocks, I'm realizing that the next light isn't going to turn red. The driver doesn't know you're on the back. You have no choice but to keep hanging on till he stops. There are things you do that when you get older, you realize how stupid they were.

SOME PEOPLE SAY, "New York's a great place to visit, but I wouldn't want to live there." I say that about other places.

YOU HAVE NO IDEA that, years later, people in cars will recognize you on the street and shout, "You talkin' to me?" I don't remember the original script, but I don't think the line was in it. We improvised. For some reason it touched a nerve. That happens.

MARTY SCORSESE LISTENS. He's open to unexpected things on that—this is a flowery way of saying it—on that voyage. He takes ideas, and he's not afraid to try them.

THERE'S NO SUCH THING as not being afraid.

MONEY makes your life easier. If you're lucky to have it, you're lucky.

I LEFT A MEETING right after they hit the World Trade Center. I went to my apartment, which looks south, and I watched it out my window. I could see the line of fire across the North Tower. I had my binoculars and a video camera—though I didn't want to video it. I saw a few people jump. Then I saw the South Tower go. It was so unreal, I had to confirm it by immediately looking at the television screen. CNN was on. That was the only way to make it real. Like my son said, "It was like watching the moon fall."

I DIDN'T HAVE a problem with rejection, because when you go into an audition, you're rejected already. There are hundreds of other actors. You're behind the eight ball when you go in there.

AT THIS POINT in my career, I don't have to deal with audition rejections. So I get my rejection from other things. My children can make me feel rejected. They can humble you pretty quick.

IT'S TRUE: I spent lunchtime in a grave during the filming of *Bloody Mama*. When you're younger, you feel that's what you need to do to help you stay in character. When you get older, you become more confident and less intense about it—and you can achieve the same effect. You might even be able to achieve more if you take your mind off it, because you're relaxed. That's the key to it all. When you're relaxed and confident, you get good stuff.

THE HARDEST THING about being famous is that people are always nice to you. You're in a conversation, and everybody's agreeing with what you're saying—even if you say something totally crazy. You need people who can tell you what you don't want to hear.

MOVIES ARE HARD WORK. The public doesn't see that. The critics don't see it. But they're a lot of work. A *lot of* work.

WHEN I'M DIRECTING a great dramatic scene, part of me is saying, "Thank God I don't have to do that." Because I know how fucking hard it is to act. It's the middle of the night. It's freezing. You gotta do this scene. You gotta get it up to get to that point. And yet, as a director, you've got to get the actors to that point. It's hard either way.

WHAT'S THE DIFFERENCE between sex and love? Hmm. That's a good question. Hey, you interviewed Al Pacino. How'd *he* answer that?

WHEN A PARENT DIES, it's the end. I always wanted to chronicle the family history with my mother. She was always interested in that. I wanted some researchers I'd worked with to talk to my mother, but my mother was a little antsy about it. I know she would've gotten into it. It would have been OK with my father, too. But I wasn't forceful, and I didn't make it happen. That's one regret I have. I didn't get as much of the family history as I could have for the kids.

AS YOU GET OLDER, the more complicated things get. It's almost therapeutic to be doing simple things with the kids.

IF YOU DON'T GO, you'll never know.

Interviewed by Cal Fussman | Photograph by Sam Jones

BORN NEW YORK, NEW YORK—08.17.43

> DE NIRO WON ACADEMY AWARDS FOR *THE GODFATHER, PART II* (BEST SUPPORTING ACTOR, 1975) AND *RAGING BULL* (BEST ACTOR, 1981). HE ALSO RECEIVED AN OSCAR NOMINATION FOR *THE DEER HUNTER* (1978).

> IN 2002, HE ORGANIZED THE FIRST TRIBECA FILM FESTIVAL, A SHOWCASE FOR FILMMAKERS AND PART OF THE REVITALIZATION OF LOWER MANHATTAN.

Johnny Depp { ACTOR—LOS ANGELES }

> **ONE TIME** a guy told me that he brought his wife to see *Pirates of the Caribbean*. She had lost her motor skills. I forget what you call it. It's not autism. Jesus, they made a movie about it. You know, where you recede and your functions start to go. Anyway, they're watching the film, and when Captain Jack Sparrow came on the screen, she started to laugh. This guy said he hadn't heard that laugh in years. And so he took her back to see the film repeatedly. For some reason, Captain Jack made her laugh every time. That's right up there.

MY MOTHER taught me a lot of things. The first thing that comes to mind is: "Don't take any shit off anyone, ever." When I was a little kid, we moved constantly. Bully picks on you in the new place? Don't ever take any shit off anyone, ever. Eloquent and right.

MY LIFE is my life because of Tim. Definitely.

THIS IS TIM BURTON in a nutshell: We were doing *Charlie and the Chocolate Factory,* and I was on the set. We were shooting, working, working, working. All great. Everything's cool. One of my pals comes up and says, "Helena [Bonham Carter, Burton's partner] just called. When you get a moment, she'd like you to give her a call back." "OK," I say. "As soon as I'm done on set, I'll go back to my trailer and give her a call." So I go back to the trailer, call Helena, and say, "Hey, what's going on?" I thought maybe Helena had a question about little boys because Billy was a little baby then and I've got two kids. So I say, "Is everything all right?" And she says, "Billy's fine. Everything's fine. But, well, you know how Tim is. He wants to know if you'd be . . . he'd like for you to be Billy's godfather." I say, "But I was just with Tim. I was with him three minutes ago. I had to leave him to walk back to the trailer to call you." So she called me to ask because Tim just couldn't. That was his way of asking. I went back to the set and said thank you, told him that I was honored. It doesn't get heavier than saying I'd like you to be the godfather of my son. But he's not ever going to put himself into a corny kind of situation with a pal. He's like, "Good, yeah, yeah." Boom. "Let's get back into the work."

LOOK, see this little carrot near the dip? Watch. I'll put it in my mouth as if it were a cigarette holder. Now I'm Raoul Duke. I spent so much time with Hunter Thompson, it just became second nature. As soon as I put anything resembling a cigarette holder in my mouth, he starts to come out. It's so natural and it's so strange. It sounds kind of ridiculous to even say it.

THE CHARACTERS are always there and, depending on the situation, not far from the surface. So they show up every now and again. It can't be good for you. It just can't. Then again, who knows?

I DON'T THINK anybody's necessarily ready for death. You can only hope that when it approaches, you feel like you've said what you wanted to say. Nobody wants to go out in mid-sentence.

I'M IN A VERY PRIVILEGED POSITION. And I'm certainly not going to bite the hand that feeds me. I like doing the work. But I'm not a great fan of all the stuff that goes along with it. I don't want to be a product. Of course you want the movies to do well. But I don't want to have to think about that stuff. I don't want to know who's hot now and who's not and who's making this much dough and who's boffing this woman or that one. I want to remain ignorant of all this. I want to be totally outside and far away from all of it.

I REMEMBER one time I had done some television interview, and they asked about my family life and kids. I talked about how I'm a proud father and how much I love my kids and how they're fun and what we do and how it's great. I was thinking that if in twenty-five, thirty years my kids watch old footage, I'd be proud for them to see their dad saying how much he loves them. Well, the show aired, and I get a phone call. "What the fuck are you doing?" I said, "Marlon, what are you talking about?" He said, "That's none of their business!" I tried to say, "Marlon, listen, man, I only wanted my kids to . . ." And it was like he gave me this sort of once-over. "You don't do it, man. That's your world and it's nobody else's business. It's not anybody's entertainment." And he was right.

PEOPLE ARE SUPER-NICE in the street. If they want me to sign something, that's great; I don't mind that at all.

THERE'S NO LIMIT to the possibilities of what I could do to the paparazzi if I catch them photographing my children.

YOU DON'T GO THROUGH THE FRONT DOOR of hotels anymore, you go through the garage. Or you go through the kitchen of a restaurant. Some people want to think that's cool, that's exciting. But it'll definitely make you a little weird if you're constantly being stared at.

PART OF THE PROCESS THAT I'VE ALWAYS ENJOYED is being the observer. You know, just watching people and learning. At a certain point, the reversal took place. I was no longer the observer—I was being observed. That's obviously very dangerous because part of an actor's job is to observe.

MY DEFINITION OF FREEDOM is simplicity, really. Anonymity. I'm sure it will be a possibility someday again. Maybe when I get old. They get tired of you.

"DIDN'T YOU USE TO BE JOHNNY DEPP?" That will be the clincher.

Interviewed by Cal Fussman | Photograph by Marc Hom

BORN OWENSBORO, KENTUCKY—06.09.63

> TO DATE, DEPP HAS TEAMED UP FOR SEVEN FILMS WITH DIRECTOR TIM BURTON, INCLUDING *EDWARD SCISSORHANDS* (1990), *ED WOOD* (1994) AND *CHARLIE AND THE CHOCOLATE FACTORY* (2005).

Marriage

> **THE LESS JEWELRY,** the better the marriage.
—HEATHER LOCKLEAR

> **GETTING MARRIED** probably stunted my growth.
—LORETTA LYNN

> **FIRST TIME** I laid eyes on my wife, what went through my mind was "That could be my woman." It was in the Fox Hills Mall in L.A., 1989. August 5. I was an unknown member of N.W.A. then. Am I happy I met her before I became known? Hell, yeah. I know a lot of famous dudes who are bachelors, and they're miserable. The parties get old. They don't know who to trust. They think they've got somebody, and after a few months, the real person comes out. It's just a mess. To be with somebody who supports me 100 percent, is good to my kids, keeps herself up, keeps the house up—she's the perfect mate. And she can handle things when I'm out of town—never falls apart. She's tough. All those qualities . . . Man, I'm lucky. —ICE CUBE

> **I'VE BEEN MARRIED** twice. Most women would rather not be married to a traveling blues singer.
—B.B. KING (PICTURED, ABOVE LEFT)

Pain

> **NOTHING** can make you more humble than pain.
—LARRY FLYNT

> **IF YOU DON'T KNOW** about pain and trouble, you're in sad shape. They make you appreciate life.
—EVEL KNIEVEL

> **PAIN** is a state of mind. —CONRAD DOBLER

> **I NEVER THINK ABOUT** the fire. I don't have nightmares about it. I only think about it when somebody like you asks a question. Today, we all know what to do in a fire. There was no education back then. They used to have fire drills in school that taught you nothing. I made the classic mistake. I was in a room in Boston's Copley Plaza when I smelled smoke. I opened the door and the flames swept in. The fire shot up my legs. The pain was seething, yet I can remember standing in the middle of this room, surrounded by flames, thinking, "What a way to die." I got to one window, and it wouldn't open. Somehow I got to another window and climbed outside. I was kneeling on a tiny ledge barely big enough to put one foot on. I'm three stories up. If I jump, I'm dead. Flames were shooting out of the window, and I just crouched there, hanging on to the windowsill, with my fingers cupped and my right hand and arm in the fire. The heat and flames burned off my pajamas and peeled away my skin. My legs had been burned to the arteries, and my arm was charring. I hung out the window by my right arm for a long time. How long? Forever. Finally, a hook and ladder came and a fireman climbed up, cradled me in his arms, and carried me to the ground. They say that people can't remember pain. Well, I felt nothing right after—the nerves were gone. But in order to cover the wounds, they needed to take skin off the rest of my body. Having to strip half of your body of skin and use it to cover the rest of your body is very painful. I can remember that pain. I remember it like yesterday.
—SUMNER REDSTONE

Family

> **CHILDREN CAN AGE AN ADULT** faster than ten years in prison. Parents can have the same effect on children. —DAVID BROWN

> **MY FATHER** didn't raise his voice. I didn't get disciplined in the traditional sense, and a lot of times I wish I had. I wished he'd just yell and get it over with, like the other kids' parents. But it was this kind of stern, serious look into your eyes, and this "Do you realize what you've done?" With me, it had to do with not wanting to disappoint. And there's a lot more power to that than, you know, the Archie Bunker way of discipline.
—LUCINDA WILLIAMS

> **WHEN I WAS ABOUT** to become a father, my friend Burgess Meredith said, "You're gonna find something wonderful—someone you love more than yourself." For self-centered people, it's a great blessing. —PETER BOYLE

> **THERE'S A BIT** of my dad in me, and there's a bit of me in my son. It's occasionally maddening to see your children doing the things that you did that were stupid. I say, "God, why doesn't he learn?" But then, why hadn't I learned? —GEORGE MARTIN

> **I NEVER SAW MY DAD** cry. My son saw me cry. My dad never told me he loved me, and consequently I told Scott I loved him every other minute. The point is, I'll make less mistakes than my dad, my sons hopefully will make less mistakes than me, and their sons will make less mistakes than their dads. And one of these days, maybe we'll raise a perfect Caan. —JAMES CAAN

> **I DON'T EXPECT** the human race to progress in too many areas. However, having a child with an ear infection makes one hugely grateful for antibiotics. —DAVID BOWIE (PICTURED, ABOVE CENTER)

> **THE LAST TIME MY MOTHER** was upset with me was when she saw me talking with my children and opening my mail at the same time. She despised multitasking. She believed it was a way to miss life, to miss the gifts that come only when you give 100 percent of yourself to a moment. —ARIANNA HUFFINGTON

> **JUST BEFORE KATRINA**, my daughter had been to a birthday party and gotten this fish. She wanted to take it with her during the evacuation, and I told her I didn't think she could get it on the plane. So she asked me to take care of it. She said, "I want to see my fish the next time I see you." So here I am in the middle of this crisis—no air-conditioning, the hotel room's 110 degrees, the water in the tank is practically bubbling—and I have to take care of this fish. Every night I'd come back to my room totally exhausted to get my two hours of sleep, and I'd feed this fish. It was a huge connection, and I was really concerned that this fish was gonna die. Incredibly, somehow it survived. I was setting off to see my family for the first time two weeks later, and, as I got to the helicopter, I realized I forgot the fish. So I held up the helicopter and got the damn fish. I took it to my daughter, and it's still alive today. —C. RAY NAGIN

Love & Sex

> **LOVE IS NOT ENOUGH** to save a relationship. —GARRY SHANDLING

> **IF I COULD FIND A WAY** to have sex with myself that was as exciting as it is with a lady, I'd live in a white tower and never come out. —ROD STEIGER

> **WOMEN AND TIGERS** are exactly alike. They have the same temperament, emotions, and vulnerabilities. They must be spoken to softly—but it doesn't hurt to carry a big stick just in case. —ROY (OF SIEGFRIED AND ROY)

> **SEX** is the driving force on the planet. We should embrace it, not see it as the enemy. —HUGH HEFNER

> **YOU SHALL NOT COVET** thy neighbor's wife? Well, how about if she goddamn covets *me*? What do you think about that? —GENE SIMMONS

> **YOU'RE DOWN BY FIVE** with thirty seconds left in the game. This is going to be amazing. You're screaming at the top of your lungs. The quarterback sends a long, smooth pass to the end zone. Your star receiver's open; the ball is sailing straight toward him; he waits in the end zone for his moment of glory. The ball's flight is interrupted as it grazes his fingertips and falls to the ground. He's missed it. You stop screaming. You feign being a good sport, but deep down, you're disappointed. No matter how loud, how convincingly you cheered, you didn't get yours. This is exactly what faking an orgasm feels like. —NATALIE KRINSKY, YALE UNIVERSITY SEX COLUMNIST

> **SOMETIMES,** sex gets in the way of a relationship. —PAMELA ANDERSON (PICTURED, ABOVE RIGHT)

Snoop Dogg { RAPPER—LOS ANGELES }

▶ **MY MOMMA** gave me the name. I used to love *Peanuts* and Charlie Brown—Snoopy was my favorite cartoon character growing up. I watched so much, I started to look like him.

A LOT OF PEOPLE like to fool you and say that you're not smart if you never went to college, but common sense rules over everything. That's what I learned from selling crack.

LOVE GOES UNAPPRECIATED a lot of times, but you still gotta keep giving it.

THE FIRST TIME I got high off marijuana was in the seventies, with one of my uncles. They had these little roaches on the table—these part-way-smoked marijuana cigarettes—and there was some Schlitz Malt Liquor Bull. I went in there and sipped the Schlitz, and my uncle asked me did I wanna hit that roach. And I was like, "Yeah." He put it on the roach clip for me and lit it up, and I hit that motherfucker. I was about eight or nine years old.

WEED: It makes me feel the way I need to feel.

IN JAIL, you're either gonna be the toughest motherfucker or you gonna be the softest motherfucker or you gotta find some other shit to be.

I WENT TO AN ELEMENTARY SCHOOL that was basically a white elementary school, but they accepted you if you were a black, gifted athlete from the inner city. They had gymnastics, they had swimming, they had track and field, they had music classes—they had all this shit we wasn't getting in the 'hood. It opened my mind up. It showed me how to interact with white people. When I started making music, it wasn't a surprise to me that white people loved my music as much as black people. I knew how to relate.

ALL YOU NEED is a kick start from somebody who can stamp your shit.

YOU CAN'T BLAME a nigga for getting paid.

FAME is a dirty game.

IT'S HARD TO SAY GOODBYE to the streets. It's all how you do it. You can pass by and say, "What's happening?" and keep it moving, but it's a certain element that'll never be able to roll with you once you get to this level, because that's the separation of it all.

TO ME, jealousy is a form of flattery. When you jealous of me, that means you love me for what I do.

IN THE BLACK CULTURE, certain kids are given nicknames that they roll with forever; the nicknames outweigh their real names. I'm one of those scenarios.

FATHERHOOD is more than a job; it's more than a responsibility. It's a lifestyle. You gotta be prepared to live it.

YOU HAVE TO COACH each kid differently. My younger son, Cordell, a.k.a. Lil Snoop, loves me like a fan loves Snoop Dogg. He's inspired by making me happy. My older son, Corde, a.k.a. Spank, does everything I say, with effort and determination—but he does it for himself. He gets his thrill out of seeing his own results on the football field. He's gonna be able to play for any high school he wants.

SPANK WAS REALLY my first love—not that I didn't love my wife, but when he was born, it was like my first love was him. I never knew about those kinda feelings and shit before.

YOU DON'T EVER hear about me doing a half-assed performance or coming halfway. I always go full speed.

I HATE LOSING. I'm a sore loser. When I was a kid, I used to cry when I lost. I cried like a baby—for real. Niggas used to pick on me behind that.

AS A BLACK MAN, you definitely have to be cocky, but not conceited. You got to have that kind of swagger, 'cause there's so much against you, and there's so many people that's just as good as you, if not better than you. You gotta push a little harder to make yourself shine.

BARACK OBAMA makes me feel good to be a black man. Just seeing him up there representin' intelligently and really knowing what he talking about and defending his shit even when they try and shoot at him. The old president and baby girl—Bill and Hill—they tried to double-wop on him—*boo bop*. But he have enough game to get out of that.

I KNEW the job was dangerous when I took it.

I USED TO HAVE A FLATTOP. I had a bald head. I had a lot of different hairstyles. Then James Brown told me one day, he said, "Don't ever cut your hair, 'cause your hair is your strength." For a while now, I've been lettin' it grow. It's just me.

I PERFORMED at a bar mitzvah. And I'm telling you, man, these little motherfuckers, they were singing my shit, they was cussin', they were singing the dirty version. I'm talking about twelve- and thirteen-year-old little white kids singin' this real gangsta shit. Man. I was shocked. I just gave them the mic and let them motherfuckers go.

IT MIGHT LOOK EASY, but it ain't.

Interviewed by Mike Sager | Photograph by Chris Buck

BORN LONG BEACH, CALIFORNIA—10.20.72

> HIS FIRST RECORD, *DOGGYSTYLE*, WAS RELEASED WHEN HE WENT BY THE NAME SNOOP DOGGY DOGG. HE SHORTENED IT TO THE MORE-DIGNIFIED SNOOP DOGG IN 1998 WHEN HE LEFT DEATH ROW RECORDS, WHICH HE HAD HELPED CREATE.

> HIS REALITY SHOW, *SNOOP DOGG'S FATHER HOOD*, BEGAN AIRING ON THE E! CHANNEL IN 2007.

Faye Dunaway { ACTOR—WEST HOLLYWOOD }

> **I'M A BIT HIGH MAINTENANCE,** but it gets your attention. A little hot and cold never hurts.

I REGRET SO MUCH. I've made mistakes. I've hurt people. I've done things I'm not proud of. But on the other hand, that way lies madness, you know?

THE IMPULSE toward perfection is more important than perfection itself.

IT DOESN'T REALLY MATTER what other people think.

GREAT ARTISTS never know if they're making the right choice.

I'M A NEW CATHOLIC. I love the church; I love Mass. I go every morning at six thirty. When I'm on the right track spiritually and emotionally, things happen in my life. It's mysterious.

HOLLYWOOD is a hard town to survive.

THE THING I LOVE MOST about men is their sweetness. They're so cute.

ONCE YOU REACH a certain age, you realize that men aren't as important as you once thought they were.

IT'S AWFULLY HARD to make marriage work. I've tried twice and I don't know how. To have to think of somebody else so much of the time—it's such a compromise.

THE MINUTE you start believing your own success, you're on the road to ruin.

FEAR is a pair of handcuffs on your soul.

THE WHOLE ERA when I was busy being a big movie star was terribly disconcerting. I was cared for and cosseted, and yet I was totally dependent. I didn't know where the cornflakes were kept. I didn't know how to turn on my own washing machine. That might sound very chic, but, I'm telling you, when you don't know how your own life works, you get disconnected.

IF YOU want something done correctly, do it yourself.

PEOPLE SELL the common man short. Among most people, there is a real impulse toward decency, love, affection, and kindness.

WHEN SOMEONE IS SUCCESSFUL, there's always a feeling that they were lucky. Luck plays a part, sure, but to be successful, you must have iron discipline. You must have energy and hunger and desire and honesty.

TIME is enemy number one. Beat time, I say. Kick it!

WITHOUT MONEY, there is no freedom. Without money, there is no art. Say what you want, but it's true: when you walk in the door with the money in your hand, people start listening.

THE STAGE MIGHT BE the only place I really feel at home. I like the greasepaint, the lights, the romance of it all. I like going backstage. I like the ensemble: it's the family that you've always wanted to have; it's like a perfect love, a relationship that is always growing and changing and deepening.

BONNIE PARKER was the first role, the one that was closest to me in many ways. She was just this small-town southern girl, coming out of nowhere, hungry, and wanting to get ahead, wanting to do something meaningful, wanting to succeed. She had a kind of poetry in her soul. She's a part of me to this day.

THE LENS IS MAGIC. You can love it. It can love you. It captures your innermost feelings and secrets.

ART SHOULD predict life.

SEX is emotional. It's connection; it's intimate. It's looking into somebody's soul. It's naked in every sense of the word. It's the hardest thing in the world.

YOU CAN'T TAKE RESPONSIBILITY for everything. You can't have that kind of control. At some point, it's all out of our hands.

Interviewed by Mike Sager | Photograph by Nigel Parry

BORN BASCOM, FLORIDA—01.14.41

> THE DAUGHTER OF A CAREER ARMY OFFICER, DUNAWAY ATTENDED SCHOOLS IN TEXAS, ARKANSAS, UTAH, AND GERMANY BEFORE STUDYING THEATER AT THE UNIVERSITY OF FLORIDA ON A FULBRIGHT SCHOLARSHIP.

> FAME CAME TO DUNAWAY WHEN SHE COSTARRED OPPOSITE WARREN BEATTY IN *BONNIE AND CLYDE* (1967) AND APPEARED IN ROMAN POLANSKI'S *CHINATOWN* (1974), EARNING BEST ACTRESS NOMINATIONS FOR BOTH.

Clint Eastwood { ACTOR, DIRECTOR—LOS ANGELES }

> **IN THE FIRST PLACE,** I was taller than most kids in my classes. In the second, we were always moving. Redding. Sacramento. Pacific Palisades. Back to Redding. Back to Sacramento. Over to Hayward. Niles. Oakland. So we were constantly on the road, and I was always the new guy in school. The bullies always thought, "Here's this big gangly guy. We gotta take him on." You know how kids are. We gotta test him. I was a shy kid. But a lot of my childhood was spent punching the bullies out.

I KIND OF had a feeling "Make my day" would resonate, based upon "Do you feel lucky, punk?" in the first movie. I thought that Smith & Wesson line might hang in there, too. But "Make my day" was just so simple. I still get it a lot.

AS YOU GET OLDER, you're not afraid of doubt. Doubt isn't running the show. You take out all the self-agonizing.

WHAT CAN THEY DO to you after you get into your seventies?

EVEN IN GRAMMAR SCHOOL they taught you to go with your first impression. It's like multiple-choice questions. If you go back and start dwelling, you'll talk yourself out of it and make the wrong pick. That's just a theory. I've never seen any studies on it. But I believe it.

AS JERRY FIELDING USED TO SAY, "We've come this far, let's not ruin it by thinking."

MY FATHER had a couple of kids at the beginning of the Depression. There was not much employment. Not much welfare. People barely got by. People were tougher then.

WE LIVE in more of a pussy generation now, where everybody's become used to saying, "Well, how do we handle it psychologically?" In those days, you just punched the bully back and duked it out. Even if the guy was older and could push you around, at least you were respected for fighting back, and you'd be left alone from then on.

THE BAND GUYS were looked down upon when I was a kid. I remember playing the flügelhorn, and everybody said, "What the . . .?"

I DON'T KNOW if I can tell you exactly when the pussy generation started. Maybe when people started asking about the meaning of life.

IF I'D HAD good discipline, I might have gone into music.

YOU WONDER sometimes, "What will we do if something really big happens?" Look how fast—seven years—people have been able to forget 9/11. Maybe you remember if you lost a relative or a loved one. But the public can get pretty blasé about stuff like that. Nobody got blasé about Pearl Harbor.

I REMEMBER BUYING a very old hotel in Carmel. I went into an upper attic room and saw that all the windows were painted black. "What was going on here?" I asked the prior owners. They said they thought the Japanese were off the coast during the war.

THE KOREAN WAR was only a few years after World War II. We all went. But you couldn't help but think, "Shit. What the hell? What have we gained?" One minute you're unleashing the tremendous power of nuclear fission, and then, a few years later, you're jockeying back and forth on the thirty-eighth parallel. It seemed so futile.

IN *CHANGELING*, I tried to show something you'd never see nowadays—a kid sitting and looking at the radio. Just sitting in front of the radio and listening. Your mind does the rest.

I REMEMBER going to a huge waterfall on a glacier in Iceland. People were there on a rock-platform overlook to see it. They had their kids. There was a place that wasn't sealed off, but it had a cable that stopped anybody from going past a certain point. I said to myself, "You know, in the States they'd have that hurricane-fenced off," because they're afraid somebody's gonna fall and some lawyer's going to appear. There, the mentality was like it was in America in the old days: if you fall, you're stupid.

YOU CAN'T STOP EVERYTHING from happening. But we've gotten to a point where we're certainly trying. If a car doesn't have four hundred air bags in it, then it's no good.

MY FATHER DIED very suddenly at sixty-three. Just dropped dead. For a long time afterward, I'd ask myself, "Why didn't I ask him to play golf more? Why didn't I spend more time with him?" But when you're off trying to get the brass ring, you forget and overlook those little things. It gives you a certain amount of regret later on, but there's nothing you can do about it. So you just forge on.

>>

BORN SAN FRANCISCO, CALIFORNIA—
05.31.30

> EASTWOOD WAS ELECTED MAYOR OF CARMEL-BY-THE-SEA, CALIFORNIA, IN 1986 AND SERVED A TWO-YEAR TERM.

> HE SPENT TWO YEARS IN THE U.S. ARMY AS A SWIMMING INSTRUCTOR AFTER BEING DRAFTED INTO THE KOREAN WAR IN 1951.

> HE IS A TEN-TIME OSCAR-NOMINATED DIRECTOR/ACTOR/PRODUCER, WITH FOUR WINS: BEST DIRECTOR AND BEST PICTURE FOR *UNFORGIVEN* (1992), AND BEST DIRECTOR AND BEST PICTURE FOR *MILLION DOLLAR BABY* (2004).

> HE HAS SEVEN CHILDREN, AGES 11 TO 44.

> EASTWOOD'S FAMOUS LINE FROM *DIRTY HARRY* IS OFTEN MISQUOTED AS, "DO YOU FEEL LUCKY?" IN FACT, HE SAID, "YOU'VE GOT TO ASK YOURSELF ONE QUESTION: DO I FEEL LUCKY? WELL, DO YA, PUNK?"

SMALLER DETAILS are less important. Let's get on with the important stuff.

I'VE GOT A GOOD CREW that is very familiar with me. I don't have to say a lot to 'em. We just set up the shot, and I depend on everybody to do their parts. I just say, "OK . . ."

WHAT HAPPENED IS I was going to college in 1950. L.A. City College. A guy I knew was going to an acting class on Thursday nights. He started telling me about all the good-lookin' chicks and said, "Why don't you go with me?" So I probably had some motivation beyond thoughts of being an actor. And sure enough, he was right. There were a lot of girls and not many guys. I said, "Yeah, they need me here." I wound up at Universal as a contract player.

PEOPLE LOVE WESTERNS worldwide. There's something fantasylike about an individual fighting the elements. Or even bad guys and the elements. It's a simpler time. There's no organized laws and stuff.

THE LAST ONE I DID was in '92. *Unforgiven*. That was a wonderful script. But it seemed like it was the end of the road for me with the genre, because it sort of summarized everything I felt about the western at that particular time.

I HAD AN ISSUE before the council. I remember getting up, and there was a lady who sat and knitted the whole time, never looked up. "No, no, no," she said. And I thought, "This can't be. When you're elected, you have to at least pretend like you're interested in what people are there for. How do you have the chutzpah to just sit there, not pay attention, not interact at all?" It needed to be corrected.

WINNING THE ELECTION is a good-news/bad-news kind of thing. OK, now you're the mayor. The bad news is, now you're the mayor.

IT'S MAKING SURE that the words "public servant" are not forgotten. That's why I did it. 'Cause I thought, "I don't need this." The fact that I didn't need it made me think I could do more. It's the people who need it that I'm suspect of.

BARACK OBAMA was unimaginable back when I was a kid. Count Basie and a lot of big bands would come through Seattle when I was young. They could play at a club, but they couldn't frequent the place.

WHEN YOU LISTEN TO RAY CHARLES, there's never any doubt whose voice that is.

YOU SHOULD really get to know somebody, really be a friend. I mean, my wife is my closest friend. Sure, I'm attracted to her in every way possible, but that's not the answer— because I've been attracted to other people and I couldn't stand 'em after a while.

I'M PAST DOING one chin-up more than I did the day before. I just kind of do what I feel like.

Smaller details are less important.
Let's get on with the important stuff.

Smaller details are less important.
Let's get on with the important stuff.

I HAVE CHILDREN by other women. I gotta give Dina the credit for bringing everyone together. She never had the ego thing of the second wife. The natural instinct might have been to kill off everybody else. You know, the cavewoman mentality. But she brought everybody together. She's friendly with my first wife, friendly to former girlfriends. She went out of her way to unite everybody. She's been extremely influential in my life.

I'M NOT ONE OF THOSE GUYS who's been terribly active in organized religion. But I don't disrespect it. I'd never try to impose any doubts that I might have on anyone else.

A GOOD JOKE is a good joke whenever. But my kids make me laugh now.

CHILDREN TEACH YOU that you can still be humbled by life, that you learn something new all the time. That's the secret to life, really—never stop learning. It's the secret to career. I'm still working because I learn something new all the time. It's the secret to relationships. Never think you've got it all.

AS YOU GET OLDER, you like kids a lot more.

THE INNOCENCE OF CHILDHOOD is like the innocence of a lot of animals.

KIDS PIERCING THEMSELVES, piercing their tongues—what kind of masochism is that? Is it to show you can just take it?

NO, I DON'T HAVE TO practice that grunt. You just do it. Once you're in character, you're in character. You don't sit there purposely thinking, "Well, I'll grunt here, or I'll groan there."

THAT'S WHY I don't rehearse a lot and why I shoot a lot immediately. I have ideas of where I'd like to take the character, but we both end up going together.

WE WERE DOING *In the Line of Fire*, and John Malkovich was on top of the building, and he has me in a real precarious situation. My character is crazed, and he pulls out a gun and sticks it into John's face, and John puts his mouth over the end of the gun. Now, I don't know what kind of crazy symbol that was. We certainly didn't rehearse anything like that. I'm sure he didn't think about it while we were practicing it. It was just there. Like Sir Edmund Hillary talking about why you do anything: because it's there. That's why you climb Everest. It's like a little moment in time, and as fast as it comes into your brain, you just throw it out and discard it. Do it before you discard it, you know?

IT KEEPS COMING BACK to "We've come this far, let's not ruin it by thinking."

YOU LOOK AT VELÁZQUEZ in his dark years and you wonder, "How the hell did he get that way?" I'm sure he didn't say to himself, "I'm in my dark period right now, so I'm going to paint this way." He just did it. That's when real art gets a chance to come into play.

MILLION DOLLAR BABY won the Academy Award. That was nice, that was great. But you don't dwell on it. An awful lot of good pictures haven't won Academy Awards, so it doesn't have much bearing. *Letters from Iwo Jima* was nominated for an Academy Award. We didn't win it, but that picture was still as good as I could do it. Did it deserve it less than some other picture? No, not really. But there are other aspects that come into it. In the end, you've just got to be happy with what you've done. There you are.

Interviewed by Cal Fussman | Photograph by Nigel Parry

MGW
TARE
NET
CU.CAP.

24.000 KG
52.910 LBS
2.290
5.05
21.71
47.8
3
1.1

Eminem { RAPPER—DETROIT }

> **DON'T CALL** it a comeback.

PEOPLE CAN TRY to reinvent themselves. I don't think you can really change who you are, though, because who you are is pretty much where you came from and what you've done up to now. You can change your image and all that—you can change your fucking clothes, your underwear, your hair color, all that shit—but it's not going to mean you're a brand-new person.

YOU WANT TO SAY, "I don't give a fuck what anybody says." Yeah, you do.

I'M SURE PEOPLE think I've vanished off the face of the earth.

I WENT FOR NINE, ten years straight, without taking a break at all. I needed to rejuvenate.

I'M A T-SHIRT GUY now. But wifebeaters won't go out of style, not as long as bitches keep mouthing off.

I LIKE IT when people talk shit—because if people weren't talking shit, there would be nothing for me to come back with. I need that. If I don't have any ammo, what am I going to say?

THERE'S OBVIOUSLY a limit to the things you want people to know, but I've pretty much put most of it out there. Maybe people don't know what kind of underwear I wear, what color.

BOXERS. Pink.

IT'S FUN to take a step back and hear other people do it, say shit I wish I would have thought of. I'm still a fan of rap.

WHEN PEOPLE BUY a CD, you don't get to sit in the car with them and watch their faces and watch their jaws drop.

THE GUY behind the counter notices me, but I haven't put an album out in four years. "How you doing Marshall?" "What's up Em?" You pay for the gas, buy a bag of chips, and leave. But I put a record out, and that same person is going to be behind the counter with a camera and a piece of paper. "Can you sign this?"

IT'S NOT LIKE I'M GOING to be a prick to everybody I meet. I keep it cool.

YOU'RE NOT going to say anything about me that I'm not going to say about myself. There's so many things that I think about myself; if someone really wanted to get at me, they could say this and this and this. So I'm going to say it before they can. It's the best policy for me.

TRUST IS HARD to come by. That's why my circle is small and tight. I'm kind of funny about making new friends.

I DON'T KNOW WHERE to go to meet a nice girl. If you've got any tips, clue me in.

THE EMOTIONS in a song—the anger, aggression—have got to be legitimate.

WHEN I'M IN THE STUDIO with Dre, I don't have to worry about the beat. I can just go. That's the only thing I got to concentrate on. When I'm trying to produce a song myself, I'm thinking about the high hat. Is it loud enough? The snare drum. Is it clear enough? This piano in the chorus. Is it too loud? That can be time consuming.

WITHIN THE LAST YEAR, I started learning how to not be so angry about things, learning how to count my fucking blessings instead. By doing that, I've become a happier person, instead of all this self-loathing I was doing for a while.

THE MUSIC, I wouldn't say it's gotten happier, but it's definitely more upbeat. I feel like myself again.

DON'T get me wrong, the aggression will still be there.

I DON'T KNOW if I've fully accepted Proof's death, but I think I've come to terms with it a little bit, knowing how to cope. There was a good two years that I was pretty down in the fucking dumps. I just lay in bed and stared at the fucking ceiling. One day, I didn't get up until seven-thirty that night.

NOT THAT I DON'T guide them at all, because sometimes I do, right from wrong. Hailie's twelve now, and she still thinks it's really bad to stick up your middle finger. I think I'm doing pretty good, with what my music is about and being able to raise little girls at the same time.

I WOULD SAY I'm an excellent dad, not to toot my own horn. *Toot.*

IF YOU DON'T OVERLOOK the fact of what you look like, then no one else will. I had a complex back then: if I get booed off stage, it's probably because I'm white. There comes a time when you gotta stop thinking like that and just be you.

I WANT TO SAY I'd be a comic-book artist. That was my dream as a kid. I used to paint and draw. If I wouldn't have had rap, I would have strived to—the past tense of *strive*, is it *stroved*?—I would have *stroven* to do something like that. Who knows? Maybe I would have.

NOBODY LIKES TO FAIL. I want to succeed in everything I do, which isn't much. But the things that I'm really passionate about, if I fail at those, if I'm not successful, what do I have?

SHIT HAPPENS. Fucking happens to the best of us. Really does.

Interviewed by Brian Mockenhaupt | Photograph by Karin Catt

BORN KANSAS CITY, MISSOURI—10.17.73

> EMINEM'S *MARSHALL MATHERS LP* (2000) SOLD 1.76 MILLION COPIES IN ITS FIRST WEEK. TO DATE, IT IS THE FASTEST-SELLING HIP-HOP AND SOLO ALBUM OF ALL TIME.

> HE IS RAISING HIS THREE DAUGHTERS—TWO ADOPTED AND ONE OF HIS OWN— LARGELY BY HIMSELF. THEY LIVE IN MICHIGAN.

Michael J. Fox { ACTOR—NEW YORK CITY }

> **RIGHT NOW,** I'm feeling pretty good. It's just one little thing in my brain.

IF I LET IT AFFECT EVERYTHING, it's gonna own everything. I don't deny it or pretend it's not there, but if I don't allow it to be bigger than it is, then I can do everything else.

MY BODY is an isometric exercise, because I'm always putting pressure against things. Whatever I'm doing at any given time, I'm also doing something else—I've always got this thing going on.

THE THING I MISS MOST is spontaneity—just kind of saying, "Fuck it, let's go to Vegas." I can't really do that.

I GOT a '67 Mustang, but I'm not driving it much. My wife gave it to me for my thirty-fifth birthday, so I've had it for eleven years, but even when she gave it to me, it came with vintage plates, which was kinda distressing—a car that's six years younger than me is a registered antique.

THERE WAS THIS IMAGE of me as this kind of cute 'n' cuddly guy, which, in as far as it got me laid, I didn't mind it too much. It made me party harder.

PEOPLE SAID, "Does it bother you that girls want to sleep with you because you're famous?" That's a tough one. Lemme think about that. *No.*

I KNEW I HAD SOMETHING MORE going on than just being cute. What was tough about that for me was growing up playing hockey, coming from Canada, leaving at eighteen, all that stuff. I was a beer drinker and a chain-smoker, and I'd been in my share of scraps when I was a kid. So I kinda saw myself as a little bit of a hard guy, you know?

I CAN'T ALWAYS CONTROL my body the way I want to, and I can't control when I feel good or when I don't. I can control how clear my mind is. And I *can* control how willing I am to step up if somebody needs me.

THAT'S ONE OF THE THINGS the illness has given me: it's a degree of death. There's a certain amount of loss, and whenever you have a loss, it's a step toward death. So if you can accept loss, you can accept the fact that there's gonna be the big loss. Once you can accept that, you can accept anything. So then I think, "Well, given that that's the case, let's tip myself a break. Let's tip everybody a break."

MY HAPPINESS grows in direct proportion to my acceptance and in inverse proportion to my expectations.

ACCEPTANCE is the key to everything.

WHICH ISN'T TO SAY that I'm resigned to it or that I've given up on it or that I don't think I have any effect on the outcome of it. It's just that, as a reality, I get it.

WHO GIVES a shit how it looks? It doesn't matter. I look like what I look like.

IF YOU DON'T HAVE someone calling you on your shit, you're lost.

I CAN'T BE SMUG, because I know that you can lose anything at any point. And I can't be angry, because I haven't lost it.

MY WHOLE LIFE, meeting people is like a blind date, because I feel like they've already seen the video on me.

I SAY TO MY SON, "My tattoo is that I don't have a tattoo." I just about got a tattoo when my dad passed away because he had one, a horse's head surrounded by a horseshoe with roses—he was a jockey before he went into the military. So when he passed away, I just about went downtown and got a tattoo of a horse with roses. I'm glad I didn't—because I was drunk outta my ass.

DISCIPLINE is just doing the same thing the right way whether anyone's watching or not.

I WAS NEVER big on lunch boxes and all that stuff, and I look at it now and think, "God, how much money I turned down." Oh, fuck, I'd do it in a heartbeat now.

I REALIZED VERY QUICKLY that I had no idea what the hell was good for me to do. You have no idea. The things you do—you do some things for money, you do some things for free. It's a very difficult place to be. But on the other hand, it's so much fun. You realize, "There's no way I should be allowed to do it, and I'm gonna watch everybody let me do it—and I can get a giggle out of how it's killing them."

I MAKE NO BONES about the fact that I stopped drinking. That was the key to everything. Until I did that, I just couldn't have the clarity.

>>

BORN EDMONTON, ALBERTA, CANADA—06.09.61

> FOX WON THREE EMMY AWARDS AND A GOLDEN GLOBE DURING THE SEVEN YEARS HE PLAYED ALEX P. KEATON ON *FAMILY TIES*. HIS FILM HIGHLIGHTS INCLUDE THE *BACK TO THE FUTURE* TRILOGY (1985, 1989, 1990), *BRIGHT LIGHTS, BIG CITY* (1988), *LIGHT OF DAY* (1987), *TEEN WOLF* (1985), AND *CASUALTIES OF WAR* (1989).

> FOX WAS DIAGNOSED WITH PARKINSON'S DISEASE IN 1991.

> AFTER FOX FILMED A SERIES OF TV ADS ENDORSING DEMOCRATIC CANDIDATES IN THE 2006 CONGRESSIONAL ELECTION, RUSH LIMBAUGH SAID OF FOX'S VISIBLE SHAKINESS, "EITHER HE'S OFF HIS MEDICATION OR HE'S ACTING."

> FOX CONTINUES TO ACT AND IN 2006 WAS NOMINATED FOR AN EMMY FOR HIS GUEST APPEARANCE ON *BOSTON LEGAL*.

I HAD TO CHOOSE not to party anymore. I could've chosen to continue doing that, but that would've been destructive. Who wants to be a cliché?

I'M DRIVING the Ferrari down Ventura Boulevard ninety miles an hour and the cop goes, "*Mike!* C'mon, take it easy. You're gonna hurt somebody." I remember sitting there after the cop walked away, going, "This is just seriously fucked up. This is really crazy." It's one of those moments when you realize that the only thing that's ever going to stop me from doing whatever I want to do is me—and I don't want the job.

NO MATTER HOW MUCH MONEY you have, you can lose it.

NO MATTER HOW MUCH FAME you have, it's not something that belongs to you. If I'm famous, that doesn't belong to me—that belongs to you. If you can't remember who I am, I'm no longer famous.

I SEE *Us* magazine and *People* magazine and all these tabloids—they have the same story over and over again. It's the same every week, and I get all kind of smug about it, and I think, "Come on, really? You care about this shit?" But then cut to me going, "Get outta the corner! Get the fuckin' puck up! What the fuck are ya doing?" It's tough to stay off the subject of the fact that we're all gonna die. We all need our subject changers. That's what it all comes down to.

THE THING WITH LIMBAUGH was so interesting. I didn't even have to say anything. People said to me, "Don't ya hate the guy?" I was like, "I can't get it up to hate the guy." I know it's a racket, I know it's a job—it's show business, and that's fine. Let's take it as show business.

PEOPLE WANTED ME to rip him apart. The truth is, Limbaugh is ripping himself apart well enough for all of us.

SIX MONTHS in the jungle with Sean Penn is tricky, but he's a real talented guy. I sent him a note at the end of it saying, "I can't say that it was a pleasure, but it was a privilege."

I HAVE THIS BOSE SIRIUS RADIO, and I put it on Classic Vinyl and get my guitar and just play along with it—it's all twelve-bar blues—and for hours I just do that.

I'm not in the widget business anymore. I have no widgets to sell.

I HAD LUNCH WITH SEAN when I was trying to decide whether to go back and do *Spin City*. I said, "I just want to pick your brain." He's a brilliant guy and a great artist and an honest fella in a great way. I said, "I'm trying to figure out whether to go back and do this TV show," and he gets this smile on his face and he goes, "Well, it is the most successful part of your gift." Brilliant. What I love is that I could hear that and laugh my ass off and say, "Fuck you"—but I so appreciate people that think on that level.

I ALWAYS WANTED to do a short film about Petomane, the flatulist. Petomane was the guy who could do the "1812 Overture" out of his ass.

WHEN I SEE PICTURES of Lindsay Lohan in the car or Paris Hilton—the level of glee and the level of viciousness—wow. We've got a *war* goin' on. We've got people *dying*. And we're all up in arms about this girl.

I HAVE SUCH EMPATHY for all these young women. I was there, and I did all that crap. We'd rip it up, y'know? And we never got busted on any of that stuff.

"SHE DESERVES IT," and "Who does she think she is?" *Who does she think she is?* She doesn't think—she doesn't know what she had for breakfast this morning. Who gives a shit? Relax, everybody. Calm down.

WHATEVER TERRIBLE THING IS GOING ON, it's going on until you find out that it's not. So get to that part as quickly as possible.

I DON'T KNOW of anyone that's had a perfect run.

I'M AN AMERICAN CITIZEN since '99. I'm happy because I get to vote. There's a lot of years that I paid for a lot of stuff that I didn't like; I like having a say in it.

I'M NOT LOOKING AT POLLING; I don't have to play any of these games; I don't have to worry about whether I'm on-message or off-message. I'm just saying, "Hey, can we look at this for a second?"

I DON'T REALLY CONSIDER MYSELF a political animal. I try not to be grandiose about that. It's like the barn is burning down, and you've got the bucket of water. I don't know how I got this bucket of water; I don't remember going to get it; but it's in my hand, so I guess I've gotta throw it.

I HAVE TO THINK OF MYSELF as a regular human being.

Interviewed by Scott Raab | Photograph by Steve Pyke

Joe Frazier { CHAMPION—PHILADELPHIA }

> **I GREW UP IN BEAUFORT, SOUTH CAROLINA,** in a six-room farmhouse with a couple of leaning posts to keep it from fallin'. I came up in a time when men were men. They didn't wear no earrings.

WHEN I WAS BORN, people came to the house and gathered round to see if I was missin' an arm. See, my dad was missin' his left hand and part of his left forearm. And those people didn't realize that my dad's missin' arm didn't have nothing to do with genes. I never asked him what happened. Don't know what exactly. But the story I heard was that another man tried to kill him in an argument over a woman.

YOU COULD SAY that was the root of my left hook. When I was a boy, I used to pull a big cross saw with my dad. He'd use his right hand, so I'd have to use my left.

I GOT A BURLAP SACK, put a brick in the middle, and filled it with rags, corncobs, some Spanish moss, and sand. I hung that sack off the branch of an oak tree. I'd wrap my hands with a necktie of my daddy's and punch at it. My mom gave me an hour a day. My brothers and sisters said, "Nah." I said, "You'll see."

WHEN YOUR MOM DIES, that's you.

HAD MY OWN CAR at twelve years old. Left school in the tenth grade. Married when I was sixteen. Ain't hard to figure out; I was a man at a very young age.

I CAME UP in Martin Luther King's time, and it was really rough. Remember those boys wiped out in Mississippi? There was a problem with a black kid on the farm where my daddy and I worked, the Bellamy farm. The boy had screwed up one of the tractors without meaning to, and one of the Bellamy brothers took his belt off and beat the child in the field. I didn't think it was right. "Well, if you keep talkin', boy," the older Bellamy brother said, "I'm gonna take my belt to you." And I told him, "You better keep that belt on to hold your pants up." He didn't do nothin'. But I had to leave, get on the Dog, and head up north. Greyhound. If I stayed, there was nothin' ahead but bad times.

NOTHIN' WRONG WITH AN ASS WHUPPIN' every now and then. You take away the ass whuppin's, and what do you get? You get people wearin' pants below their belly buttons. I'm tellin' you, you go out these days and see the crack of a young lady's butt. It's crazy, man. They should be locked up for indecent exposure. Look here. See? Suspenders! *And* a belt! I ain't takin' no chances.

NOBODY KNOWS where the nose goes when the door's closed.

THERE ARE PLACES on a man's head that are as hard as a rock. Your head's actually stronger than your body. And you don't have too many instruments up there workin'. But you got a lot of tools workin' in that body: the liver, the kidneys, the heart, the lungs. You soften that up and see what happens. I lived by the body shot.

FRIDAYS AND SATURDAYS are holidays for black people.

ALI'S PROBLEM was that he knew I wasn't afraid. That's why he was always looking for those little things that would set me off. He did a damn good job of it, too. Called me ugly. Said I was ignorant. Said I was too small. Called me a gorilla. Ever see the poster promotin' the fight in Manila? Look at the drawings by LeRoy Neiman. Look at me on that poster and then look at *Planet of the Apes*. And you tell *me* what's goin' on.

I SAID SOME THINGS in the past, but the truth is I love to see the Butterfly these days. He says, "We're two *baaaaaad* brothers." But after all this time, there are some things I'll never understand. Why'd he say, "I am *thee* greatest"? You would never say, "That is thee picture." You'd say, "That is the picture." I am *thee* greatest. Every word he said about himself: "I am *thee*."

I WASN'T A BIG GUY. People thought the big guys would eat me up. But it was the other way around. I loved to fight bigger guys. Only one big guy I didn't like to fight. That was George. Fightin' George Foreman is like being in the street with an eighteen-wheeler comin' at you.

I DON'T SEE ANY DIFFERENCE in sex drive from the time I was twenty until now. A man ordinarily can have sex anytime. Ain't that right?

I HAD MY OLYMPIC GOLD MEDAL cut up into eleven pieces. Gave all eleven of my kids a piece. It'll come together again when they put me down.

Interviewed by Cal Fussman | Photograph by Andrew Hetherington

BORN BEAUFORT, SOUTH CAROLINA—01.12.44

> FRAZIER WAS TWENTY YEARS OLD WHEN HE WON THE HEAVYWEIGHT GOLD MEDAL AT THE TOKYO OLYMPICS IN 1964. HIS CAREER RECORD IS THIRTY WINS (TWENTY-SEVEN BY KNOCKOUT), FOUR LOSSES, AND ONE DRAW.

> HE WON HIS FIRST TITLE DEFENSE AGAINST MUHAMMAD ALI IN 1971. HE LATER LOST TO GEORGE FOREMAN IN KINGSTON, JAMAICA.

John Kenneth Galbraith { ECONOMIST, AMBASSADOR, PROFESSOR—CAMBRIDGE, MASSACHUSETTS }

> **A GOOD RULE OF CONVERSATION** is never answer a foolish question.

GIVING AN OPINION that people don't want to hear can work both ways. If it's a person you like, it can be very hard. If it's a person for whom you have a major distaste, it can be extremely enjoyable.

I WOULD HOPE I LAUGH quite a few times a day. I don't seek to add to the solemnity of life.

FOR ANY SENSIBLE PERSON, money is two things: a major liberating force and a great convenience. It's devastating to those who have in mind nothing else.

MODESTY is an overrated virtue.

ONE OF THE CHARACTERISTIC FEATURES of John F. Kennedy was his wonderful commitment to the truth. We had breakfast together on the day I left to be ambassador to India in 1961. The *New York Times* was on the table, and there was a story on the front page about the new ambassador to India. Kennedy pointed to it and said, "What did you think of that story?" which, needless to say, I had read. It wasn't unfavorable. I said I liked it all right but I didn't see why they had to call me arrogant. Kennedy said, "I don't see why not. Everybody else does."

I HAVE NO CAPACITY to cook. It's a field of ignorance, which I have carefully cultivated.

FRANKLIN D. ROOSEVELT was good on great issues or small. A great war. A great depression. He presided over both. No question about it—he's the person who most impressed me. In my life, he had no close competitor.

I MET Winston Churchill once. I went to a gathering that he assembled one night for a discussion on European union. I was principally impressed by the way his wife grabbed his arm every time he reached for another drink.

I'VE ALWAYS THOUGHT that true good sense requires one to see and comment upon the ridiculous.

KITTY AND I were married in 1937. No question—there is a secret to maintaining a marriage over time: each partner must systematically subordinate himself or herself to the other. That is the only formula for a happy marriage.

IS IT GOOD TO HAVE FRIENDS whom you don't agree with? Temporarily. But it has always been my purpose to get them to change their minds.

I HAVE MANAGED most of my life to exclude religious speculation from my mode of thought. I've found that, on the whole, it adds very little to economics.

THE TERRIBLE TRUTH with which we must all contend is that the day may come when nuclear arms fall under the control of some idiot someplace in the world. And that will be the day of reckoning.

I'VE LONG BEEN AN ADMIRER of Adam Smith, who's greatly praised by conservatives—who unfortunately have never read him. They would be shocked to find some of the things Smith advocates.

STRONG GOVERNMENT, to some extent, is in response to huge problems.

IN RICHER COUNTRIES such as ours, I want to see everybody assured of a basic income.

I SAW JOHN KENNEDY on the Cape a few weeks before his death. We spent a day together. Much of that was on a) that he was going to get out of Vietnam, and b) the pressures that he was under from the military.

LBJ AND I WERE BOTH from rural backgrounds—he in Texas and I in Canada. That was the origin of a closer relationship than if I had spent my life as a Harvard elite. We'd been friends for many years, back when he was in Congress. It was very sad that we clashed on Vietnam, but it was an overriding issue. Johnson had one answer which was not entirely unpersuasive. I recall his exact words: "Ken, if you knew what I have to do to contend with the military, you would be glad for what I do." The pressures of the military were very powerful. More powerful than most of us then realized.

IF I HAD TO PICK OUT perhaps the greatest achievement that I've seen in all my years, it is in the diminishing role of race and discrimination. We have made greater progress there than I ever anticipated.

A SHIELD AGAINST NUCLEAR WEAPONS is foolish. It owes much to the fact that the people advocating it are the people who would be benefiting from the effort.

HOW MUCH MONEY should a man carry in his wallet when he goes out of the house? I never thought of that.

Interviewed by Larry Getlen | Photograph by Ken Schles

BORN IONA STATION, ONTARIO, CANADA—10.15.1908
DIED CAMBRIDGE, MASSACHUSETTS—04.29.2006

> GALBRAITH BECAME AN ECONOMICS PROFESSOR AT HARVARD UNIVERSITY IN 1949.

> IN 1958, HE WROTE *THE AFFLUENT SOCIETY*, A BESTSELLER THAT HAS BECOME A CLASSIC.

> PRESIDENT KENNEDY APPOINTED HIM THE U.S. AMBASSADOR TO INDIA, WHERE HE SERVED FROM 1961 TO 1963.

Ted Giannoulas, *a.k.a. The Chicken*

{ ENTERTAINER—SAN DIEGO }

> **I'M JUST A GUY** in a chicken suit.

IT STARTED OFF AS A LARK for a radio station in San Diego in March 1974. They were doing a small advertising campaign with a cartoon chicken, and they decided to have somebody dress up in a chicken suit and give away candy Easter eggs. Nobody at the station wanted to wear the suit, so they decided to go to the campus of San Diego State and find someone who would agree to do it. There we were, at 1:30 p.m. the Friday before Easter break, with the campus virtually deserted, just five of us sitting around. Guy walks in and says they want to hire somebody to do some work at the station for a week. Said they were paying two dollars an hour. He looks around the room, points at me, and says, "You, you're the shortest. You'll fit the costume. You start tomorrow."

I'VE BEEN PLAYING THE CHICKEN for twenty-nine years. There are television shows that don't even last twenty-nine episodes.

MY FATHER taught me to always deliver more than you promise and you'll be surprised how opportunities open up for you.

I'M NOT FAMOUS. The chicken suit is famous.

THE PHILLIE PHANATIC is going to the Hall of Fame. Now they're taking laundry in there. There are four or five people who have worn that outfit! They didn't have any formal ceremony for me, because, I think, the Hall of Fame was afraid that the purists would be outraged.

WHAT YOU SEE at Disneyland—that's not me. I have a show; I have gags and routines. It just happens to be in the context of a live sporting event. I'm an entertainer that can entertain an audience and connect with them. I'm a comic.

THE GREATEST MOMENT of my life was my Grand Hatching in June of 1979. We sold out the Murph. I was brought in in a ten-foot Styrofoam egg on top of an armored truck, escorted onto the field by California Highway Patrol. All the ballplayers came out and took me off the roof, and I hatched out of the egg. Ten-minute standing ovation, and, I'll tell you, I know how Lou Gehrig felt at that moment. I made $40,085. That night I was the highest-paid athlete in the world.

WHY DID THE CHICKEN cross the road? To get away from stupid questions.

THE SUIT ITSELF is worth no more than a grand. It's very old-school, nothing high-tech about it. It's just genuine synthetic fur.

MONEY CHANGES EVERYTHING. But it only changes those who have no backbone and who are weak in the mind. I've come across a little success, but I'm the same person I was in college. I will always be.

IF IT'S DNA that makes the ballplayer, it sure didn't work for John Henry Williams.

SOME PLAYERS WERE BORN to give you the red ass. One time there was a Padre, Dane Iorg, who was normally a mild-mannered player. But he starts yelling at me, "Get off the field!" Everyone was laughing at first, but then everyone's jaws dropped: "Is he really giving the Chicken the razz?" I told him, "You're just upset because I'm getting more playing time out there than you are."

TONY GWYNN is a very self-centered, egocentric individual. He's as two-faced as they come.

THE PRESS IS INTIMIDATED by athletes, and it's unfortunate.

I CAN'T SAY that the Yankees are bad for baseball. But if the king wins every hand, you'll stop showing up at the poker table.

I SEE GOOD SERVICE and I'll tip 50, even 100 percent. But I'm not afraid to tip zero.

GOD? I'm sure there is one, and I hope he likes me.

HAD I WORKED WITH TED TURNER, the Chicken would have been bigger than Mickey Mouse. Ted called me to his seats in the middle of a ball game in September of '78. He literally makes the offer sitting there in the seats. He whips out this business card, and he writes on the back our contract. His initial offer was fifty thousand dollars. He said, "I'm gonna give you your own TV show. I'm gonna make this TBS thing really big." But too many people loved me in San Diego, and I wasn't mature enough to make the move. Let me tell you something, when it was leaked out that I was considering this offer—and it was big news in San Diego, it was big news—it led off newscasts. I had school kids as class projects write me letters saying, "Stay in San Diego."

I THINK IT WOULD HURT the illusionary aspect if I was photographed without the suit. It's like seeing Santa without the beard.

ON A HOT DOG? Mustard, relish, onions, and jalapeños, too. No ketchup.

UNDER THE SUIT I have a T-shirt, my leotard, and my briefs. I gotta go with briefs because they keep my nuggets intact.

TRUST IS THE SECRET to making people laugh. Everything else comes out of that.

DOING SOMETHING that nobody thinks is gonna work and sticking with it—that's my life.

Interviewed by Daniel Torday | Photograph by James Smolka

BORN LONDON, ONTARIO, CANADA—08.17.53

> GIANNOULAS'S WEB SITE QUOTES THE LATE SAN DIEGO SPORTSWRITER JACK MURPHY AS WRITING, "THE CHICKEN HAS THE SOUL OF A POET. HE IS AN EMBRYONIC CHARLES CHAPLIN IN CHICKEN FEATHERS."

> THE *SPORTING NEWS* NAMED GIANNOULAS ONE OF THE HUNDRED MOST POWERFUL PEOPLE IN SPORTS IN THE TWENTIETH CENTURY.

John Goodman { ACTOR—LOS ANGELES }

> **ST. LOUIS WAS A WORLD** of kids. All playing. Playing in the rain. Playing till after the sun went down and you got called. *"John-nnnnnny!"* And then you listened to the Cards at night. Jack Buck and Harry Caray. *"Ba-da-da-da-dum.* St. Louis baseball Cardinals are on the air! Brought to you by Anheuser-Busch!"

I WENT BACK TO THE HOUSE where I grew up the other day. I didn't want to go inside. It would be like going back to grade school and going to the urinal.

THE BEST LESSON my mother taught me? Wear clean underwear. For some reason she was obsessed with me getting hit by a car and having clean underwear in the ambulance.

SHE ALSO TAUGHT ME persistence. My dad died a month before my second birthday. She didn't have a shot in hell, and she just kept doing what she did: taking in laundry, babysitting kids, working at the drugstore, working at the barbecue joint. And she raised her kids.

THE FIRST MOMENT was in eighth grade. Doing a play. I forgot my lines. I couldn't look down and say I forgot my lines. So I got up from the dinner table, walked around, improvising, until I got the thread back. It just seemed natural. We had a good-looking acting teacher, and she gave me a big hug and a kiss.

JUNIOR HIGH SCHOOL'S TERRIBLE. I had the tape on the glasses, the acne, and the what was the name of that shit? English Leather.

YOU DON'T WANNA MEET a lot of your heroes. That can turn out bad.

I WENT TO TAKE my physical. But they measured me two inches shorter than I am. They measured me at six foot instead of six foot two. I was eleven pounds overweight for that height. They told me to lose weight and come back. By the time I was scheduled to come back, the draft was abolished.

THERE ARE NO coincidences.

I JUST IDOLIZED AL PACINO, and I was afraid that, you know, he was gonna wipe his feet on me or put a cigarette out on my neck or something. But he was so full of fire. He had such passion for acting. It's nice to meet someone like that.

GIVING UP a lot of yourself isn't really that hard when you realize that you get more than you give up.

SHE'S BEEN THROUGH a lot. New Orleans is the old broad that's sitting at the corner of the bar, listening to Patti Page, and remembering better days. But you can't quite get rid of her.

MY DAUGHTER taught me to see things with a fresh slant. She has a vitality of spirit that I've traded in for a lot of cigarettes and beer over the years.

ROSEANNE BARR knows what's funny. If she believes in something, she'll take it by the neck like a terrier and shake it to death.

GETTING A SCRIPT from the Coen brothers is like getting what you want for Christmas.

THERE AREN'T MANY BENEFITS that I can see in having a large frame. It's hard to sit on airplanes. It's hard to get into really cool cars. It's been hell on my knees. It's never really done me any good.

MY TASTES have changed radically. You can't dump as many things into the old Dumpster as you could in the old days and still have it smell fresh.

WHITE CASTLE? Oh, yeah! Sliders. They taste better when you're drunk.

I WOULD'VE LIKED to have met Hemingway. We probably would've gotten into a fight or something.

THE QUALITY of sex improves, but the quantity not so much.

WHEN I LOOK AT MYSELF on film, I just see shit I should've done. I'm incapable of watching myself objectively. Unless it's *The Big Lebowski*. The writing is so goddamned good, you can just enjoy it, go along for the ride like everybody else.

BABE RUTH is one of those things I wish I could go back and do over. It's like being in that dream where you're in the subway with no clothes on.

I ALWAYS OVERTIP—because, at the end of the night, your feet hurt and you get to count it up and there's a nice feeling when you've gotten tipped well. I know what it's like. My mom lived on tips.

HOW QUICK TIME goes by now, compared to when you were a kid. Summer used to last forever. Now it's twelve weeks.

THERE'S NO FORMULA to life. If I figured one out, I'd probably have to check out the next day. "Oh, Mr. Goodman, your seven o'clock stroke is here, sir."

IF THE MORTAR and bricks are laid right, the building will last for a while.

Interviewed by Cal Fussman | Photograph by Chris McPherson

BORN ST. LOUIS, MISSOURI—06.20.52

> FOR TEN YEARS, GOODMAN PLAYED ROSEANNE'S HUSBAND, DAN CONNOR, ON *ROSEANNE*.

> HE HAS APPEARED IN FIVE MOVIES MADE BY JOEL AND ETHAN COEN: *RAISING ARIZONA* (1987), *BARTON FINK* (1991), *THE HUDSUCKER PROXY* (1994), *THE BIG LEBOWSKI* (1998), *AND O BROTHER, WHERE ART THOU?* (2000).

> GOODMAN HAS HOSTED *SATURDAY NIGHT LIVE* ELEVEN TIMES.

Mikhail Gorbachev ⟨ LEADER—MOSCOW ⟩

I WAS JUST A BOY. My father was going off to fight in World War II. We were all saying goodbye to him. It was very emotional. Everyone was crying. Just before he left, my father bought me some ice cream. It came in an aluminum cup. I can still remember that ice cream.

WE WILL HAVE PEACE for all, or we will have no peace at all.

TRUST is when there is no place for lying.

THE POLITICIANS IN AMERICA sometimes act in a way that seems disrespectful toward our country and our people. The Russians are people who value their dignity. You better not mess with that.

YOU HAVE TO CONSIDER that Reagan was twenty years older than I was. He was the age of my mother. So there was a generation gap. During one of our talks, he tried to lecture me and moralize. I said to him, "Mr. President, you are not my teacher, and I am not your student. You are not a prosecutor, and I am not a defendant. So let's not subject each other to lectures. Let's talk frankly and address the issues. If you want to lecture, we might as well wrap it up, because there's really nothing to talk about." He got a little upset. Not long after that, he said, "Why don't we go on a first-name basis? You call me Ron and I'll call you Mikhail." That was an important step.

YOU KNOW, many urban people have the impression that muffins grow on supermarket shelves. Homemade bread is best.

WITHOUT THE FOUNDATION OF THE FAMILY, it's very hard to be a good human being.

I GREW UP in the hinterlands. I never saw bananas when I was a young man. I never saw a pineapple.

WHEN I WAS ABOUT FIFTEEN years old, some frontline soldiers gave me a glass with liquid in it, but they didn't tell me that it was vodka. I didn't know anything about alcohol at the time. I gulped it down, and these guys had a good time watching my baptism by fire. After that, I became a lot more cautious as regards alcohol. To this day, I'm not a big drinker.

THE DAY AFTER I announced that I was stepping down, I was scheduled to come to the Kremlin for an interview with a Japanese reporter. I got a call beforehand from one of my assistants, who said that Yeltsin was in my office with his entourage, finishing off a bottle of whiskey. These people were almost like savages, celebrating their big victory over a bottle in my office. I told myself: "That office has been desecrated. I will never set foot in that room again."

THAT LOUIS VUITTON AD? The proceeds go to Green Cross International and its American counterpart, Global Green. Also, I travel a lot, and a good bag comes in handy.

WE ARE HALFWAY toward a democratic transition. When Putin became president, the country was in chaos. People were struggling to survive, just to live, and the West was ignoring it. The West liked Yeltsin, so the Russian people were thinking, "Why in this time of trouble is the West supporting Yeltsin?" It was very frustrating. You need to understand that Putin rescued the country from chaos.

HAVE PATIENCE. Like I say to my American friends, it took you more than two hundred years to get where you want us to get in two hundred days.

A RURAL PERSON feels a connection to the environment not just on a daily basis, but hourly.

THE MEMBERS of the nuclear club are not setting a good example for other countries. They insist that other countries cannot develop nuclear weapons, while at the same time they strive to perfect their own.

LOOK AT WHAT HAPPENED in New Orleans. Look at how big the blow was and how difficult the consequences are in dealing with such a blow. Imagine what would happen in a situation where nuclear weapons were used. Imagine the effect of the radiation. It's been years since the Chernobyl accident, and there are towns and villages where people do not live. The towns are still there. They haven't been torn down, but not a single person lives there. So this is a very serious matter—more than serious.

NUCLEAR WEAPONS need to be abolished.

Interviewed by Cal Fussman | Photograph by Henry Leutwyler

BORN PRIVOLNOYE, RUSSIA—03.02.31

> GORBACHEV RESIGNED AS PRESIDENT OF THE SOVIET UNION ON DECEMBER 25, 1991, SIX YEARS AFTER BECOMING ITS LEADER. HE WAS AWARDED THE NOBEL PEACE PRIZE IN 1990.

> HE APPEARED IN A 1997 TELEVISION COMMERCIAL FOR PIZZA HUT WITH HIS GRAND-DAUGHTER, ANASTASIA.

> GORBACHEV IS A FOUNDER OF GREEN CROSS INTERNATIONAL, A GLOBAL ENVIRONMENTAL ORGANIZATION.

Merv Griffin { GAME SHOW CREATOR, ENTREPRENEUR— BEVERLY HILLS }

> **I'M NOSY.** Just plain old nosy.

I'VE BEEN VERY FORTUNATE with my health. I smoke. I drink—not heavily, but I like my wine. I don't exercise. I take a cab to a cab. It's all in your DNA.

BETTE DAVIS said, "Old age is not for sissies." I love that.

HOW DOES IT FEEL to be the guy who gave Vanna White to America? It feels *wonderful.* She's crocheted me two comforters. I think she thinks I sleep all day.

I WAS EIGHTEEN, and I was walking along the railroad tracks, and I just started crying. I don't know what it was. No words were spoken to me—I'm not saying that. It was a sudden realization that from then on, my life would not be my own. And a year later, I was singing on the radio in San Francisco.

LUCK COMES IN if you're well equipped to deal with it. By the time I took over for Jack Paar, luck just happened to be a wrong entrance on a stage by Paar. He didn't think anyone was in the studio. I was taping a game show, and he walked through the curtain, at the peak of his career. I said, "What're you doing here?" He said, "I'm coming through *my* studio." And I said, "Well, it's my studio." And it went on. It was a very funny interview. It happened by accident. He went to his agent and said, "Who was that boy? Give him one of my Monday nights." And that was the beginning of everything.

WHAT HAVE I LEARNED from talking to all these famous people? That there's a major story behind *everyone.*

ROSE KENNEDY was the only guest who ever intimidated me.

I WON'T STOP WORKING. I see people in powerful positions who retire and either contract Alzheimer's or just die of boredom.

I REFUSE to be bored.

THERE ARE THREE THINGS I do: I do three or four crossword puzzles every morning. It really keeps you sharp. Whenever I have time, I'll do transcendental meditation. But most of the time, I do a kind of exercise that's my own, and it's very weird: I pick a show from my past or a period of time in my past, and I try to remember everyone who was involved at that time—their names and everything about them. That's my mental exercise, and I hope that's the thing that'll keep me from Alzheimer's.

IT'S A BETTER TEXTBOOK, looking at those clips, than historians could write, because you saw the principal people being interviewed. Martin Luther King! No one had an interview with Martin Luther King. To see him sit down there—he makes the audience laugh, and you see a whole person instead of a podium and a million people in front of him at the Lincoln Memorial.

IT'S ALWAYS BEEN my philosophy: Turn the page. If something falls through, turn the page. It's over with, get used to it, get on with it. Very simple. It's always worked for me.

I WATCH A LOT OF TV. I love *American Idol.* Whether I would hire those singers if I owned a casino, I don't know. I might put 'em in the lounge, but not the main room.

I GET MY CONFIDENCE from being prepared. At eighty-one years old, I could be the whole reference library for *Jeopardy!* I think you just *know everything.* How could you not?

MY DIVORCE—we just couldn't live together. My show was a hit. I was spending all my time working on the show, and she's at home cooking. Very talented, gifted woman with wild, wonderful ideas. But she had no avenues to express herself, and I was out expressing myself all over the damn place. And in California, it didn't work. The thing to do is move to California and get a divorce.

GREAT LOSSES come from the same place as great joys. The things that please you also terribly disappoint you.

WHEN EVA GABOR was still alive, she'd get up early at the ranch, and when I'd get up an hour later, I'd walk down to the stable, and every horse in the pasture would have red lipstick on it.

I'VE OUTLIVED all of my diet doctors. My first diet doctor was Dr. Atkins. And then I went through Dr. Stillman, the water diet. I think he drowned on his own diet. And I had Dr. Tarnower, and his girlfriend shot him. So I gave up dieting.

PEOPLE SAY I've reinvented myself so many times. I haven't! I just sit here in my big leather chair, and people come in with offers I really like. I don't reinvent myself; it just follows me.

"WHAT'RE YOUR HOBBIES?" Jeez, I would *never* ask that.

I KNOW THAT when I get bored, no matter what I do on television, they're gonna get bored.

THERE ARE NO bad guests.

Interviewed by Scott Dickensheets | Photograph by Catherine Ledner

BORN SAN MATEO, CALIFORNIA—07.06.25
DIED LOS ANGELES, CALIFORNIA—08.12.07

> GRIFFIN CREATED *JEOPARDY!* WHICH FIRST AIRED IN 1964, AND *WHEEL OF FORTUNE*, WHICH PREMIERED IN 1975.

> HIS SYNDICATED TALK SHOW, *THE MERV GRIFFIN SHOW*, LAUNCHED IN 1965 AND RAN FOR TWENTY-ONE YEARS.

> HE WAS AN HONORARY PALLBEARER FOR PRESIDENT RONALD REAGAN.

Merle Haggard { SINGER—REDDING, CALIFORNIA }

> **I'VE LIVED AT THE VERY END** of what must have been a wonderful country.

THEY'VE LEFT THE REDWOODS up alongside the highway so we'll think they're all there. But go up in an airplane, and you'll see that they've clear-cut everything behind.

THE KIDS just don't know how big the tear on the rip-off was. If they had any idea, I believe they could do something about it. But it may be too late. We'll see. They're smarter. They can talk to one another. I don't look for a politician to bullshit his way in this time.

WHEN I WAS NINE YEARS OLD, right after my dad died, my mother got me some violin lessons with this big heavyset lady. It took nine lessons before this lady said to my mother, "You're wasting your money. He's got too good an ear. He's not going to fool with learning to read when he can play something that he hears on the radio." When I heard her say that, I knew I had something.

WE WEREN'T THIEVES by nature. Pranksters. Practical jokers. We were without a car one time, Dean Holloway and I. We just went out and started borrowing cars. Sometimes we'd bring 'em back. Put gas in 'em. Clean 'em up. Leave a little note: "THANKS FOR THE CAR." Like the Phantom.

I'M IN A VERY SMALL percentage of people ever in the joint who beat it. It's like 2 percent of 2 percent. If you've ever been to the joint, you're going back.

I'LL TELL YOU WHY IT'S DIFFERENT when somebody else is singing "Mama Tried": They're reading the words. I'm telling the story.

I GOT OUT SOMETHING like nine that morning—February 3, 1960. There's a big metal security device at the main door coming out of San Quentin. When they open that door, it comes up and you have to step over it. Just as I was stepping over that device, a Hank Snow record came on: "The Last Ride." My foot just stopped in midair. The song was coming from a radio near this guard who was standing there with his gun. He said, "What, did you change your mind?" I said, "No, that's a really great song." I stayed there and listened to the rest of the song.

COULDN'T HAVE DONE the music without it. Wouldn't have thought of it. Wouldn't have been part of me.

WILLIE NELSON IS AN IDOL for me. The music is sort of immaterial. Willie is seventy-four. A lot of people don't realize how healthy he is. He doesn't eat any strict diet. But he doesn't eat very much of anything. He understands the value of water.

SEVENTY IS A BIG MARK. I'm feeling good. But Bing Crosby felt good, too, and he came off the eighteenth hole, just kind of laid down in the grass, and that was that.

FREEDOM is what prohibition ain't.

I PROBABLY HAD AS BAD a sex urge as anybody when I was younger. I remember an old guitar player, Eldon Shamblin, told me, "When you get pussy off your mind, you can go ahead and learn something." Isn't that great?

WILLIE NELSON'S THE ONE who told me the reason it costs so much to get divorced is because it's worth it.

I REMEMBER going to a dance when I was a kid—my older brother took me in. Roy Nichols was playing. My brother said, "Hey, there's a little guy in there playing guitar. He don't have to pick cotton or go to school." Roy Nichols became my idol on the guitar. Many years later, he went on to play for me for half price. But he and I could never look directly at each other. I never knew why. At first, I thought it was because I admired him too much. But it was Roy, too. Anyway, late in his life, Roy had a stroke. Paralyzed him on one side. Right down the middle. Half of his nose he could blow, the other half was dead. After his stroke, I went over to Roy's house. He looked me right in the eye and said, "Look here, I love you." I got chills. He said, "That old shit went down the hole with this stroke."

THEY GOT LAWS for the white man and laws for the black man—we all know that.

LEFTY FRIZZELL said you don't have to experience everything to sing about it. But you've got to believe it.

I THINK what we're lacking in music today is it seems like all the good stories have been already taken. "Stardust" has already been written. "Your Cheatin' Heart." "Imagine." God almighty, lightning may never strike again like that.

IF ONLY somebody could come up with something different—start a new trend. Real music. If only somebody could sing a song, had something to say, had a good melody, and could do it in person, without help from any electronics. I think the people would go nuts. It's bound to happen. There's got to be a guy out there somewhere. A natural.

Interviewed by Cal Fussman | Photograph by Kurt Markus

BORN BAKERSFIELD, CALIFORNIA—
04.06.37

> HAGGARD HAS HAD THIRTY-EIGHT NUMBER-ONE COUNTRY HITS, WAS ELECTED TO THE COUNTRY MUSIC HALL OF FAME IN 1994, AND WON THE GRAMMY LIFETIME ACHIEVEMENT AWARD IN 2006.
> HAGGARD WAS ARRESTED AND SOMETIMES JAILED FOR A STRING OF CRIMES IN THE 1950S AND SENTENCED TO TEN YEARS IN SAN QUENTIN PRISON.
> IN 1972, HAGGARD WAS PARDONED FOR HIS PREVIOUS CRIMES BY CALIFORNIA GOVERNOR RONALD REAGAN.

Woody Harrelson { ACTOR—HAWAII }

> **WHEN I HAD JUST STARTED** *CHEERS*, my nerves were ajangle, to put it mildly. I was absolutely terrified. What you're learning is to not show the fear and to ultimately overcome it so that the level of relaxation is commensurate with the level of tension.

IT'S AN ODD BEAST, fame. It's got multiple personalities.

"YOU'RE GREAT, MAN." "Oh, dude, you were so *great*." "You're the man!" You'll hear it all, and that's fine. But if you start to believe it, that's a dangerous thing.

NATURAL BORN KILLERS is really a misunderstood romantic comedy.

I DID IT JUST LIKE I DO anything. I research the occupation, so I looked up everything I could on serial killers. I didn't want to fire any guns. But I guess it's a testimony to how effective the immersion was that, probably halfway through the movie, I went from having a strong aversion to firing a gun to enjoying it. Enjoying the chaos and twistedness of what was going on.

JESUS, in my mind, was saying, "We're all children of God. These miracles that I can do, you can do also." I don't think he was trying to separate himself by saying, "I am the way, the truth, and the life, and no one cometh under the father except by me"—like, I'm the son of God; I'm the man; if you've got any issues, you gotta come through me. That was a distorted version of God.

I REMEMBER MY DAUGHTER Deni coming along, and she was so pure and caring of everybody and everything. And somehow, this little being managed to get around all the obstacles—the gun turrets, the walls, the moats, the sentries—that were wrapped around my heart. My heart at that time needed her.

I THINK IT'S THE BEST THING going, parenthood.

I THINK it's a cool thing to just wake up and write. It was beautiful earlier today—the sky was outrageous. Rembrandt, Picasso, van Gogh, they don't have a palette like that. That firmament that God gets to work with every day, even on a lazy day, just blows your mind. I came in and just started writing this: "A new day, trembling with potential / I am the potentiate, and my life is equal to the task of living of loving, of moving my love"—that's my name for Laura: my love—"Yesterday I wallowed in me-hood, following a well-worn path / Today, I jump from bridges, dance on tiny windowsills high above the ubiquitous crowd of unsuspecting faces / Combative. Angry. Hostile. Those were the bedrock of this body's previous tenant and now I, nameless, unnameable, ergo mysterious, incorrigible, march to the musical manifestations, the bass and harp of distant angels, calling me with their many magnificent mouths: Dance, creature! Put down your pen, lift up your limbs, and dance to greet another golden morning." Anyway, that was today.

EXPECTATIONS are pretty tough on relationships.

THE OTHER DAY, we were all three sitting playing cards—me, Willie, and Kris Kristofferson—and Kris says, "If you love them more than they love you, it's bad. But if they love you more than you love them, it's even worse."

WHEN I WAS IN MY TWENTIES and just so sexually prolific, the first time I went to Machu Picchu, this guy, a spiritual teacher, says to me, "When you make love, you must be making love." I thought that was the greatest advice I had ever heard.

LAURA—I don't know, I just, I love her.

LARRY FLYNT AND I stayed in touch. I was going through turbulent times with Laura. And Larry, out of this incredible compassion, just invites her to dinner, unbeknownst to me, sits and talks with her, and just tries to help. He tried to help! And I don't know how much help he was, but it meant a lot to me that he tried.

THE WHOLE CONCEPT of the raw-food thing is any food you heat over 118 degrees, you kill all the enzymes and most of the nutritional value of the food. The enzymes are as much or more important than the various nutritional things that are always getting all the good PR. But to eat only raw food, you've got to love a salad. You've got to just *love* a salad.

HERE YOU GO, try this. Ice cream. Mint chip. Good, right? It's raw. No dairy.

DOES ACTIVISM WORK? That's a good question. Me climbing the Golden Gate Bridge was about stopping them from cutting down the redwoods. What I noticed was, you try to get them to stop cutting down this forest, and maybe you succeed, well, they just go cut *that* forest down.

I'M A LITTLE BIT OPTIMISTIC. I like seeing one of our own—I'm speaking as a Hawaiian—get into the White House.

HEMP WAS NEVER ABOUT marijuana. Marijuana's about marijuana. That's consensual, victimless crime. That's saying, "I think I should have the freedom to do whatever the hell I want to do if I'm living in a so-called free country, as long as I'm not hurting someone else." That's freedom. If I'm gonna hit myself in the head with a hammer, so be it. That's freedom.

HERE, YOU FINISH the ice cream.

Interviewed by Ryan D'Agostino | Photographs by Deni and Zoe Harrelson

BORN MIDLAND, TEXAS—07.23.61

> HARRELSON STARRED AS WOODY BOYD ON *CHEERS* FOR NINE YEARS.

> HIS FILM HIGHLIGHTS INCLUDE *WHITE MEN CAN'T JUMP* (1992); *NATURAL BORN KILLERS* (1994); *THE PEOPLE VS. LARRY FLYNT* (1996), FOR WHICH HE EARNED AN ACADEMY AWARD NOMINATION FOR BEST ACTOR; *KINGPIN* (1996); AND *NO COUNTRY FOR OLD MEN* (2007).

Werner Herzog { FILMMAKER—LOS ANGELES }

> **I DO NOT MAKE** documentaries or features. My films are something else.

FACTS DO NOT INTEREST ME much. Facts are for accountants. Truth creates illumination.

I KNOW the heart of men. It may sound pretentious, but it's true.

NOT A GOOD QUESTION. You are trying to deduce if I am obsessed like the subjects of my films. Let's not get into that. I am a professional person. Others would not do what I do, but I am trying to be a good soldier of cinema.

I WAS SHOOTING a film with an entire cast of midgets, and one caught fire and was run over by a car. He was completely unhurt, and I was so astonished, I told the cast that if they all escaped filming unscathed, I would jump into a cactus for their amusement. And they did, so I jumped into a cactus.

THERE IS NO SMALL TALK in the Sahara.

YOU LOOK at the footage of Timothy Treadwell, you look into the abyss of human nature.

IT'S VERY MYSTERIOUS. Amie Huguenard, Treadwell's girlfriend, wanted to leave him for good. But at the end, she does not run away, she tries to defend him. You hear quite clearly that she attacks the bear with a frying pan, beating it over the head.

I DO NOT KNOW WHY people who are in love do what they do.

WE ARE OVERCONCERNED with the well-being of whales, panda bears, and tree frogs. But cultures are dying with incredible speed. There are six thousand languages still alive, many of them spoken by very few speakers. By the end of the century, there may be only 10 percent left. I met an aborigine in Australia who was eighty years old and the only speaker of his language. He was considered mute because he had nobody left to talk to. He is certainly dead now.

WHY AMERICA? I got married.

LOS ANGELES is the city with the most substance in the United States—cultural substance. There is a competition between New York and Los Angeles, but New York only consumes culture and borrows it from Europe. Things get done in Los Angeles.

I WILL NOT BECOME A CITIZEN of a country that has capital punishment. It is a question of principle.

I MADE A FILM where I hypnotized the entire cast. People who are psychotic should not be hypnotized.

IT IS SILLY to believe human life is sustainable on this planet. We've got maybe twenty thousand years, maybe fifty thousand years, maybe five hundred thousand years.

RESPECT the natives.

THE STUDIO wanted it to be a plastic miniature boat pulled over a garden hill, but I said we will pull a real ship over a real mountain, and it will be a grandiose event in a magnificent opera. I wanted the audience to be able to trust their eyes.

MORE THAN IN ANY OTHER historical epoch, our sense of reality is severely challenged. It is the Internet, Photoshop, digital effects in cinema, video games—tools that have arrived with instant impact. It is like warfare. For centuries, warfare was the same: the medieval knight with a sword in combat. Suddenly he was confronted with firearms and overnight was never the same. It is now a moment of the same magnitude for us.

SCHOOL has not given me anything. I have always been suspicious of teachers. I do not know why.

I DO NOT GET LOST. Sense of direction is a missing skill among modern men.

TOURISM is a sin. Traveling on foot is a virtue. The moment people understand that you have come on foot and are trying to engage and understand them, there is an immediate change in attitude. On foot, no one chases you away or does not allow you to use their resources. They tell you stories they have not told anyone else.

IF I OPENED A FILM SCHOOL, I would make everyone earn their tuition themselves by working. Not in an office—out where there is real life. Earn it as a bouncer in a sex club or as a warden in a lunatic asylum. And travel on foot for three months. And do physical, combative sports, like boxing. That makes you more of a filmmaker than three years of film school. *Pura vida*, as the Mexicans say.

I WAS SHOT a year ago. It did not impress me because I had been shot at before. Once, with an elite unit of insurgents crossing over from Honduras into Nicaragua, we came under fire in the middle of the river, which was unpleasant because we were so visible and the jungle hid the shooters.

SUNGLASSES. Good boots. Binoculars. And a mosquito net.

IT IS SIGNIFICANT that neither the Sherpas nor any of the other mountain people ever thought about climbing the Himalayas until bored English aristocrats in the nineteenth century came in. You do not have to be on the summit of Mount Everest to appreciate it. To speak of "conquering" a mountain is not right.

I WON'T ANSWER THAT. The meaning of life does not belong in a magazine. A magazine should know its limitations.

Interviewed by Matthew Belloni | Photograph by Sam Jones

BORN MUNICH, GERMANY—09.05.42

> GROWING UP IN RURAL BAVARIA, HERZOG HAD NO EXPOSURE TO MOVIES OR TELEVISION. HE MADE HIS FIRST TELEPHONE CALL WHEN HE WAS SEVENTEEN YEARS OLD.

> HIS FILM HIGHLIGHTS INCLUDE *SIGNS OF LIFE* (1968), *FITZCARRALDO* (1982), *GRIZZLY MAN* (2005), AND *RESCUE DAWN* (2006).

Dustin Hoffman { ACTOR—LOS ANGELES }

> **I DON'T UNDERSTAND BOREDOM.** All you have to do is walk around the house as if you were blind. How could you be bored? Depressed, yes. That's a different ball game. I know depression. I know every degree of it. But not boredom.

YOU TAKE THE LAUGHS out of *Rain Man*, and it's not the same movie. When we're in the phone booth, and I fart—that was a fart. That wasn't written in the script. We were waiting to do the shot, and Barry Levinson had the earphones on. The door closed, and I snuck one out. We're tight in there, you know. And Cruise looked at me and said, "Did you fart?" And I said, "Yeah." But I stayed in character. "Fart." Barry heard it and he came running over in hysterics and said, "That's in the scene. Put it in, wherever you want." That's a good director: someone who takes advantage of accidents.

SEEING BAD WORK is one of the most painful experiences, because you realize how easy it is to do.

YOU LOOK AT SOME GREAT WORK, and you wonder, "How did they know what they knew when they were twenty-five?"

AT ONE POINT when I was in my twenties, I became addicted to a derivative of morphine called Demerol. I'd been burned and was in the hospital for a month. When I was healing, everything was fine. And this yoke was lifted off me, and there was this Zen feeling that people shoot for when they go into meditation. There was this sense of peace. I remember thinking, "Why weren't we constructed this way?"

I LIKE TO MIMIC my grandkids. I'm trying to understand the intensity of fixation on a leaf. Kids don't need anything else in their life.

ONCE THE REVIEWS CAME IN, the play got longer and longer, because the pauses were dramatic and the actors were milking every moment. Suddenly, it was running twelve minutes long. Arthur Miller was very sensitive about this. "The audience is like a fish on a hook. I don't want them sitting back. I want them at the edge of the seat." I said, "But Arthur, sometimes the audience is laughing. They're going to lose the dialogue." He said, "Fine, lose it. I don't care. You've got to keep the play going. Do it right, and you'll have ambulances lined up around the block."

CERTAIN PROFESSIONS are not given their due. Costume designer is one of them.

YOU HAVE TO UNDERSTAND, they suck the life out of the set once you're ready to shoot. "OK, quiet now! Quiet! Quiet!" Suddenly, they've artificialized the ambience, and this feeling of natural behavior is out. Brando would refuse to go along. He'd be talking with someone close to the camera: "What'd you do this weekend? You grilled? What'd you grill?" Action! Then he'd step right into the scene. He wanted the same reality.

THERE'S ONLY ONE THING that doesn't date. Poverty is not dated. Homeless people have looked the same since the thirteenth century. Go back to the times of Tolstoy and Dostoyevsky. Look at photographs. It's amazing. The face on a homeless person is timeless.

MIDNIGHT COWBOY was done on a low budget. You gotta have money to pay for a scene that includes a bunch of people on the street in midtown Manhattan. So Jon Voight and I were walking in regular traffic and being filmed by a camera hidden in a van across the street. That's a stolen shot. That was a cab that almost hit us. In my brain, I wanted to say, "We're making a movie here, asshole!" But your brain knows that would ruin the take. So "I'm walking here!" really means "We're shooting a film here!"

I JUST STARTED JUMPING ROPE again. I like to do it to "La Bamba." Record it over and over and over again so that it runs for an hour. It's best if you can do it like a boxer, with your feet moving up and back so that they're not jumping up and down. It's easier on your knees. And it's great just to listen to "La Bamba."

COURAGEOUS? How's this? Jake was a month premature. The placenta had torn off the wall, and Lisa was hemorrhaging. Like in one of those TV shows, the doctor got her on a gurney and said we had to hurry. "I need anesthesia! I need this! I need that!" Later we were told that we had a twelve-minute window. Lisa would have expired, and Jake would have gone with her. Lisa could sense the urgency of it. She said quietly to the doctor, "If you have a choice, you make sure to save the baby." Just like that. Simple. I don't know anything more courageous. If a man was in that situation, the guy would say, "There's got to be a way to save both of us." Men would negotiate. *There has to be a way.*

HOW HAS GOD CHANGED FOR ME since the time I was six years old? He got older.

I'M SURE YOU'VE HEARD what George Burns said when somebody asked him what it's like to have sex when you're ninety. He said, "Did you ever shoot pool with a piece of rope?" You can't do any better than that.

THE BETTER YOU ARE as a parent, the richer the nest you've built, the more difficult it is for your kids to leave. So they have to invent things to dislike about you. And they're brilliant at it.

I'VE GOT A FEW BLUEBERRIES LEFT. That's a good metaphor for life.

Interviewed by Cal Fussman | Photograph by Bryce Duffy

BORN LOS ANGELES, CALIFORNIA—08.08.37

> BEFORE WINNING THE BEST ACTOR ACADEMY AWARD FOR *KRAMER VS. KRAMER* (1979), HOFFMAN HAD BEEN NOMINATED THREE TIMES BEFORE: FOR *THE GRADUATE* (1967), *MIDNIGHT COWBOY* (1969), AND *LENNY* (1974). HE WAS NOMINATED AGAIN FOR *TOOTSIE* (1982) AND *WAG THE DOG* (1997) AND WON FOR *RAIN MAN* (1988).

Jesse Jackson { SOCIAL CONSCIENCE—SOUTH CAROLINA }

 SUCCESS needs no explanation. Failure does not have one that matters.

WHEN I GREW UP in Greenville, every white man was a deputy sheriff.

I WAS NEVER TAUGHT to be inferior in my home. I was taught that something was wrong with them. It's not that we weren't ready. They were not fair.

WE HAD FAITH. We had hope. But faith is spiritual. Hope is spiritual. At some point, you have to have the law.

AFTER WE WON *Brown v. Topeka Board of Education* in 1954, most folks where I lived couldn't understand what that really meant. Civil rights had no meaning to a lot of the older generation. I remember sitting on a porch in Greenville with my grandparents and their friends. Somebody said, "What does integration mean?" I said, "Well, you take salt and pepper, put 'em together, and shake 'em up—that's what it means." Somebody said, "No time soon." Oh, that got some laughter. "No time *sooooon*."

A MAN WHO CANNOT BE ENTICED by money or intimidated by the threat of jail or death has two of the strongest weapons that anyone has to offer.

MY HIGH SCHOOL FOOTBALL COACH taught me to bark signals with authority, or the other ten players will not be inspired. You cannot get a team to move with precision on a weak signal.

PEOPLE are screaming for the running back who scored the touchdown. But the lineman knows how he got there.

WHAT WAS FUNNY at one point ain't funny no more. One of my mama's favorite jokes was "How do you name all them Chinamen? Drop the silverware. Ting-tong. Ching-chong." That ain't funny no more.

EVERYBODY has a best.

OUR GOAL WAS NOT FREEDOM. Freedom was the necessary prerequisite to get to equality.

UNEQUAL school funding will not end on the day of Barack's inauguration.

IF YOU THINK black people have a motivation problem, open up a Wal-Mart and advertise a thousand jobs. Watch five thousand people show up.

THIS IS WHAT YOU HEAR: "Kobe made it." "The Williams sisters made it." "Why don't you work harder?" Well, working harder did not solve the problems when the levy collapsed in New Orleans and two hundred thousand people were sent into exile.

SOMETIMES it's the context. If Michael Richards is sincere, then you forgive. You redeem, and you move on.

WHEN YOU'RE BEHIND, get up earlier.

STORMS COME, and they are so personal they seem to know your address and have the key to your house.

IF A BLACK DOCTOR discovers a cure for cancer, ain't no hospital going to lock him out.

I SUPPORTED BARACK in the state senate. I made his case before people knew who he was. There was no plan to attack him. I was talking about a philosophical difference. I had no idea it was being recorded. But locker-room trash talk has no place in the domain for responsible leaders. I was sincerely pained by the error and quick to apologize.

WHEN ALL THE DUST SETTLES, love covers all.

Interviewed by Cal Fussman | Photograph by Eric Johnson

BORN GREENVILLE, SOUTH CAROLINA 10.08.41

> JACKSON LED OPERATION BREADBASKET, THE ECONOMIC ARM OF THE SCLC, MARTIN LUTHER KING JR.'S SOUTHERN CHRISTIAN LEADERSHIP CONFERENCE.
> JACKSON ATTENDED THE UNIVERSITY OF ILLINOIS ON A FOOTBALL SCHOLARSHIP BEFORE TRANSFERRING TO NORTH CAROLINA A&T, WHERE HE GOT INVOLVED IN THE CIVIL RIGHTS MOVEMENT.

> **THE GRASS** may always be greener on the other side, but who knows what chemicals that guy is using?
—VINCENT O'KEEFE, AVON LAKE, OHIO

> **PUT YOUR BLUE** socks on the opposite side of the drawer from your black socks.
—JOE CASSIDY, EAST AURORA, ILLINOIS

> **THERE IS A POKER** analogy for just about everything.
—JE BANACH, UNIONVILLE, CONNECTICUT

> **BY THE TIME** it was all said and done, I spent almost $200,000 on my college education. By the time it was all said and done, the U.S. government spent $2,435.98 on my ceramic body armor, Kevlar helmet, and flak jacket. As the cadence says, "I love working for Uncle Sam / Lets me know just who I am." It also lets me know what I think I'm worth and what they think I'm worth.
—FIRST LT. TIMOTHY HECK, USMC, CAMP FALLUJAH, IRAQ

> **NEVER TRUST** a man who wears gloves with the fingers cut off. —COLIN KIETZMAN, ST. LOUIS, MISSOURI

> **THE SOUND OF LAUGHTER** coming from a room does not necessarily mean everyone is having a good time. Same is true of group photos where everyone is smiling.
—JOHN GACCIONE, DIX HILLS, NEW YORK

> **STEP 1:** Put keys in pocket. Step 2: Open door to trash chute. Step 3: Drop trash bag down chute. Step 4: Close door to trash chute. Step 5: Remove keys from pocket.
—CHRISTOPHER HEAD, SEATTLE, WASHINGTON

> **A GOOD DRINK**, one good drink, can really help you let go of a crappy day.
—RICK VAIL, HILLSBOROUGH, NEW JERSEY

> **YOU CAN TELL** a lot about a person by the way they karaoke. —STEVEN RAMIREZ, HOUSTON, TEXAS

> **IF AT THE END** of an anecdote you have to say, "It was so funny," it wasn't. —BRIAN GOTTA, SAN DIEGO, CALIFORNIA

> **VONNEGUT** said the existence of music is proof of the existence of God. Don't agree? Go see Springsteen on Saturday night and go to church on Sunday morning, then tell me which event made you feel more alive. —
TIMOTHY McGANN, SOUTH YARMOUTH, MASSACHUSETTS

> **NEVER LET PEOPLE** roll you down hills inside of things.
—HUGH ROSS, LOS ANGELES, CALIFORNIA

> **SHORTLY AFTER** I got my driver's license, I defied my strict Catholic parents and drove to the Baskin-Robbins across town instead of Sunday evening services. While I haven't been back to church since, I had my doubts back then and was worried about the sudden possibility of getting struck by lightning or falling down dead of unknown causes. To ease my fears, I came up with this rationalization about heaven while sitting on the hood of my brother's '78 Camaro and eating a hot fudge sundae: I like who I am, and while I'll make mistakes, if I don't get into heaven because of what I believe, then that's not the place I want to be. I still believe that.
—CHRIS HEAD, SEATTLE, WASHINGTON

> **IF A WAITER** in France looks at you and tells you that you won't like what you just ordered, trust him. Ditto Spain.
—TODD LOWE, HONG KONG

> **THE PRETTY GIRL** you just held the door open for? Go back and introduce yourself. That's how I met my wife. Best thing I ever did.
—STEVE SCHNIER, TORONTO, CANADA

> **IF WE PUSH CLOSER:** more and harder. If we pull back: less and lighter. The simplest formula too often forgotten. —CHRISTY WEATHERS, AUSTIN, TEXAS

> **IF A WOMAN** asks you how many sexual partners you've had, the only answer is twelve.
—MARK MOTRONI, MANHASSET, NEW YORK

> **I DIDN'T ASK** for my 38Ds, but I sure wouldn't give them back. —ANDREA CRAIG, BIRMINGHAM, ALABAMA

> **RELIGION** is in many ways like a good pair of shoes. It gives support, a little bit of a lift in your days, and it separates us from the other animals. But personally, I prefer to go barefoot. —GORDON HATHERLEY, LAKE STATION, INDIANA

> **SOME THINGS** are best left un-Googled. —GREG ROBICHEAUX, LAFAYETTE, LOUISIANA

> **FUCK SUBTLETY.** —DANIEL WILD, NEW YORK CITY

> **ALWAYS** approach the intimidatingly attractive woman. If you get turned down, who cares? You aren't having any less sex with her. —JON LEGG, NORMAL, ILLINOIS

> **I HAVE** cerebral palsy. That means my muscles don't work the way I want them to. My dad is helping me write this. Here's what I've learned: To make friends, smile. A dog makes you cool. The Three Stooges crack me up. And a roller-coaster ride is an amazing experience, especially if you can't move around much by yourself. —JASON GACKSTETTER, AGE 6, SAN DIEGO, CALIFORNIA

> **I WASH MY SHEETS** every Thursday. It's just an optimistic way of going into the weekend. —CHRISTOPHER HERBERT, MINNEAPOLIS, MINNESOTA

> **THE BEST PART** of the party is where the smokers are. —GARRETT PHILLIPS, ATLANTA, GEORGIA

> **IF YOU WONDER** whether your tie is too short or too long, retie it. —JAMES FELICIANO, TOKYO, JAPAN

> **OUR SYSTEM** of government may be the greatest in the world, but it doesn't work very well. Politics makes it impossible. In 1994, I was in Senator Joe Biden's office and saw an enormous portrait of him. That sums it up. It should have been a wall-sized portrait of the citizens of Delaware. —ANDREW GLOVER, OSKALOOSA, IOWA

> **LISTEN TO** the quiet, nagging doubts. —JASON HUBBERT, OKLAHOMA CITY, OKLAHOMA

> **YOU CAN'T LIVE OFF** of yesterday's orgasms. —MIGGS BURROUGHS, WESTPORT, CONNECTICUT

> **ONE** of the things women claim is most important in a man is a sense of humor. In my years as a comedian, I've learned that they're usually referring to the humor of guys like Brad Pitt, Tom Cruise, and Russell Crowe. Apparently, those guys are hilarious. —JIMI MCFARLAND, DENVER, COLORADO

> **NEVER PARTY** with people wearing rented clothes. —DAVE KESSLER, RICHMOND, INDIANA

> **"NO" MEANS NO**, "Maybe next Saturday night when the kids are sleeping out" means no, and "That's disgusting" means never, at least not without a major credit card. —ROBERT CHANNICK, DEERFIELD, ILLINOIS

> **WHEN TELLING** the world what you've learned, bear in mind that most people couldn't give the remotest shit about what you've learned unless it qualifies as inside information under the Securities Exchange Act of 1934 or will help them get laid. —JEFFREY S. LISABETH, LLOYD HARBOR, NEW YORK

> **NEVER UNDERESTIMATE** the pleasure of warm socks. —PAUL STERN, EDMUNDS, WASHINGTON

Ted Kennedy { SENATOR FROM

MASSACHUSETTS—WASHINGTON, D.C. }

> **IF I COULD** have a meal with anybody, living or dead, who would it be with? My brothers who left too early. My sisters. My parents. I always associated the times when we were together—and there weren't that many times when we were all together—as the happiest times. There'd be magnificent conversation. It would be blueberry season, and my mother would ensure that we'd have blueberry muffins. We'd have blueberry pancakes. We'd have blueberry pie. We'd have blueberry *everything*.

THERE ISN'T A DAY that goes by when I don't think about my brothers.

MY FATHER WOULD SAY, "Do the best you can. And then the hell with it." He always looked at the effort grade rather than the final grade.

WHEN I WAS SEVEN, I had the honor of receiving my first holy communion from the pope when my family went to Rome for his coronation. There were seven seats allocated to the United States and each of the major world powers. My parents arrived at St. Peter's with nine children. So there were eleven of us in seven seats. I, being the youngest, was squeezed to the far end of a very small bench. I remember one of the central thoughts I had during the whole ceremony: being squeezed in but still not being separated. That had a lot of significance to me over the course of my life.

WHEN I WAS A BOY, I used to look up at the sky at night and stare at the stars. I thought they were little pinpricks in a big covering and that the bright light that came through was really heaven on the other side.

MY MOTHER WAS THE SAFE HARBOR for our family. The gift of faith came from her.

THERE ARE TOO MANY people being left behind and left out.

I LIKE TO HAVE TWO DOGS in my office. Splash, here, is wonderful company. He's got a great personality. He's been known to bark when people speak too loudly or for too long. Some have asked that we make him a permanent member of our Democratic party caucus so that speeches will be shorter.

MY FAVORITE RESTAURANT? Dunkin' Donuts. Uh-oh. Better not say that. Besides, that's not a restaurant. Make it . . . Legal Sea Foods.

YOU MUST be prepared for good luck.

IF YOU MAKE A MISTAKE, recognize it, learn from it, and move on.

A GOOD MARRIAGE is loving someone in a lot of different circumstances. Respect for them and their views and ideas and the life that they're leading with you. Shared values and interests. A good sense of humor. And a little volatility along the way.

I SAID THAT I *knew* the first time I set eyes on Vicki. But then she brought out a picture. She had worked in my office as an intern years before I thought I saw her for the first time. So it wasn't really love at first sight. We still have that picture. It says, "To Vicki, Thanks for your work." And it's signed *Ted Kennedy*.

I GET UP VERY EARLY in the morning. I enjoy the quietness, the stillness, the rawness in the winter and fall. It's a special time.

HAVING A CHILD with cancer reaches to the very depths of your soul. Particularly because there is so little you can do, yet certainly more that you can do now than when Teddy had it. We were fortunate to have access to good health care. Secondly, fortunate to have health insurance. Many of the parents I met at the hospital had children who were taking a similar treatment. That treatment was to last for two years. Some parents sold their houses to pay for it. Some could only afford twelve or fourteen months of the treatment. They were asking the doctors, "What percent does that reduce my child's chances of being able to survive?" So, you ask me why I'm for health care. I didn't need a reason before, but that's a reason I'll never forget.

WHEN YOU'RE OLDER, FAITH is a very powerful factor and force in helping you look for the hopeful aspects of life. It gives you a sense of purpose and resolution. It's a matter of great solace and strength.

I'VE ASKED MY CHILDREN to make their presents to me on birthdays and holidays—and I do the same—related to shared experiences. See up there on the wall? That picture of me and Patrick sailing. Patrick was a boy at the time. The boat is being blown very hard. You can barely see him because he was small, but he's sitting next to me and being carefully protected. He accompanied the picture with that note, a quote from one of my speeches: "Should the storm come, we shall keep the rudder true."

THERE WERE NINE KENNEDYS. Thirty-two in the next generation. And sixty-two in the next generation. Forty-four of those sixty-two are aged thirteen or younger. I'm very blessed. I took forty-two of them camping last summer for two days. We had a great time, but, well, what's the best way to say this? I'm not sure when we're going on the next camping trip . . .

Interviewed by Cal Fussman | Photograph by Gerald Förster

BORN BROOKLINE, MASSACHUSETTS—02.22.32

> KENNEDY WAS FIRST ELECTED TO FINISH THE TERM OF HIS BROTHER, JOHN F. KENNEDY, AFTER JFK BECAME PRESIDENT.

> HE RAN FOR PRESIDENT IN 1980, BUT WAS DEFEATED FOR THE DEMOCRATIC NOMINATION BY INCUMBENT JIMMY CARTER.

> IN JUNE 2008, KENNEDY UNDERWENT SURGERY FOR A MALIGNANT BRAIN TUMOR.

Kris Kristofferson { SINGER, ACTOR, WRITER—

SANTA MONICA, CALIFORNIA }

> **YOU DON'T PADDLE AGAINST** the current, you paddle with it. And if you get good at it, you throw away the oars.

NEVER GIVE UP, which is the lesson I learned from boxing. As soon as you learn to never give up, you have to learn the power and wisdom of unconditional surrender and that one doesn't cancel out the other; they just exist as contradictions. The wisdom of it comes as you get older.

IF YOU CAN'T get out of something, get into it. If you can't fix it, fuck it.

TELL THE TRUTH. Sing with passion. Work with laughter. Love with heart. 'Cause that's all that matters in the end.

THERE ARE POINTS IN YOUR LIFE, especially if you have creative ambitions, where selfishness is necessary.

IF GOD MADE ANYTHING better than women, I think he kept it for himself.

I BELIEVE IN THE HERB, and if it were up to me, it would be legalized.

THE NUMBER ONE RULE of the road is never go to bed with anyone crazier than yourself. You will break this rule, and you will be sorry.

I'VE BEEN TRYING to think of things to tell my kids, something that I could pass down, and it's like, gee whiz, I maybe never learned anything that didn't contradict itself.

THE CLOSEST I'VE COME to knowing myself is in losing myself. That's why I loved football before I loved music. I could lose myself in it. Music and drugs and rock 'n' roll—all of it is for you to lose yourself.

KISSINGER had his reasons.

THE OLDER I GET, the less conservative I become.

DENNIS HOPPER playing golf is one of the first signs of the apocalypse. It's true—he's become a Republican.

IT'S HARD TO TURN AWAY when you feel like you are getting paid more than you deserve.

WHEN I WAS THIRTY and a long time after that, I felt like I had to leave home to do what I had to do. Now, it's just the opposite.

THE ONE THING I REGRET is missing the time with my older children when they were young. I think of it when I'm carrying my little four-year-old around. We'd already split up by the time my son was born, and I rarely got to hold him, but, fortunately, we are very close now. In fact, if I had to live with one person on an island, I'd probably live with him, 'cause he's the funniest son of a bitch I know.

I WAS A SLOW STARTER. I mean, I grew up in the fifties, and, jeez, I wasn't even laid in high school. Looking back on it, I didn't know anything, which was kind of unfortunate for my first couple of wives. When I found out that girls like sex as much as guys, I was, for many years, feeling like that was my function. I mean, I wasn't as bad as Clinton, but I was led by the pecker.

I'M SURE YOU SLOW DOWN a little bit, but I'm also sure that you'll probably be getting a hard-on until they throw dirt on you.

BEING IN LOVE with a lot of people is incompatible with a stable family life.

THE DESIRE to be fucked up probably leaves you, but the desire to be high never does.

I'VE TRIED to be more self-sufficient as I've gotten older. I'd like to not worry about whether they're going to sell my next album or book. Hell, William Blake wasn't even published in his lifetime.

WHEN WAS THE LAST TIME you looked at the stars with the wonder they deserve? That they're out there is totally a mystery.

FREEDOM IS JUST ANOTHER WORD: It seems to get truer the older I get. It makes me think about the time when my apartment got robbed and everything was gone and I was disowned by my family. I owed money to a hospital, and I owed my wife five hundred a month for child support, and I thought, "I'm losing my job." I hadn't any money, I hadn't anything going for me, but it was liberating. I was in this Evangeline Motel, like something out of *Psycho*, a filthy place, just sitting there with this neon Jesus outside the door, in the swamps outside of Lafayette, Louisiana, and I thought, "Fuck. I'm on the bottom, can't go any lower"—and from then on, man, I drove my car to the airport, left it there, and never went back to get it. Went to Nashville and called this friend of mine, Mickey Newberry, and told him I'd just got fired, and he said, "Great. Johnny Cash is shooting a new TV show. Come up, and we can pitch him some songs." The next moment, they cut three of my songs, and they were hits. I never had to go back to work again.

Interviewed by Scott Carrier | Photograph by Anton Corbijn

BORN BROWNSVILLE, TEXAS—06.22.36

> KRISTOFFERSON WON A BEST ACTOR GOLDEN GLOBE IN 1977 FOR HIS ROLE IN *A STAR IS BORN,* OPPOSITE BARBRA STREISAND, AND WAS NOMINATED FOR AN OSCAR FOR HIS ORIGINAL MUSIC IN *SONGWRITER* (1984).

> HE WROTE "ME AND BOBBY MCGEE," WHICH BECAME A HIT FOR HIS FORMER GIRLFRIEND, JANIS JOPLIN.

Jack LaLanne { GURU—MORRO BAY, CALIFORNIA }

I'M GOING TO BE NINETY in September. Everybody else can have a piece of the birthday cake, but not me. I have rules, and I follow 'em. No cake, no pie, no candy, no ice cream! Haven't had any in seventy-five years. It makes me feel great *not* eating birthday cake. That's the gift I give myself.

FORGET ABOUT WHAT YOU *USED* TO DO. This is the moment you've been waiting for.

DON'T ASK ME about politics. I don't like to get into Barbra Streisand-ism. Let's stick to what's important.

WHEN I WAS YOUNGER, I drank a quart of blood a day for about six weeks. I'd get it at the slaughterhouse. I'd heard about those Masais, you know, those seven-foot African guys; they'd drink cattle blood for strength. Then one day a little clot got stuck in my throat, and that was it for me.

AS LONG AS THE EMPHASIS is on winning, you're gonna have steroids.

IF MAN MAKES IT, don't eat it.

OF COURSE I HAVE FEARS. But what good is thinking or talking about them? Billy Graham is about the hereafter. I'm for the here and now.

YOU'VE GOT TO SATISFY YOU. If you can't satisfy you, you're a failure.

I WORK OUT for two hours every morning, seven days a week—even when I'm traveling. I hate it. But I love the result! That's the key, baby!

THE ONLY WAY you can hurt your body is if you don't use it.

LOOK, are you a suckling calf? Name one creature on earth that uses milk after it's weaned. Man's the only one. And man's the only one who lives out only half his life span. A cow has four stomachs. You don't. You can't handle whole milk.

I'D LIKE TO TALK TO JESUS about those twelve disciples. They were a great public relations team.

IF YOU WANT TO CHANGE somebody, don't preach to him. Set an example and shut up.

SCALES LIE! You lose thirty pounds of muscle, and you gain thirty pounds of fat, and you weigh the same, right? Take that tape measure out. That won't lie. Your waistline is your lifeline. It should be the same as it was when you were a young person.

IF YOU LOSE A COUPLE OF INCHES off your stomach, your business down there will look an inch longer.

SEX IS GIVING, giving, giving. The more energy you have, the more you're going to please.

NOW, I'M NOT as sexually active as I was when I was younger. But look at my wife—she's still smiling!

THE GUY WHO'S MOST IMPRESSED ME is Paul C. Bragg. He completely saved my life. When I was a kid, I was addicted to sugar. I was a skinny kid with pimples and boils. Used to eat ice cream by the quart. I had blinding headaches. I tried to commit suicide. And then one day, my life changed. Bragg was a nutritionist. My mother and I were a little late getting to his lecture. The place was packed, and so we started to leave. But Bragg said, "We don't turn anybody away here. Ushers, bring two seats. Put those two up on the stage." It was the most humiliating moment. There I was, up on stage. I was so ashamed of the way I looked; I didn't want people to see me. Little did I know they had problems, too. And Bragg said, "It doesn't matter what your age is, what your physical condition is. If you obey nature's laws, you can be born again." From that moment on, I completely changed my diet, began to exercise, and went on to become captain of the football team. And do you know something? Every time I get ready to lecture, I think, "If I can just help one person like I was helped . . ."

SHOW ME THE GUY who doesn't get nervous in front of a crowd and I'll show you a lousy speaker.

WOULD YOU get your dog up every day, give him a cup of coffee, a doughnut, and a cigarette? Hell, no. You'd kill the damn dog.

YOU LEARN AS YOU GO. When I first went on television in 1951, I pulled out a loaf of Langendorf's white bread, squeezed it into a ball, and threw it down—*boom*. "That's what it does when it hits your stomach!" I said. Only problem was that Langendorf's was one of the network's sponsors! Oh, jeez, the phone calls. That's the last time I ever showed a label.

GO ON, HAVE A GLASS OF WINE with dinner. What is wine, anyway? Pure grapes. A glass of wine is much better for you than a Coke.

IF I DON'T KNOW what I'm doing by now, I must be pretty stupid.

WHAT I DO ISN'T ABOUT MONEY. Can you put a price on a human life?

ANY STUPID PERSON CAN DIE. Dying's easy. Living's a pain in the butt.

I CAN'T AFFORD TO DIE. It'll wreck my image.

Interviewed by Cal Fussman | Photograph by Bryce Duffy

BORN SAN FRANCISCO, CALIFORNIA—09.26.14

> LaLANNE CLAIMS HE ATE JUNK FOOD AND SUGAR UNTIL AGE FIFTEEN, WHEN HE HEARD NUTRITIONIST PAUL C. BRAGG SPEAK.

> IN 1975, AT AGE 61, LaLANNE SWAM THE LENGTH OF THE GOLDEN GATE BRIDGE, UNDERWATER, HANDCUFFED, TOWING A THOUSAND-POUND BOAT.

Elmore Leonard { WRITER—DETROIT }

BAD GUYS are not bad guys twenty-four hours a day.

I LIKE HOMICIDE DETECTIVES. They wear hats. They wear hats so that other law enforcement people will know they're homicide.

AS A LITTLE KID, I wanted to play with a knife, and my mother wouldn't let me. I cried, and she gave me a rubber one. I said, "Mom, a rubber knife just doesn't do it."

I'VE BEEN MARRIED THREE TIMES. During the first one, I had a love affair. Then I divorced, and Joan and I were married. She died in '93, and I felt I had to get married again. Quickly. I like being married. Just then, the French-speaking landscaper showed up. Christine is twenty-four years younger than me. We started talking, and that was it. I remember saying to a friend, "I'm thinking of marriage again, but Joan's been dead for only six months. Don't you think I should wait a year?" He said, "What are you, Sicilian?"

THE BEST THING about my kids is the fact that I can count on them. I knew they'd understand when I married somebody their age.

YOU DO APPRECIATE sex more as you age. The simple fact is there will be fewer and fewer situations.

MY MATERIAL LOOKS like a movie. Then when the studio gets into it, they find out it's not quite as simple as it looks.

THE CONVICTS WHO WRITE ME assume I've done time.

A LINE OF DIALOGUE is not clear enough if you need to explain how it's said.

ONCE, I came back from Hollywood in the early seventies throwing up blood. My doctor said, "We're going to have to do an exploratory operation." He said, "Acute gastritis? That's something you see with skid row bums." I was drinking heavily.

ALCOHOL NEVER PREVENTED ME from writing. But when I quit—on January 24, 1977, at 9:30 a.m.—my fiction got better.

I WAS BROUGHT UP CATHOLIC. I don't go to receive the sacrament anymore. But it's important to me to go through this little drill about what my purpose is before I get out of bed every morning.

GOD'S WILL is not necessarily something bad that happens to you. You can become a millionaire, and that's God's will. You have to look at it this way: what are you doing to deserve God's will?

I TRIED TO ENLIST in the Marines when I was seventeen, but they wouldn't let me in because of my left eye. It was probably a good thing. I would've been shipped off to Iwo Jima, I'm sure. I'd have been pushing up that flag—or daisies.

I DON'T HAVE A COMPUTER, so I don't have to contend with e-mail. I do have—what do you call it, when you send printed messages over the phone? . . . A *fax*, yeah, that's it. I do have one of those.

A PEN CONNECTS YOU to the paper. It definitely matters.

WHEN YOU MEET SOMEBODY who bores you, you have to put up with him until he leaves. But when you meet a boring character, you turn the page.

A GOOD EDITOR is someone who knows what your problem is.

I GAVE A TALK in Florida and became friends with a judge who invited me to his home. He showed me his gardens and orchids. Then he showed me some photos. One was of a guy with a butcher knife in his head. Another was of a car that had been buried underground with a cadaver in it. After they pulled the car up, they had to park it behind an airplane with the propellers going just to blow all the corruption out. He also showed me a photograph of a dead chicken that had been sexually violated.

DON'T BE SURPRISED at anything untoward that you come across.

THERE'S A SCENE IN MY NEXT BOOK in which a character who's been traveling around with this girl leaves her in a motel room and goes out to see some buddies. The next morning, he comes back and he's hungover—terribly hungover. And he says, "I can't believe what we did with those chickens last night." And that's all he says. She wonders what they were doing with those chickens—but it's left to the imagination.

I'VE WRITTEN FORTY NOVELS. I don't know why, but my favorite is *Freaky Deaky*.

WE'VE RAISED MONEY for charities by having people bid to get their names in one of my novels. A diminutive curator at the Detroit Institute of Arts won one auction. His name is Elliot Wilhelm. So I used his name for the 260-pound gay Samoan in *Be Cool*. It's the character played by the Rock in the movie. At first I didn't hear from the real Elliot Wilhelm. But I came to find out that he loved the idea.

IF AN ADVERB became a character in one of my books, I'd have it shot. Immediately.

Interviewed by Cal Fussman | Photograph by Jeff Mermelstein

BORN NEW ORLEANS, LOUISIANA—10.11.25

> LEONARD HAS WRITTEN NEARLY FORTY NOVELS, MANY OF WHICH HAVE BEEN MADE INTO FILMS. AMONG THE MOST NOTABLE ARE *3:10 TO YUMA* (TWICE, IN 1957 AND 2007), *THE BIG BOUNCE* (1969 AND 2004), *GET SHORTY* (1995), *RUM PUNCH* (AS *JACKIE BROWN*, 1997), *OUT OF SIGHT* (1998), AND *BE COOL* (2005).

> LEONARD HAS NEVER SPENT SO MUCH AS A NIGHT IN JAIL.

Jerry Lewis { COMEDIAN—LAS VEGAS }

HEY, PENNY! Forty-three years, Penny's been in my office. She's something else. She doesn't let me get away with anything. Penny, bring me an orange soda, honey. You haven't done a goddamn thing all day.

I WILL TELL YOU about interviews: I've had them run from two and a half minutes to nine hours. Rarely anything in between. If I get to an interview and I can see they're not that interested, I tell them, "Since the surgery, I get these heart spasms." And they're gone.

EVERYBODY IS NINE YEARS OLD. Starting with me.

YOU KNOW what I'm going to be, don't ya? The big eighty! Jesus Christ, that's depressing.

IF YOU'RE NOT NERVOUS, you're either a liar or a fool. But you're not a professional.

I PERFORMED FOR SIX PRESIDENTS. I met nine. One of my most prized possessions is a plaque Jack Kennedy gave me that says, "There are three things that are real: God, human folly, and laughter. Since the first two are beyond our comprehension, we must do the best we can with the third."

DON'T come telling anybody they're wrong until you can tell them how they can be right.

ADRENALINE IS WONDERFUL. It covers pain. It covers dementia. It covers everything.

I USED TO FALL because the fall worked—because it paid off. And I had the best time. If you had told me that I would suffer from it years later, I would not have changed a thing.

WANT A LIST? Diabetes. Pulmonary fibrosis. Bypass surgery—double. I had three surgeries on my spine. My spine is a joke. Every time I took a fall, my dad would say, "You're going to pay for that one." And he was right. So every time I get a new diagnosis, I think, "Where did I get that one from?"

EGO IS NECESSARY.

PENNY! Do we have a photograph of *The Ladies Man* set?

I'VE NEVER paid a lady for her services. Even at sixteen years old, and a pretty horny kid, I just never could do that. It had nothing to do with morals. It had to do with "That lady's somebody's daughter."

I'M ABOUT TO TELL YOU SOMETHING I have never, ever told anybody: I never read anything that's written about me. Ever.

TOM SHALES in *The Washington Post* wrote about the telethon in 2003. He said, "The Jerry Lewis telethon is one of the greatest shows on earth, and one of America's greatest showmen is the guy behind it." I read that twice.

IN 1954, a child diagnosed with muscular dystrophy was given a death sentence. He was gone in a year. A child today diagnosed with any of the neuromuscular diseases can go for twenty years. So you want to talk to me about using pity? I don't care what I have to use. I used to say, "If there's a guy in a bar and you tell me that if I become a transvestite I can get a hundred bucks out of him, I'll dress up and get it if it's for my kids."

YOU DON'T HAVE TO be terribly funny to dress in drag. It's no challenge.

THAT SAID, I'm ashamed to tell you that I turned down *Some Like It Hot.* See how smart I am? I felt I couldn't bring anything funny to it. The outfit was funny. I don't need to compete with the wardrobe. So whenever Billy Wilder saw me, he said, "Good afternoon, schmuck, how's it going?" And, of course, Jack Lemmon sent me candy and roses every holiday, and the card always read, "THANKS FOR BEING AN IDIOT."

I HAD A MEETING with eight or nine studio executives recently. I told them, "You bought the option to remake *The Bellboy* in 1996, and for nine years you can't get it made? I made it in less than nine days, including writing the final draft." I said, "Come to me with a deal, and I'll write the screenplay for you." They said they'd get back to me.

THAT WAS THREE MONTHS AGO.

IN HOLLYWOOD, *control* is a dirty word. That's in granite, kid.

MY REPUTATION is that I had an affair with every one of my leading ladies. One of my leading ladies was Agnes Moorehead, so let's just put that reputation where it belongs.

MEN CAN DEMEAN THEMSELVES for a laugh. Women can, too, but it's a tougher laugh.

PENNY! I love you my darling, you old horse.

A FEW YEARS AGO, I thought I might open a chain of eulogy stores where you could go in off the street and, for twenty bucks, they'll tell you all the nice things they're going to say about you after you croak. But I don't want people to say wonderful things about me when I can't hear them. Tell me now, while I'm still here.

Interviewed by Amy Wallace | Photograph by Art Streiber

BORN NEWARK, NEW JERSEY—03.26.26

> LEWIS STARTED PERFORMING AT AGE FIVE, SINGING ON NEW YORK'S BORSCHT CIRCUIT, IN THE CATSKILLS.
> HE HAS ACTED IN MORE THAN FIFTY FILMS.
> HE WAS NOMINATED FOR THE NOBEL PEACE PRIZE IN 1977 FOR HIS EFFORTS TO RAISE MONEY TO BATTLE MUSCULAR DYSTROPHY.

John Malkovich { ACTOR—CAMBRIDGE, MASSACHUSETTS }

> **NOTHING** you do particularly matters. But I'm not sure that's a great excuse for doing it poorly.

I'VE PRETTY MUCH LEARNED not to worry about things I can't control. I often find myself with friends and acquaintances, and they're worrying about this or that. I say, "You're worried about the plane going down? What are you, a pilot?"

IT STILL INTERESTS ME to try and make a kind of perfect play. I mean, you'll never even be close. Like a great baseball player hits .320 or .318, maybe even .340 one year. We hit like .060. And it's OK. If you think you've discerned what went wrong before, by the time you apply your little brain to that, several hundred things have gone wrong. Things are flawed or damaged or corrupted or all three. But that's kind of nice because it reminds me of life and because a lot of times when people have made superexceptional things, it's really hard for them to go again.

THERE WILL BE PEOPLE who will hate anything you do. And some people will really love it. But that's not really different from the people who really hate it.

THIS IS WHAT POLITICS IS TO ME: Somebody tells you all the trees on your street have a disease. One side says give them food and water and everything will be fine. One side says chop them down and burn them so they don't infect another street. That's politics. And I'm going, "Who says they're diseased? And how does this sickness manifest itself? And is this outside of a natural cycle? And who said this again? And when were they on the street?" But we just have people who shout, "Chop it down and burn it" or "Give it food and water," and there's your two choices. Sorry, I'm not a believer.

I BELIEVE IN HUMANS.

A MOVIE IS LIKE A LINE DRAWING, but a theater performance is like a painting. It develops over what seems like an extraordinary amount of time. I did a play called *Burn This* for two years. It probably took me about six months—the accents, the vocal patterns, the rapidity, what I had in my head—to run it through my mouth—'cause it's a painting. You do a little bit each day.

I LIKE TO WORK. I go to the theater, and maybe I'm upset about something. And the play starts, and I start watching. And it's too late, I'm already lost in it—and when I say "lost in it," I don't mean lost in the magic of it, because, to me, the magic of it is the work. What went wrong? How could it be different? Why was it so good tonight and so absolutely gobsmackingly awful in the matinee? What is this great mystery?

A LOT of our wonderful actors, from Brando to George C. Scott, found it a shameful occupation and really lost interest in it. But it always interests me, and watching others do it always interests me, and I don't find it shameful. I mean, as compared to what?

TWENTY-FIVE OR THIRTY YEARS AGO, you became famous, what's the worst that could happen to you? Page Six? Cindy Adams? Liz Smith? There weren't cell phones with cameras. Waiters didn't listen to your conversations and send them to Drudge or Defamer or Gawker or Jezebel or Agent Bedhead. Now we're all Japanese. We're a nation of paparazzi. And it's OK. You make your peace with it. We get so many rewards, we're much more remunerated than other people, so I guess we should take more licks than other people, too.

IT'S HARD TO BELIEVE Michelle Pfeiffer ever said hello to me—not that she's not memorable, God knows. But I sort of blacked it out. What I'm trying to say is, when I think of the other person, I don't think of me as involved with them. They're uncorrupted by me. As if they were never troubled by my existence.

I'M ALWAYS MISTRUSTFUL of people saying they know this or that. When you think of how history is revealed, we know certain things to be facts at certain periods of time, which turn out not to be so factual as time marches on.

I DON'T REMEMBER my life before I had children.

IT WAS FANTASTIC when they were growing up. But they're not terrifically interested in either me or what I do. I remember Amandine was nine, and Nicole was trying to explain to them that I didn't work in the garden with a guy called Mark, that isn't what I did for a living. And they didn't believe it.

GETTING OLDER is just so irritating. I was never a great tennis player, but I loved to play. Now, I can't brace like that, let alone run after the ball. Playing basketball, I can't jump. It irritates me a lot. But this year, I started ferociously going to the gym—two or three hours a day and really hitting it hard. I hate not being able to do things I like to do much more than I hate going to the gym.

I'M A SORT OF NONSMOKER—let's just put it that way. I'll always be a smoker who just doesn't smoke.

Interviewed by John H. Richardson | Photograph by Jake Chessum

BORN CHRISTOPHER, ILLINOIS—12.08.53

> MALKOVICH WON AN EMMY FOR THE TV MOVIE *DEATH OF A SALESMEN* (1985) AND WAS NOMINATED FOR OSCARS FOR *PLACES IN THE HEART* (1984) AND *IN THE LINE OF FIRE* (1993).
> HE PLAYED HIMSELF IN *BEING JOHN MALKOVICH* (1999), IN WHICH A PUPPETEER SELLS TRIPS INTO MALKOVICH'S HEAD.

Arthur Miller { PLAYWRIGHT—NEW YORK CITY }

> **YOU HAVE TO LEARN** how to duck, because they're going to throw it at you.

SEX is the most compressed set of circumstances that we've got. Everything is in that collision.

WHAT I'M DOING is helping reality out—to complete itself. I'm giving it a hand. But there's some piece of reality that is a reported reality that it hangs on. It does hang on it.

WHEN I WAS IN NEVADA, I lived about sixty miles out of Reno. There was a guy who had this house on stilts. In the desert. And that was a very curious thing, looking at this house raised up about ten feet above the ground. I wondered, "Was he waiting for a flood?" Well, it turned out he had a hole in the ground under that house, and there was a silver mine down at the bottom of this hole. He would periodically go down and dig himself out some silver. That was his bank. And I think that's like a writer. He's living on top of that hole. He goes down there and sees if he can chop out some silver.

THERE'S SUCH A VARIETY of cultures in this country, we can be misled only up to a certain point. As soon as we start marching in step, somebody loses a beat somewhere.

I'VE ALWAYS DONE things physical. When I was about six, I made a go-cart. You couldn't steer it, and you'd be doing thirty miles an hour down the street, but I remember telling my brother, "Pretty good for my own making." He always used to kid me about that sentence.

I KNEW PLAYWRIGHTS, young guys my age, who were simply not prepared to face the fact that their plays weren't any good. Mine weren't. I thought, "Either I do this right or I'm gonna get out of it. I'm not gonna spend the rest of my life being a fool."

SEX IS ALWAYS trouble. That's part of why it's so pleasurable—because for a moment the cloud lifts and then descends again.

I FIND MYSELF interested in what I'm looking at.

I DON'T BELIEVE in the afterlife. I don't believe there is a God. The whole thing is accidental.

I'M A WRITER, so I write. That's my job. But it's more than a job. I just have a terrifically pleasant feeling if I create a form that completes itself and you can walk around it. It's a whole object.

SOME PEOPLE should never get married. Not everyone has that combination of dependency. You're leaning on somebody, and the desire to support somebody else, it just doesn't exist in some people.

I COULD WRITE about failure only because I could deal with it. Most of my work before *Death of a Salesman*, 98 percent of it was a failure. By the time Willy Loman came along, I knew how he felt.

SOME FAILURES ARE RIGHT. And some people fail because society isn't ready for them. That's what makes it so difficult.

YOU SHOULD READ because it's a pleasure. Or go to the theater because it's a pleasure. That's what it's about, basically—even the pleasure of misery, if that happens to be the nature of the beast.

WHENEVER I hear somebody's in touch with God, I look for the exit.

THE ONLY THING that I am reasonably sure of is that anybody who's got an ideology has stopped thinking.

WHEN PLAYS were written in verse, by the very nature of the language, it tended toward what I call prophecy. The energy of springing out of the dead level of contemporary reality. And we don't write that way much anymore, so something else has to enter— this spirit of coming disaster or coming happiness or something coming.

I BELIEVE IN WORK. If somebody doesn't create something, however small it may be, he gets sick. An awful lot of people feel that they're treading water—that if they vanished in smoke, it wouldn't mean anything at all in this world. And that's a despairing and destructive feeling. It'll kill you.

THE MORE SEX the better. It may be a good thing to get it out in the open. You turn on the television now, and they're screwing on the television. That's part of life. Why hide it in a basement someplace and get a lot of gangsters to distribute it?

POLITICIANS ARE US, which is very dangerous. If they weren't us, it would be a lot better.

WE HAVE never, in my opinion, met up with this kind of an administration, which is extremely intelligent and has terrific control over the political life of the country. They are representing the rich people in a way that I didn't think was so blatantly possible. It's almost sociopathic. As though, "OK, if you can make it, you're one of us; if you can't make it, too bad, Jack." Some of the monkeys fall off the tree.

TO WRITE ANY KIND of imaginary work, you gotta fall on your sword. You gotta be ready to be blasted out of existence. Lots of times, the blood is on the floor.

Interviewed by John H. Richardson | Photograph by Inge Morath

BORN NEW YORK, NEW YORK—10.17.1915

DIED ROXBURY, CONNECTICUT—02.10.2005

> ONE OF THE LEADING PLAYWRIGHTS OF HIS GENERATION.

> MILLER'S MOST FAMOUS WORK, *DEATH OF A SALESMAN* (1949), WON BOTH A PULITZER PRIZE AND A DRAMA CRITICS CIRCLE AWARD.

> HE WROTE THE SCREENPLAY FOR THE FILM *THE MISFITS* (1961) FOR HIS SECOND WIFE, MARILYN MONROE; IT WAS BASED ON AN *ESQUIRE* SHORT STORY PUBLISHED IN 1957.

Bob Newhart { COMEDIAN—LOS ANGELES }

SOMETIMES YOU FORGET you're famous. You wonder, "Why is that person staring at me?"

I DON'T WANT TO find the secret. I'm afraid all the joy will go out of it if I find the secret.

HUMOR'S A WEAPON if you want to make it one.

IN TODAY'S WORLD, you would call my father mostly unaccessible. I'm not sure that isn't true of most fathers at that time. He went through the Depression. I don't know what that would have done to my psyche.

I'VE BEEN MARRIED FORTY-FIVE YEARS. I think laughter is the secret. For some reason comedians' marriages seem to last longer. Think of it: Jack Benny, George Burns, Buddy Hackett, Alan King—you can go down the list.

CELEBRITY HAS TWO SIDES. For one thing, it somewhat cuts you off from the source of your material. Whereas you used to be able to just go and observe people, you aren't quite as free. The other side of it is, especially having had a television series, that you're a part of people's lives. A movie star portrays one person and then the next one and then the next one, whereas you were the same person for years on the same show. People will say, "Yeah, my whole family used to sit and watch your show, and it was a bonding experience." You're part of people's personal history.

ONE OF THE FIRST THINGS you ever learn as a stand-up is don't show fear.

THE GIANT SUPERSTARS are people whose talent is so enormous that their death wish can't destroy it.

THE CALM-DELIVERY THING started when I was an accountant. At the end of the day, I'd be really going crazy. I had this friend of mine in advertising. I'd call him up and play a character, just to break the monotony of things. I'd call and I'd say, "Mr. Stevenson, I don't mean to bother you, but I'm here at the yeast factory, and a fire broke out, and they sent over a bunch of fire engines, and they're throwing water. I gotta run up to the second floor, 'cause the yeast is rising." I'd just make a whole scenario, and he was the straight man.

THERE'S GRATIFICATION in making somebody laugh. It's a wonderful sound. I find myself, to this day, doing it, wanting to make people laugh.

I THINK OF THOSE GREAT SONGS written during the Depression—they helped cheer people up. "Pennies from Heaven," "I've Got a Pocketful of Dreams." I suppose we need a few of them now. Maybe they could be in hip-hop, but I don't know if anyone would understand the lyrics.

I WASN'T the class clown. I wasn't that obvious. There would be a circle of guys, and they're watching the class clown. And I'm standing in the back, and I turn to the guy next to me, and I say something funny to him, and he starts to laugh. And the guy next to him says, "What did he say?"

THE OTHER DAY I was listening to the radio. The Afghan minister of tourism was assassinated. I'm thinking, "What threat did he pose to the Taliban? Who even wants to go to Afghanistan?" His phone rings once a month.

YOU SHOULDN'T get too close to the truth, because then maybe you stop being funny.

Interviewed by Mike Sager | Photograph by Jeff Minton

BORN OAK PARK, ILLINOIS—09.05.29

> NEWHART LEFT HIS JOB AS AN ACCOUNTANT IN CHICAGO TO PURSUE COMEDY IN 1958.

> HE WON THREE GRAMMY AWARDS FOR HIS COMEDY ALBUMS, INCLUDING BEST NEW ARTIST AND ALBUM OF THE YEAR FOR *THE BUTTON-DOWN MIND OF BOB NEWHART* (1960) AND BEST COMEDY PERFORMANCE–SPOKEN WORD FOR *THE BUTTON-DOWN MIND STRIKES BACK!* (1960).

Jack Nicholson { ACTOR—LOS ANGELES }

> **THEY'RE PRESCRIPTION.** That's why I wear them. A long time ago, the Middle American in me may have thought it was a bit affected, maybe. But the light is very strong in Southern California. And once you've experienced negative territory in public life, you begin to accept the notion of shields. I am a person who is trained to look other people in the eye. But I can't look into the eyes of everyone who wants to look into mine; I can't emotionally cope with that kind of volume. Sunglasses are part of my armor.

I HATE ADVICE unless I'm giving it.

I HATE GIVING ADVICE, because people won't take it.

I LOVE DISCOURSE. I'm dying to have my mind changed. I'm probably the only liberal who read *Treason*, by Ann Coulter. I want to know, you understand? I like listening to everybody. This to me is the elixir of life.

I DON'T THINK many people have a very good understanding of leisure and the importance it plays in our lives. People today are too competitive about leisure, as if it needs to have some other value in order to be able to fit into our puritanical view of the world. But if you're playing golf to get a loan, it ain't golf, you know what I mean?

I WAS PARTICULARLY PROUD of my performance as the Joker. I considered it a piece of pop art.

THE CAMERA photographs what's there.

RIGHT NOW, I'm upset because I was supposed to have the weekend to play golf. I just finished, like, two straight years of work. I thought I'd take some time for myself. I figured that this weekend I'd be able to get out there on the golf course. And then, boom! There goes my hamstring. And here's the rub: Rather than just give myself a break and say, "Okay, you have every excuse in the world to lay on your ass this weekend and watch the ball games, " I have to be a Calvinist. I have to complain: "Son of a bitch! I'm here. I'm inside. When's the hammie gonna get better? I've already tested it too early and hurt it again. How long is it gonna take to heal? Have I already ruined the next two weeks?

AFTER SEPTEMBER 11, I held my tongue. All of the public positions had been taken—for, against, good, evil. I had nothing more to add. So I thought, "Bring in the clowns," you know what I mean? That's why I've done a coupla years' worth of comedies.

I'M PRETTY WELL ashamed of this, but I only read the sports pages.

THE FUEL for the sports fan is the ability to have private theories.

I'VE ALWAYS THOUGHT BASKETBALL was the best sport, although it wasn't the sport I was best at. It was just the most fun to watch. I always said, "Batman and basketball. Night games and night comics." The basketball players were out at night. They had great overcoats. There was this certain nighttime juvenile-delinquent thing about it that got your blood going.

I'M THE AGE where we didn't have television as kids. So when I saw my nieces and nephews watching *Howdy Doody*; *Kukla, Fran and Ollie*; and so forth, I thought the world had gone mad.

IF YOU THINK ABOUT about those old shows, they all had puppets. And somehow I think, symbolically speaking, that has contributed to a generational lack of ability to accept personal responsibility. It's why the baby boomers are such conspiracy theorists and I'm not. It's why everybody thinks we went to Iraq to get the oil and I don't. I see that as a minor, symbolic generational difference that all adds up to mass movements. People are so frustrated. They don't want to take responsibility for their failures. There's always an excuse, you know? It's always "I'm this and that's why" or "This happended to me and that's why." Everyone has the impulse to point their fingers elsewhere. They point at the puppet: He did it! Not me!

I ALWAYS HESITATE to say things like this in interviews because they tend to come back to haunt you, but if I were an Arab-American, I would insist on being profiled. This is not the time for civil rights. There are larger issues for Americans.

LATELY, I've been de-emphasizing what actors think of as character work. The limps and the lisps, the accents—I don't want to be bothered. You gotta make it come from the inside. It's all about who you are. That's all you can really contribute. I feel autobiographical about whatever I do.

I WAS TALKING to Sean Penn on the phone today. I told him it was interesting that they managed to leave me off this long list of Method actors they'd published in some article. I told him, "I'm still fooling them!" I consider it an accomplishment. Because there's probably no one who understands Method acting better academically than I do—or actually uses it more in his work. But it's funny; nobody really sees that. It's perception versus reality, I guess.

>>

BORN NEPTUNE, NEW JERSEY—04.22.37

> NICHOLSON ROSE TO STARDOM IN 1969 WITH THE COUNTERCULTURE EPIC *EASY RIDER*, EARNING AN OSCAR NOMINATION FOR BEST SUPPORTING ACTOR.
> HE WROTE THE SCREENPLAY FOR *HEAD* (1968), A PSYCHEDELIC SAGA STARRING THE TELEVISION POP GROUP THE MONKEES.
> IN EACH OF THE FILMS FOR WHICH NICHOLSON WON AN OSCAR, THE LEADING ACTRESS WON THE BEST ACTRESS AWARD: LOUISE FLETCHER IN *ONE FLEW OVER THE CUCKOO'S NEST* (1975), SHIRLEY MACLAINE IN *TERMS OF ENDEARMENT* (1983), AND HELEN HUNT IN *AS GOOD AS IT GETS* (1997).

BELIEVE IT OR NOT, I supported Richard Nixon on the issue of presidential privilege. How could anyone conceive of being the president of the United States and think that every single thing that you say or do can become a part of the public record? It just seems so stupid to me. A man needs a private life.

MY MOTTO IS "More good times."

I THINK I'VE DONE OKAY. I take responsibility for my successes as well as my failures. But when I look at my professional mistakes, I'm always left with the feeling that maybe I should have done more. These are my private musings. I'm such a perfectionist. I always feel overpraised or whatever. In the abstract, I know I'm a good person, a good professional. But it's nice to be noticed a little bit, ain't it?

I'M CERTAINLY NOT as tough as people think. I'm not a fighter and so forth. I'd just as soon go home.

CHILDREN GIVE YOUR LIFE a resonance that it can't have without them.

I CERTAINLY knew my father. He just didn't happen to be my biological father.

THAT IS CORRECT: I didn't know that my sister was really my mother until I was thirty-seven years old. But life has taught me that there have been a lot of things that I didn't know. If I start giving that more weight because of the half-digested view of an analytical life, it's working against you, you know what I mean? Accentuate the positive, that's what I say. It's a trick, but it works.

HERE'S ANOTHER old actor saying: "It's very easy to go down, so always live up." Incline yourself upward.

I'D PREFER if people had no impressions of me. As a kid, I had to tell my own family, "Please, just don't talk about me!" Because they always got it wrong. Always. I just didn't want them to tell anyone anything about me. God knew, they had a great opinion, and they loved me and meant well, but it was like, "Please, you don't have this right." You know what I mean?

MEN DOMINATE because of physicality, and thus they have mercy where women do not.

WHEN IT'S OVER for a woman, it's over. You're not getting an appeal.

THERE'S A TACIT AGREEMENT in the nation today that the white male is the only legitimate target for any and all satire, criticism, and so forth. And we pretty much just accept it.

A LOT OF PEOPLE in the middle of their lives have a secret yearning for more romance.

A lot of times, you gotta be there even if you don't wanna be.

I DON'T KNOW if this is a true statistic, but I heard somewhere that there are three times as many single women over forty as single men. That's what we got from the women's movement. The chickens have come home to roost.

I RESPECT THE SOCIAL GRACES enormously. How to pass the food. Don't yell from one room to another. Don't go through a closed door without a knock. Open the doors for the ladies. All these millions of simple household behaviors make for a better life. We can't live in constant rebellion against our parents—it's just silly. It's not an abstract thing. It's a shared language of expectations.

IF I HAD TO LIST the most prominent highlights in my life over the last decade or more, the things I'd write would pretty much involve moments with my children. You know how it goes: They write an essay or a poem, and your heart is in your throat. They give such stunning love. Lorraine won her soccer tournament. Ray is becoming a big guy. Jennifer has her own boutique; it's called Pearl. She's also designing clothes. I have to tell you, I did more glad-handing and arm twisting for Jennifer's fashion show than I've ever done for any picture of my own. That's what you're driven to do when you have kids.

I HAVE TO keep myself in check when I go to the kids' sports events. I sit waaay in the back. I make sure I don't do too much cheering, you know what I mean? I'm still not quite adjusted to this modern school of thought: "Oh, it doesn't matter who wins.' I'm not all the way there yet, but I accept it from the back row.

I THINK THE GREEKS invented sports as an antidote to philosophy. In sports there are absolute rules. It's not, what about this? what about that? Either you're safe or you're out. It's ten yards or it's not. It's in the hoop or out of the hoop. It's certain.

I'VE GROWN out of talking like I know something when I don't.

I'M A PRETTY LIBERAL Democrat, but I'm not after Bush the way all the rest of them are. I was alive in World War II. We turned off the all the lights, as if people might come running up the beach. In that climate, what else were you going to do? We didn't have a choice then. And we don't really have one now. I don't know what else Bush can do. We just have to see how it goes.

WHY CAN'T SOMEBODY use modern intelligence and relate it to traffic?

WHAT WOULD IT BE LIKE to fuck Britney Spears? I can answer that question: monumental. Life altering!

MY DAUGHTER IS THIRTEEN. Lately, all I've been thinking about is, Would you please get a pair of pants that's not, you know, down below your navel?

WHAT DO I DO WELL as a father? I'm there all the time. I give unconditional love. And I have a lot of skills in terms of getting them to express themselves. I'm good with handy hints—if they can tell me what their problem is—'cause I've had a lot of problems in life myself. I make an effort to expose them to things. I want them to have a deep inner feeling that it's all right to be happy, that you don't have to be constantly manufacturing problems that you don't really have.

A LOT OF MY LIFE LESSONS were learned as a child gambler on the boardwalk.

I ENVY people of faith. I'm incapable of believing in anything supernatural. So far, at least. Not that I wouldn't like to. I mean, I want to believe. I do pray. I pray to something . . . up there. I have a God sense. It's not religious so much as superstitious. It's part of being human, I guess.

DO UNTO OTHERS. How much deeper into religion do we really need to go?

I WOULD NEVER want to vilify somebody who considered abortion murder. I was an illegitimate child myself. I may not have existed today.

A QUESTION you always ask in acting is, Where were you going if this scene didn't interrupt the movements of the character?

FOR A LONG time, I was afraid to be alone. I had to learn how to be alone. And there are still times when I think, "Uh-oh! I gotta talk to somebody here, or I'm gonna go crazy!" But I like to be alone. Now I do. I really do. There's a big luxury in solitude.

I WAS INFLUENCED in golf by a plaque I read in Kyoto, Japan. It tells about this Zen archery tournament that had been held there. It's this long colonnade. At the end is a four-inch square. The participants would sit in a cross-legged position, and they'd have to shoot the arrows all the way without hitting the wall. And the world record in the event was something like 180 straight arrows. Knowing sports in the poetic way that I do, this impressed me. So I started thinking of golf as Zen archery.

I GET PEEVISH, sure. Nobody yells or screams any more than I do. But the toughest days are when I get home and realize, "Holy shit! They were right! Oy, I'm an asshole!" And this happens at least once or twice every picture, where you're just . . . you're just so sure you're such a big-time guy, you know what I mean? And then you get home, and you have that moment of holy shit.

I'M VERY FORTUNATE in the sense that outside of cohabiting relationships and so forth, I've always got on just as well with women.

I ALWAYS ASK MYSELF a theoretical question: "If I had started out today, would I have wound up doing porn pictures to make a living?"

THE LESS PEOPLE KNOW about me, the easier my job is.

ALWAYS TRY in interviews to avoid the clichés about the problems of public life.

ALWAYS try to avoid interviews.

Interviewed by Mike Sager | Photograph by Sam Jones

Buck O'Neil { BASEBALL PLAYER—KANSAS CITY, MISSOURI }

> **NO, YOU'RE NEVER** gonna see that again. Oh, no! I mean, nobody is going to pitch to Barry Bonds in the World Series. You walk him. You don't walk batters to get *to* Barry Bonds. But that's how it was. That was a different era—an era of personal competition. You *lived* to pitch to Josh Gibson. Why do you think Babe Ruth hit so many home runs? They weren't pitching around him. When Walter Johnson was on the mound, he felt it was his job to get him out. *This is how I get my kicks—pitching to the best.*

It was the second game of the World Series. We're playing at Pittsburgh. We're ahead 2-0 in the seventh inning, and Satchel Paige is on the mound. Batter knocks a triple down the left-field line. I go over to the mound and Satchel says, "You know what I'm fixin' to do?" And I said, "You're gonna get this guy out and we goin' home." He said, "No, I'm gonna walk him. I'm gonna walk the next guy, too, and pitch to Josh Gibson." Fill the bases to get to the great Josh Gibson! I said, "Man, don't be facetious." I call out to the manager, "Listen to what this fool is sayin'!" And the manager says, "All these people in the ballpark came out here to see Satchel Paige and Josh Gibson. Let him do what he wants to do."

Now, there's some history here. See, years before, Satchel and Josh played for the same team, and they had this conversation as they were travelin' through the Blue Mountains. Satchel told Josh, "They say you're the best hitter in the world, and I know I'm the best pitcher. One day we're gonna meet up on different teams and see who the best really is." So Satchel walks the first batter, and as he's walking the second he's having a conversation with Josh in the on-deck circle, saying, "Remember that time in the Blue Mountains?" As Josh heads to the plate, the crowd's feeling it, but Satchel isn't through yet. Oh, no. He's just setting the stage. He sets his glove on the mound and motions for the trainer, Jewbaby Floyd. Now it's show time. Jewbaby goes out to the mound with a glass foaming over with bicarbonate of soda. Understand, Satchel was famous for having stomach problems. So Satchel drinks that glass down and lets out a great belch. Big old belch! "OK, Josh," he says. "You ready?" So Josh steps into the batter's box with that great, great body after two guys were walked *just to get to him.* And it was scary. All you could do was hope he didn't kill someone. Satchel throws him a fastball. Josh doesn't even move his bat. Strike one. "OK, Josh, now I'm gonna throw you another fastball, just about the same place," Satchel says. "But it's gonna be a little harder than the last one." Josh doesn't move his bat. Strike two! "I got you oh-and-two, and in this league I'm supposed to knock you down. But I'm not gonna throw smoke at yo' yolk. I'm gonna throw a pea at yo' knee." Now, Satchel was about six-four, but when he wound up and kicked that leg up, he looked seven feet tall. Josh never even swung. Strike three! And let me tell you, when Satchel walked off the mound, he was *ten* feet tall. He said, "Nobody hits Satchel's fastball."

You know, I must have told that story a million times. But I never get tired of it. Why would I? Every time I tell it, I'm thirty years old again, playing in the World Series.

GATES. That's the best barbecue in Kansas City. Beef on a bun and baked beans. Hallelujah!

I'LL TELL YOU WHAT hurt me more than not being able to play major league baseball. See, you've got to realize that I thought I was playing the best baseball in the country. What really hurt me was not being able to attend Sarasota High School. I couldn't attend the University of Florida, although my father was paying taxes to support these institutions just like the white man. But the white man was thinking this: "If I keep him dumb, I can work him for a dollar a day." You understand? And right now, I'm looking at this country and I see the people coming from Mexico. I see companies sending jobs overseas. Cheap labor. There you go. There you go. Everything is geared up on the side of the rich man.

A NICKNAME means you belong.

BACK IN 1947, we had a lot of ballplayers better than Jackie Robinson. But they wouldn't have stood what Jackie stood. Had a black cat been thrown on the field at Willie Wells, Willie would have picked up that cat, walked into the stands, and shoved it down that sucker's throat. But Jackie knew that he had twenty-one million black folks riding on his shoulders. Understand now, Jackie was as fiery as any man who ever lived. Jackie would knock you on your butt. But he had to be able to play a role that wasn't in his character whatsoever. Everything got holed up inside of him. And that's why he died so young.

LIKE THE PERSON you love. That's how you have a long marriage.

EVER SINCE THEY MADE THEIR DECISION [to not vote me into the Baseball Hall of Fame], people keep callin' and asking me about it. But I can't complain. I'm having a wonderful life.

I'M GOING TO THE DOCTOR tomorrow at the University of Kansas medical center. They're doing a study on Alzheimer's disease, and they want to know how come my memory's so good. They want to see if exercise can help eliminate that disease.

CAN YOU BELIEVE IT? Fifty-seven degrees in January. I'm goin' to play some golf.

Interviewed by Cal Fussman | Photograph by Brent Humphreys

BORN CARRABELLE, FLORIDA—11.13.1911
DIED KANSAS CITY, MISSOURI—10.06.2006

> AFTER A NEGRO LEAGUE PLAYING CAREER HIGHLIGHTED BY THREE ALL-STAR GAMES AND TWO WORLD SERIES, JOHN JORDAN "BUCK" O'NEIL MANAGED THE KANSAS CITY MONARCHS TO FOUR LEAGUE TITLES.
> HE WAS INSTRUMENTAL IN ESTABLISHING THE NEGRO LEAGUES BASEBALL MUSEUM IN KANSAS CITY. HE WAS POSTHUMOUSLY AWARDED THE PRESIDENTIAL MEDAL OF FREEDOM BY GEORGE W. BUSH ON DECEMBER 7, 2006.

Peter O'Toole { ACTOR—LONDON }

ANARCHIC, ARBITRARY sexual urges—there's not a man or woman who doesn't love and has not been disturbed by them.

I'VE NEVER LOOKED for women. When I was a teenager, perhaps. But they are looking for us, and we must learn that very quickly. They decide. We just turn up. Never mind the superficialities—tall and handsome and all that. Just turn up. They will do the rest.

I WAS OBSESSED with losing it for four years. How did it happen? Alfresco, at night. On the steps of an old chapel—I shan't say where. Two semiprofessional mill girls. Me and another bloke and two girls. Exultation. Wow—it was very good!

I DON'T THINK I've changed much from my boyhood.

SIX YEARS: 1939 to 1945. It was life. One's literacy was newspapers, bombs, Germans. We didn't have a childhood. We had the war.

FROM BOTH my mother and father I learned endurance. Things were pretty tough. But things could be tougher.

LISTEN, everybody was offered the part of Lawrence of Arabia: Marlon Brando, Greta Garbo, Groucho Marx. Everybody but me. They all turned it down for various reasons. And David Lean had banked his life on that picture. David's wife was seeing a guru at the time, and this guru had seen a film called *The Day They Robbed the Bank of England*, in which I played a silly English officer. And the guru told her that he had just seen the man who should play Lawrence.

THE BEDOUIN are about five foot, so I spent two years pretending I wasn't tall. I became telescopic.

MAY I tell you a camel story? It was the charge at Aqaba—a mile and a half, and we were in front of five hundred Arab stallions. The day of the shooting, we turned up to the kickoff. And Omar—a gambling man, Omar—worked out the odds of whether he would fall off. So he tied himself to the camel. And I said, "I'm going to get drunk." So we both drank milk and brandy—it was terrifying—and a mile and a half later, horses, madness, we both finish up in the sea. And Omar was upside down with his head in the water, still tied to the camel.

I LOVE BULLFIGHTING. I love the dance, I love the courage, I love the style, I love the skill. I love everything about it.

WHEN WE WERE DRAMA STUDENTS, we imitated John Gielgud, we imitated Richard Burton, we imitated Michael Redgrave, we imitated Larry Olivier. It's language. For my generation, drama, the theater, plays, they are human speech as an art form. To turn up for material that exists and say, "No, I'm superior to that material" is a very strange attitude. I'd be very careful if I were you.

IF YOU GO TO THE WEST END theaters now, it's a graveyard. Lots of musicals, they're cheerful. But the plays? God almighty.

NEW YORK nearly fifty years ago was one of the most magical places ever. And one of its most endearing qualities was its playfulness. If you had a bit of scratch—not much, but a bit—you could do anything, go anywhere, get anything, get away with anything.

EVERYTHING YOU HEAR about the true American spirit—the matriarchy and the femininity and the toughness—you find in Kate Hepburn. She was funny as hell and brave and dotty. Kate! I gave my daughter her name.

YEARS LATER, in Ireland, daughter Kate, then nine or ten, said, "Daddy, there's an old Gypsy woman at the door!" We had a Gypsy nearby who would pinch our flowers. I went to the door and said, "No, thank you, we don't—oh, hello, Kate." She had four jackets on. One belonged to Barrymore, one to Spencer Tracy, one to me, and one to Humphrey Bogart. Khaki trousers and boots—this was her uniform.

ON RACETRACKS, green is considered unlucky. To be disobedient in a way that can't be seen, I wear green socks. I have since I was fourteen.

FOR CHRIST'S SAKE, we all have eccentricities. We're all crippled with them, aren't we?

RICHARD BURTON AND I lived around the corner from each other in Hampstead—before Elizabeth Taylor, before anything. He'd come to my place, or I'd go to his. And then we'd carry the other home. Elizabeth wasn't keen on that. She probably thought I led him astray. I don't know. She didn't approve. That was a bone of contention between me and Richard. I said, "If you now need permission to come see me, then you go fuck yourself, you old git!"

I DRINK NOW. But not like before. Christ, who could?

WE LIVE public lives. If you want to guard your privacy, stop it.

COMEDY is among the most difficult crafts. I've never known a good actor who couldn't play comedy. I know no actor who finds it easy.

MY FAVORITE SMELL? Cordite. After you've fired a gun.

GOOD PARTS make good actors. I take them as they come.

Interviewed by Stephen Garrett | Photograph by David Hurn

BORN CONNEMARA, IRELAND—08.02.32

> AFTER THE TITLE ROLE IN *LAWRENCE OF ARABIA* (1962) BROUGHT HIM STARDOM, O'TOOLE HAD AN IMPRESSIVE TEN-YEAR STRETCH: *BECKET* (1964), *WHAT'S NEW PUSSYCAT?* (1965); *THE LION IN WINTER* (1968); *GOODBYE, MR. CHIPS* (1969); AND *THE RULING CLASS* (1972).

> TROUBLES WITH ALCOHOL SIDELINED HIM FOR MUCH OF THE REST OF THE 1970S, BUT O'TOOLE WENT ON TO RECEIVE THREE MORE BEST ACTOR NOMINATIONS, FOR *THE STUNT MAN* (1980), *MY FAVORITE YEAR* (1982), AND *VENUS* (2006). HE HAS NEVER WON.

Al Pacino { ACTOR—NEW YORK CITY }

THIS WAS A GOOD ONE. I wanted to go to a baseball game. I like to go to ball games. I can remember going with my grandfather when I was three years old. Only it's a little different when you sit down to watch and they're putting your name on the scoreboard. There's nothing wrong with it. I mean, we're all in this world together. But this time there was a complication. It was an afternoon game, and I had something to do that night. I figured I'd go early, see the players practice a little, watch an inning or two. But I didn't want to make a thing about leaving early. I mean, the players are performers. Can you imagine what people would think if they saw me walking out right after the start of a Broadway play?

So I'm thinking, I'll go and just slip out. Only somehow I forget that the woman I'm going to the game with is also well known. Getting out of the car, I say to this guy who's with us, "Do we have an old hat or something in the trunk?" He takes a look. He pulls out a hat and some glasses, and then he says, "Hey, Al, look what we have here! An old beard!" I put the beard on. What I'm thinking, I don't know, because I look like one of the Smith Brothers on a cough drop box.

We go into the stadium, the game starts, and all of a sudden people in the stands are looking in my direction. Cameras are turning in my direction. People on the field are looking in my direction. I'm thinking, What the heck is going on? I got the beard. I got the hat. It's the woman I'm with, of course. Which would be fine, except, all of a sudden, the beard is sliding down my face. This is just ridiculous. What am I going to do now? What *can* I do? I take the beard off.

And, of course, the whole thing is on the eleven o'clock news. "Hey, what's Al Pacino doing at the stadium with a beard?" That beard should be in the museum of mistakes. I laughed when I saw myself on the news, but I learned. No more of that. Everywhere I go, I go. I'm just gonna be me: Al.

WHEN I WAS A KID, my great-grandmother would occasionally give me a silver dollar. She was always very affectionate toward me. When she would give it to me, the rest of the family would always scream in unison, "No! No! *Noooooooooooo!* Don't give him the silver dollar!" And they meant it, because we were really poor. And as soon as it was in my hand, everybody would scream, "Give it back! Give it back!" and so I'd feel uncomfortable about taking it.

My father and mother split up when I was very young. I was an only child in a tenement in the South Bronx with my mother, my grandmother, and grandfather. We didn't have much. So it was a big day when I found out you could get Tom Mix spurs off the back of a cereal box. Tom Mix was a cowboy hero in the movies, and he was huge. *Huge!* Just the fact that the spurs came in a box by mail made them huge. And so we sent away for the spurs.

I must have been about six years old when my great-grandmother died. I don't remember much about the funeral, only bits and pieces: you know, everybody clustered together. We come home, and the Tom Mix spurs have arrived in the mail. I get all excited. But then I remember my great-grandmother has just died. I want to be happy, but . . . On that day, I learned conflict.

I WAS HOME ALONE a lot growing up. My mother worked, but she would take me to the theater to see all the movies. And the next day, all alone, I would act out the movie at home, playing all the roles. I saw *The Lost Weekend* at a very young age. Probably too young to see something like that. But I was very impressed with it. I didn't know what was going on, but the passion was interesting to me. Ray Milland won an Oscar for that. In it, there's a scene where he's looking for a liquor bottle. When he was drunk, he hid the bottle in the apartment. Now he's sober, and he wants to find it. He knows it's somewhere, but he forgets. He looks for it and finally *finds* it. I used to do that scene. On occasion, when my dad used to visit me, he'd take me to his relatives in Harlem and say, "Show 'em the bottle scene." I'd act it out, and they'd all laugh. And I'd be thinking, "Why are they laughing? It's a very serious scene."

I WAS AT A STREET CARNIVAL when I was a kid and threw the ball and knocked down a couple of bottles, but they didn't give me the prize. To this day, I can't *believe* that they would do that. The injustice! I went back to the apartment and told my grandfather. And that look on his face, it comes back to me even now. It said, "You're not expecting me to go down six flights, walk five blocks, and try to prove to some guy at the carnival that you knocked down the bottles and should get the prize." I saw all that on his face. At the same time, he tried to tell me how sometimes this happens in life. And he was right. It happens in life.

MY MOTHER DIED before I made it. You know, here's what I really remember about my mother: We're on the top floor of our tenement. It's freezing out. I have to go to school the next day. I'm maybe ten years old. Down in the alleyway, my friends are calling up to me. They want me to go traveling around with them at night and have some real fun. My mother wouldn't let me. I remember

>>

BORN EAST HARLEM, NEW YORK—04.25.40

> PACINO DROPPED OUT OF NEW YORK'S LEGENDARY HIGH SCHOOL OF THE PERFORMING ARTS AT AGE SEVENTEEN TO PURSUE HIS ACTING CAREER.

> HIS FILM HIGHLIGHTS INCLUDE *THE GODFATHER* (1972), *DOG DAY AFTERNOON* (1975), *SCARFACE* (1983), *FRANKIE AND JOHNNY* (1991), *GLENGARRY GLEN ROSS* (1992), AND *CARLITO'S WAY* (1993). PACINO'S PERFORMANCE IN *SCENT OF A WOMAN* (1992) FINALLY LANDED HIM AN OSCAR FOR BEST ACTOR.

being so angry with her. "Why can't I go out like everyone else? What's wrong with me?" On and on I screamed at her. *She endured my wrath.* And she saved my life, because those guys down in the alley—none of them are around right now. I don't think about it that much. But it touches me now as I'm talking about it. She didn't want me out in the streets late at night. I had to do my homework. And I'm sitting here right now because of it. It's so simple, isn't it? But we forget, we just forget.

ONE OF THE MOST STRIKING THINGS I've ever experienced was in the South Bronx, in one of those vaudeville houses that had been turned into a movie house. It seated thousands, and this traveling troupe came through. I was fourteen and had never seen grown-ups act on a stage, though I'd been onstage myself. In elementary school, I was in a show where there was a big pot—the melting pot—and I was the representative from Italy, stirring. I can remember the kids in school asking for my autograph, and I would sign it "Sonny Scott." It was catchy, you know.

By the way, **I don't recommend tap dancing on logs over cold water in a cold place.**
And if you do try, I hope they pay you well...

Anyway, this troupe was doing *The Seagull* by Chekhov. There were about fifteen or twenty people in the audience, all of us clumped together in the middle of a theater that seated thousands. The play started, and then it was over. That's about how fast it went for me. It was magical. I remember thinking, "Who was the person who wrote this?" I went out and got a book of Chekhov's stories. Then I went into the High School of Performing Arts. And one day I go into the Howard Johnson's near the school for something to eat, and the star of that show is pushing coffee behind the counter. My jaw dropped. I was in awe of this guy. I had to tell him. I remember that exchange. He was so grateful in a way, kind and understanding. He had to be all of twenty-five. There he was, waiting on me at the Howard Johnson's. Things are relative.

MY BIG BREAKTHROUGH came when I was twenty-one. I was doing *Creditors*, a translation of an August Strindberg play. My friend Charlie Laughton directed it in an obscure theater in the bowels of SoHo, which at the time wasn't SoHo but just a bunch of warehouses.

The play takes place in Sweden at the turn of the century, and the character I played is named Adolf. It was the first time I had the opportunity to explore a world that I hadn't come in contact with—and then to find myself actually inhabiting that role. It wasn't the literal thing of being Swedish, but the feeling that I was connected to the metaphor. It was a transforming experience, tantamount to falling in love. It felt like I didn't need to do anything else in life but that. It was like discovering you could write. Suddenly you had an outlet. The concern was no longer whether you were going to get paid for it or whether you were going on to be successful or famous. It was, as they say, no longer the destination but the journey.

I was homeless at the time. I would sometimes sleep at night in the theater where I performed. Sometimes Charlie would put me up at his place. It was hard, but at that age you can sleep anywhere. At the time, I even thought it was cool. I was alive to what I was doing.

There's a time in your life when that happens to you if you're lucky enough to have it happen. Then it goes. You start to make a living. But, you know, from time to time I try to think about life back then . . . and to stay in touch with it.

THE FIRST TIME I felt like I had money was in Boston, when I was in a repertory company. Before that, the closest I'd come was bus transfer slips. When I was a kid, they had these transfer slips that came in yellow and pink and blue. There was a place where these rejected slips were, and we would stuff our pockets full of them. Even though they were valueless, there was a kind of value to them. You could imagine what it was like to have a pocket full of bucks.

Later on, I got a job delivering a trade paper called *Show Business* to the newsstands. Rain, sleet, and snow, I delivered. I'll never forget—I got twelve dollars for it. A ten and two singles. I would always cash my ten so I had twelve singles. Then I could peel off the singles at a bar, and it looked like a bankroll.

I must have been twenty-five when I got that paycheck from the repertory company in Boston. I went into a bar and had a martini *and* a steak. And afterward, I *still* had money.

YOU KNOW WHAT the difference between acting in a play and a movie is? I'll tell you. Acting's like being a tightrope walker—and there's a difference between doing it onstage and in a movie. Onstage, the tightrope is way up high. You fall, and you *fall*. In a movie, the wire is on the floor. You fall, and you get up and do it again. Acting in a play is a different state of being. You wake up knowing that you have to walk the wire at eight o'clock.

I WAS A YOUNG MAN when I went to shoot *The Godfather*. I remember being in Sicily, and it was so hot. If you haven't slept and you're not feeling well and it's 120 degrees and you're dressed in all wool, well, you just want to go home. You start feeling, "What am I doing? I'm just shooting this over and over again, and I don't know what this is anymore."

All these Sicilian extras were lined up. They all got wool clothes on, too. This one guy, this Sicilian extra, says in Italian, "We've been out here all day. It's hot. I'd like to take a break." And the production guy says, "You take a break, and you're off the picture." Now, the extra obviously has no money, which is why he's doing it in the first place. He looks at the production guy, shrugs his shoulders, says, "Mah!" and walks away. And I said to myself, "This guy, he's my hero."

These are the things that stay in my head. I loved that guy. Could I have done that? No. Could I do it now? *Nahhhhhhhh.* That was freedom. For a moment, that guy made me feel good. Suddenly, the wool was OK.

I didn't know what was gonna happen with that movie—and then, the most amazing thing happened. We were in New York, doing the burial of Don Corleone. We'd shot all day. It's six at night and I'm going home. I see Francis Coppola sitting on the gravestone, and he's crying. Literally bawling. "Francis," I say. "What happened? What's the matter?" And he says, "They won't give me another setup." Meaning, they wouldn't let him shoot the scene again. So he's sitting on the gravestone crying, and I thought, *This guy is going to make a movie here.* If he's got that kind of passion, that kind of feeling about *one* setup . . . That was the moment. I could feel it then. This guy *cares.* And that's it. That's the way to live—around people who *care.* It may be a tough ride, but something is going to come out of it.

I DIDN'T KNOW HOW TO DRIVE until I was twenty-four or twenty-five. I didn't need to, growing up in New York. But I had to learn for films. The money was coming in, and finally I got a car. I went with my friend Charlie and got this white BMW right out of the dealership. We get in the car and drive to my apartment in Manhattan. As we're driving, I'm thinking, "Y'know, this just isn't me." It just didn't *feel* right. But I said to myself, "What the hell, you'll get used to it." I parked it in front of the apartment, and we went up for a cup of coffee. When we came down to drive Charlie home, the car is gone. I remember looking at that space where the car used to be, looking at Charlie, and laughing.

And I had a flashback. Years before, Charlie and I were riding bikes, and we went into Katz's Deli on Houston Street. Now, the relationship I had with my bike was much different from the one I had with the car. I'd had that bike for a couple of years and used it to get from the Bronx to Manhattan. I didn't have money at the time, and it was not only my form of transportation but also a great source of fun and amusement. It was one of the few things I could do for free. Anyway, Charlie and I park our bikes on the street and go in the deli and get some hot dogs. Every other bite I would turn around to check on the bikes. I must have put mustard on the dog or something, because the next time I turned around, the bikes were gone. I remember running outside, and they were nowhere in sight. It wasn't funny that time.

I WAS AT A STREETLIGHT ONCE, and I looked over at a young woman and smiled. She said, "Oh, hi, Michael." You know, Michael from *The Godfather.* It was as though she'd stripped me right there of my anonymity. Just stripped me. I wasn't Michael when I said hello. I was me smiling at a young woman on a street corner. I was seen, but I wasn't, you know what I mean?

You're always nervous before the start of a play. It shows there's something you're going to reveal.

Until you are famous, you can never understand the haven of anonymity. There's a line from the play *The Local Stigmatic* that goes like this: "Fame is the perversion of the natural human instinct for validation and attention." That's a bit of a hard line. But I'll tell you this: fame really complicates personal relationships. And when you put together fame and success, that can be a bit of a headache. But as Lee Strasberg, my friend and mentor, once said to me, "Darling, you simply have to adjust."

I DIDN'T WIN AN OSCAR the first seven times I was nominated. I would like to be able to talk about it in a way that gets at some of the feelings. Now I look at all the nominees and think, "What if they were all brain surgeons? Which one, if you needed brain surgery, would you let operate on your brain? That's the one you should give the Oscar to." But back then, it depended on what state of mind I was in.

One year, I was into whatever altered my mood—a lot of booze, a lot of pills. I've long since stopped. But as I was sitting there during that show, I was thinking, "If I get this award, I don't know if I'll be able to get to the stage." That thought paralyzed me. Also, I didn't have anything prepared to say. I truly could not believe I was going to win. However, it was a vague thought creeping in the back of my mind. "Knowing you, Al . . ."

I was young and had my whole future in front of me. Parts were coming, and I hadn't learned how to be appreciative of the things that come to you. The reality is, at the time, I was out of sync with what was happening to me. I hate to say it because it sounds like I'm bullshitting, but it's the truth. I hope they had the camera on me after Jack Lemmon won, because I was smiling and applauding like the happiest man on the planet.

I HAD A DEAR, DEAR FRIEND who died of cancer at age thirty-five. We were the same age. I went through the whole thing with him—saw it all. There was a moment I will never forget. It was outside his room. His father and mother came to visit him. I was very close to him, and I'd never once heard him talk about his father. He had a relationship with his parents that was complicated, and they hadn't seen him for a while. But there was love there somewhere. Anyway, his father was in the room with him, and I was in the hall. And his father came out and looked me straight in the eye and said, "What are we gonna do?" I hesitated, but he had my arm. He looked at me and said, "If I could take his place . . ." Not only was this guy ready to die, ready to go right there on the spot for his child, but he really was asking me if I knew how he could do it. It was very powerful. And then I had children, and I understood.

I DIDN'T KNOW MY DAD WELL. He was an accountant. Finally, he got himself a little bar in California with a music stand. It was his place, which he felt good about. I went to visit him. I remember excusing myself to go to the bathroom. As I was going, I just felt a sense of somebody covering my back.

My father was married five times. What does that tell me? That he liked married life. OK, what does it *tell* me? It tells me we're creatures of habit.

I've never married. On women, I can be funny and glib. Or I really can try to tell you. Where to start? I have always enjoyed the company of women. I have very close women friends. I could probably sit here for a long time and tell you why that is or why I think it is. But to say a lot would be an understatement, right?

We'll let it ride there.

I WENT FOUR YEARS without doing a movie toward the end of the eighties. It wasn't a conscious decision. It just happened after I was unhappy with the results of a couple of movies I'd made.

I don't want to mention the movies. But it bothers you when something that is potentially worthwhile doesn't come through. You know how actors have recurring dreams about not knowing their lines? Well, I have a recurring dream where I'm in one of those movies that doesn't work. In my dream, I'm saying, "But I didn't know I was doing that movie. It was a mistake. Really. I didn't know I was being filmed."

It was time in my life to take a break and look around. I found myself wanting to get back to some of the things that I'd done earlier in my life, to observe more.

An actor with too much money will usually find a way to get rid of it. I poured my money into my own film, *The Local Stigmatic*,

Everywhere I go, I go.
I'm just gonna be me: Al.

which I never released. I did some plays. All of a sudden the years passed, and suddenly I owed some back taxes and the mortgage was due and I was broke. But you know what really hit me? I was walking through Central Park, and this guy comes up to me—didn't know him at all—and he says, "Hey, what *happened* to you? We don't see you, man." I said, "Well, I . . . uh, I . . . uh," and he said, "C'mon, Al, I want to see you up there!" And I recognized that I was lucky to have what I've been given. You gotta use it.

I WENT TO SEE FRANK SINATRA in a concert. This was about twenty years ago. His opening act was Buddy Rich. So Buddy Rich came out, and I wondered about him because Buddy Rich was in his sixties and he was playing the drums. I know he's a good drummer. But I'm thinking, "Now I'm going to sit here and listen to him drum for a while and twiddle my thumbs until Frank Sinatra comes out." But once he started and then kept going and going and going, he transcended what I thought he was gonna do tenfold. And it became this *experience*.

He did things I've seen great ballet dancers do. It really took me by surprise, and not only me, but everyone else, too, because in the middle of this riff, the entire audience stood up in unison and started screaming.

When Sinatra came out, he said, very simply, "You see this guy drumming? You know, sometimes it's a good idea to stay at a thing." Buddy Rich stayed at a thing. Not only did he stay at drumming all those years, but as he was playing that night, he stayed at it. It was like he was saying, "I went this far, lemme see if I can take it further and further." And then suddenly it took itself. That's why we do this. To find that place. But it's not enough to have found it. You gotta keep going. What's that saying? He who persists at his folly will one day be wise.

IT SURPRISED ME, the feeling I got when I won the Oscar for *Scent of a Woman*. It was a new feeling. I'd never felt it. I don't see my Oscar much now. But when I first got it, there was a feeling for weeks afterward that I guess is akin to winning a gold medal in the Olympics. It's like you've won a race and everybody knows you won. It's a wonderful feeling, a complete feeling. I wish I had better words for it.

THERE'S A SCENE in one of the movies I've got coming out—*Insomnia*—where I'm chasing a character played by Robin Williams over logs floating on cold water. You know, it's what the loggers do, sort of a cross between rodeo and tap dancing on logs. A scene like that shouldn't be perfect. It should be *spontaneous*. That's what it's about.

I like to avoid the word *perfection*. There's the real apple. And then there's the apple that looks like the perfect apple. The problem is when you bite into the perfect apple, it doesn't have the taste or nourishment of the real apple.

YOU KNOW, I'M A LITTLE concerned now. I'm going to do my next part, and I've got to cut my hair and beard off. And my twins, my fourteen-month-old twins, have never seen me any other way. So I have this plan. I've got to get a beard and a wig made, to get them accustomed gradually—because if I come home with a bald head and no beard . . .

Then I'm wondering, "Should I put the fake goatee on and the fake hair on and have them pull them off? But that might freak them out. *Hmmmmmm*. Maybe I should have them help me shave it off."

Interviewed by Cal Fussman | Photograph by Platon

Roman Polanski { DIRECTOR—PARIS }

❯ I LIKE SHADOWS in the movies. I don't like them in life.

MEMORY DOESN'T LAST. When Kosovo started, they had already forgotten about Bosnia, let alone World War II. I remember after the war was over and my father returned from the concentration camp. He said, "You'll see—fifty years from now, people will have forgot all about it."

AFTER SHARON'S DEATH, I definitely had a strong desire to give up. Your next question will be, what prevented me? But I can't answer it. I just survived. I was simply born this way. My father survived the concentration camp. I've been asked, why did he survive? Well, I don't know. He wanted probably more than the others to survive. It can be anything. It can be the desire for revenge. It can be a longing to see your loved ones. Truly, I don't know, and I never asked myself the question.

I THINK YOU should not ask yourself too many questions. It's the centipede syndrome, you know? The centipede was asked which foot he puts after which, and he couldn't walk anymore.

WORK HAS ALWAYS sustained me.

SEX is not a pastime. It's a force, it's a drive. It changes your way of thinking.

FOR A LONG TIME, I didn't want children. After what happened, I didn't particularly want to get married. Children without a partner with whom you intend to share the rest of your life doesn't make much sense to me. Can you understand the way one can feel after an event like that? After losing someone who is everything to you?

DEALING WITH ADVERSITY is like the brake pedal in the car. It just happens instinctively. You go through it, or you perish.

KIDS JUST ACCEPT REALITY as it is, because they have no way of comparing it with anything else. I'm much more sensitive now to all this, having a child that goes through all these stages that I went through. She's now six: that's the age I was when the Germans walked into Poland. She's five: that's the age when my parents took me for the last holiday in the country. You see? She's seven: that's when I was running in and out of the ghetto through the hole in the barbed wire. I see it through her eyes, and it's only now that I realize that I was in harm's way. But at the time when I was a kid, no. The only tragic thing was the separation from my parents. *This* was something that made me cry, not that the food was bad, not that I had lice, not that there were fleas in the bed, not that there were bedbugs. And I think, you know, how tragic it would be for my daughter to go through that.

TOUTES PROPORTIONS GARDÉES.

I THINK THE PILL altered female thinking. When you think that millions of women were taking daily hormones, you cannot deny that it must have changed their personalities. I truly don't think that feminism would reach such absurd proportions if there were no Pill. It must have had an effect.

I DON'T THINK that Hollywood people like making movies. They like making deals.

AFTER THE PARTY, you either clean up the mess or move the apartment. In general, I clean up.

THERE'S A DIFFERENT JUSTICE for people who are public figures than for those who are not.

THERE WAS NO PLOT against me. There was no setup. It was all my fault. I think that my wrongdoing was much greater than Bill Clinton's.

PLEASURE is a carrot. And a stick.

I THINK, in America, people are getting too big.

DRUGS TAKEN FOR RECREATION may be justified. Taken for any kind of positive output, I think it's laughable. Drugs alter perception, and you have to be an observer as well as a creator. You have to have a handle on what you do. If your sense of touch is impaired, you may break the handle. Or you might take it for your wife's ass.

FILMS are films, life is life.

FLATTER ACTORS. It's irresistible to them.

NEVER PULL A HAIR from Faye Dunaway's head. Pull it from somebody else's head.

I'M NOT A MASOCHIST, but I always take a cold shower in the morning. It's a great beginning of the day, because nothing can be worse afterward.

Interviewed by John H. Richardson | Photograph by Alastair Thain

BORN PARIS, FRANCE—08.18.33

> POLANSKI'S MOTHER DIED IN A NAZI CONCENTRATION CAMP. HE AVOIDED CAPTURE AND WAS EDUCATED AT THE FILM SCHOOL IN LODZ, POLAND.

> IN 1969, POLANSKI'S WIFE, ACTRESS SHARON TATE, WAS MURDERED BY THE SO-CALLED MANSON FAMILY. TATE WAS EIGHT MONTHS PREGNANT AT THE TIME.

> IN 1977, MORE TRAGEDY: POLANSKI WAS ARRESTED AND CHARGED WITH THE STATUTORY RAPE OF A 13-YEAR-OLD GIRL. AFER FIRST DENYING THE CHARGES, HE ENTERED A PARTIAL GUILTY PLEA. FREE ON BAIL, HE FLED TO FRANCE.

> HIS FILM *THE PIANIST* WON ACADEMY AWARDS IN 2002 FOR BEST DIRECTOR, BEST ACTOR, AND BEST ADAPTED SCREENPLAY. POLANSKI COULDN'T ATTEND THE AWARDS, AS HE STILL FACES CRIMINAL PROCEEDINGS IF HE EVER RETURNS TO THE UNITED STATES.

Iggy Pop { SINGER—MIAMI }

THE FIRST MOMENT? Driving down a nice two-lane highway, summer day, Ann Arbor, Michigan. I'm in the backseat of a '49 Cadillac. Always had a good car, my dad. Frank Sinatra's singing: "Fairy tales can come true / It can happen to you / If you're young at heart." My dad's singing along. From that moment on, when people asked me what I wanted to be, I would say, "A singer." As I got older, I realized that might not be realistic. So then I thought, "I'll become a politician."

THE MORE walking-around money I have, the less I walk around.

SEX may be a little more factual than love. You know whether it was good or not. You know whether you liked it or not. You're not going to change your mind about it ten years later.

TRY TO FIND some ground that hasn't been covered.

THE PEANUT BUTTER, the shards of glass—I look back upon those moments kind of like a proud parent.

WE LIVED IN A TRAILER. My parents gave up their bedroom, and I moved in with my drum set. My dad just sat there, with his quarter-inch military haircut, reading the newspaper. My parents wanted to light my artistic candle. But over time, the definition of "the arts" began to stretch. And as I got older, they suddenly realized, "Oh, my God, we're the parents of Iggy Pop."

I BECAME IGGY because I had a sadistic boss at a record store. I'd been in a band called the Iguanas. And when this boss wanted to embarrass and demean me, he'd say, "Iggy, get me a coffee, light." And that really pissed me off, because in those days a cool nickname was Tab or Rock. I had a nickname that I couldn't escape around town, and it was torture. Then my band opened for Blood, Sweat & Tears. I think the entire band got fifty dollars total. But we had a lot of new ground. And afterward, a huge piece was written about us in the *Michigan Daily*. In this story, the writer calls me Iggy. I was like, "Oh, fuck. We got all this press, but they're calling me Iggy." What could I do? I knew the value of publicity. So I put a little "Pop" on the end. Took me thirty years to make what I wanted out of the name.

MY MOM WAS A SAINT. She taught me to be terminally nice.

YOU MUST'VE HAD a night where you did two grams of nasty blow in New York City and a fifth of Jack Daniel's and been with not the greatest chick you ever slept with and you got two hours' sleep and you wake up and it's the morning rush and you're hearing *honk! honk! honk!* out your window and it's gray and it's cold and you just want to die. At that moment, yeah, I regretted what I'd done the night before. But big-picture regrets? Nah.

I'M NOT a one-trick pony. I've had my picture in *People* magazine vacuuming the floor. I do a little vacuuming, a little bleeding.

A LOT OF PEOPLE tried to out-Iggy Iggy. G. G. Allin. He was just doing every awful thing onstage: having sex, going to the toilet. He took that detail and ran with it. That didn't put me in a position to compete with him. Just the opposite. It made me embarrassed.

I WAS LUCKY. I'd seen my own vomit, and it was green. It was some sort of bile, and it told me this is too serious. Can't go on. The green vomit gave me a chance to step out and get a little perspective on the world.

THE DRUGS WENT AWAY gradually. The outbursts got fewer and farther between. The big turn for me came when my body began to remember all the times it felt bad. Then I became very, very strong. I really don't want to crawl under the table and shiver and see little mice running under my eyes for the next fourteen hours. I don't want my confidence for the next twenty-two gigs fucked with.

QIGONG is such a powerful form of energy that some of the masters in China can walk on tissue paper. You know—twelve large men cannot push me. There are guys who can do that shit. I've learned enough of the qigong to deal with the musician's lifestyle.

NOTHING'S SHOCKING anymore. The transfer of information has become so fast, we're at the point where even the straightest little old lady in Jonesville, South Carolina, is saying, "Ah, we've heard about that Marilyn Manson, and we know what he does at night . . ."

ALMOST ALL COOL-ASS ROCK front guys are incredibly huge assholes. It would be nice to meet one who wasn't.

I FIND IT HARD TO FOCUS looking forward. So I look backward. What was I doing when I was thirty-nine? That was the first time I woke up and thought, "You're about to decease unless you get some sort of plan going." I did, and that worked out pretty well. So there's hope for twenty years from now.

THE BEST PIECE OF WISDOM my father gave me came fairly recently. I was trying to decide on a new woman in my life. He said, "Well, just listen to your medulla oblongata. It'll tell you what to do." So I listened to my medulla oblongata, and it said, "Get with that Nigerian-Irish chick. Go with the hottie."

I HAVE NO IDEA why a guy would bring a jar of peanut butter to a concert.

THERE WILL ALWAYS BE explosions. But there will always be a vestige left.

Interviewed by Cal Fussman | Photograph by Jeff Minton

BORN MUSKEGON, MICHIGAN—04.12.47

> POP IS OFTEN REFERRED TO AS THE GODFATHER OF PUNK BECAUSE OF THE NUMBER OF ARTISTS THAT HAVE COVERED HIS SONGS OR BEEN OVERTLY INFLUENCED BY HIM AND HIS BAND, THE STOOGES.

> HIS ACTING CREDITS INCLUDE *THE COLOR OF MONEY* (1986), AND THE VOICE OF NEWBORN BABY IN *THE RUGRATS MOVIE* (1998).

Christopher Reeve { SUPERHERO — BEDFORD, NEW YORK }

> **WE ALL HAVE** many more abilities and internal resources than we know. My advice is that you don't need to break your neck to find out about them.

MANY PEOPLE AT FIFTY think they've already started to go downhill. I actually think the opposite. I nearly died at forty-two; a neurosurgeon literally had to reconnect my skull to my spinal column. So I survived the accident, survived the surgery, survived ulcers, pneumonia, blood clots, broken bones, and a severe allergic reaction to a drug that almost killed me in July 1995. I've been to the edge much sooner than I ever expected. The fact that I'm still here, gaining rather than losing ground, is very rewarding.

ABE LINCOLN put it very simply in 1860: "When I do good, I feel good. When I do bad, I feel bad. That's my religion."

WE HAVE A GOVERNMENT that, generally speaking, does not respond to the people. Seventy percent of the American public supports embryonic stem cell research. And yet it's already been banned by the House and is stalled in the Senate. And we have no federal policy. All the excitement generated in 1998, when embryonic cells were first identified, has pretty much died down—because scientists don't know what's going to happen in the future. Probably the saddest thing is that most young doctors who would like to go into stem cell research say, "I can't go into that because this may not be going anywhere for a while, and I've got to pay off my student loans."

NEVER ACCEPT ULTIMATUMS, conventional wisdom, or absolutes.

SUPERMAN is a big fish in a small pond. He's Superman on Earth only because he's in a different solar system. If he'd grown up on Krypton, if Krypton had not been destroyed, he might have been average—nothing special about him. That allowed me to underplay the character and make him quite casual.

I'VE NEVER HAD A DREAM in which I'm disabled.

SOME PEOPLE are walking around with full use of their bodies, and they're more paralyzed than I am.

IN THE FIRST FEW YEARS after the accident, people were almost *too* respectful. I remember going on *Letterman*. He was so serious, almost reverential, that I had to crack jokes to keep the interview alive. But over the years, that's virtually disappeared, because people see that I'm living a full and active life. Now it's almost the other way around. What happened to the pity?

IN REHAB, I saw both extremes: good relationships grew stronger, and ones that were in trouble fell apart.

I USED TO SAY to my wife, Dana, all the time, "I really put the marriage vows to the test. This is not what we meant by 'in sickness and in health.'"

YOU GET USED to the need to be taken care of in the bathroom.

I'M OFTEN ACCUSED of being too aggressive with researchers, saying, "Why can't you go faster? Why can't you get to the human trials sooner? Please appreciate the fact that the patient population is willing to accept reasonable risks."

LIVING IN FEAR is not living at all.

I HAD THE PRIVILEGE of playing Katharine Hepburn's grandson in a play. Perhaps because she'd never had children of her own, I felt that I'd been adopted for the time that we worked together, which was about eight months in '75 and '76. She was very loving, but also very demanding. She set a high standard not only for herself but for the people she cared about. So I was drawn in more deeply than I thought I would be. At the time, I sometimes felt overwhelmed by the challenge of living up to her expectations. Her mantra was "Be fascinating!" I remember thinking, "That's sort of like Babe Ruth saying to Little Leaguers, 'Just hit the ball.'"

SUCCESS IS FINDING SATISFACTION in giving a little more than you take.

IT'S BEEN RELATIVELY EASY to get the support of politicians who have an emotional connection to disease and disability. For example, Senator Harkin has a nephew with a spinal cord injury. Now you see Nancy Reagan working behind the scenes, lobbying for stem cell research beyond the limitations imposed by Bush in August 2001, and you think back to the early '80s, when she and her husband were in office and opposed federal funding for AIDS research. Thousands of people died. It's helpful that she's asking senators to back therapeutic cloning to create more stem cell lines. But the way I see it, she's doing it now only because Ronnie doesn't recognize her. Why do people wait until it hurts?

I'VE LEARNED to ignore my moods.

TO REALLY BECOME FREE inside takes either courage or disaster. Certainly to my kids, I recommend courage.

IF YOU CAME BACK here in ten years, I expect that I'd walk to the door to greet you.

Interviewed by Cal Fussman | Photograph by Chris Floyd

BORN NEW YORK, NEW YORK—09.25.1952

DIED MOUNT KISKO, NEW YORK—10.10.2004

> REEVE'S STARRING ROLE IN *SUPERMAN: THE MOVIE* (1978) ONLY SERVED TO INTENSIFY THE TRAGEDY OF HIS JUNE 1995 ACCIDENT, WHEN HE FELL FROM A HORSE DURING A STEEPLECHASE RACE, LEAVING HIM PARALYZED.

> IN 1996, REEVE HELPED ESTABLISH THE UCI REEVE-IRVINE RESEARCH CENTER, WHICH SPECIALIZES IN SPINAL CORD INJURIES.

Burt Reynolds { ACTOR—JUPITER, FLORIDA }

> **I WAS NUMBER ONE** five years in a row at the box office. But what's really stunning is that no one until me had ever gone from number one to number thirty-eight in one year.

THE GREATEST ACTORS in the world are the people around you when you're at the top of the mountain.

GOD FORGIVE ME, but I love the attention of people.

YOUR BULLSHIT DETECTOR gets better with time.

I'VE HAD TO reinvent myself four or five times. And I'm now working on the most challenging reinvention: survivor.

I ONCE SAID to my friend Ossie Davis, "You know, I was first-team all-state when I was in high school." And he said, "How many blacks were on that team?" I said, "None."

FOR A WHITE GUY, I was fast. I ran a 4.4 forty on grass in football shoes.

WHEN I TOLD MY DAD I was going into show business, he said, "If you ever bring any of those sissy boys around here, I'll shoot 'em and make a rug out of 'em for your mother." At the end of his life, whenever he saw Charles Nelson Reilly, who's rather flamboyant, he'd kiss him on the cheek.

WHEN MY DAD said something to me, I said, "Yes, sir." I didn't question him. And I was forty years old.

MY SON SAID, "If you go to an actor's house, there's a picture of the actor and other actors. If you go to a producer's house, there are Picassos. I think I'll be a producer."

I COULD HAVE WON millions of dollars in lawsuits about the AIDS rumors back in 1984. I survived it by my father's philosophy: I'll piss on your grave.

NOWADAYS, instead of saying, "He's a prick," I'll say, "He's complicated."

BANKRUPTCY? It's not pleasant. There are some people who look at you like you've got leprosy and their bank account might drop if they touch you.

I DON'T PLAY GOLF. I don't have a hobby. I'm pretty passionate about my work, even though I sometimes have this realization on the second day of shooting that I'm in a piece of shit. So I can do one of two things: I can just take the money, or I can try to be passionate. But the name of the boat is still the *Titanic*.

PAUL NEWMAN is the personification of cool.

I'D RATHER BE SHOT IN THE LEG than watch an Ingmar Bergman picture.

THE BEST DIRECTION I EVER GOT was on *Deliverance*, when John Boorman said, "Stop acting. Just behave. We'll wait for you, because we can't take our eyes off you." I didn't know he said the same thing to Jon Voight and Ned Beatty.

I CAN TELL a young person where the mines are, but he's probably going to have to step on them anyway.

FOR A LONG TIME, if you were seeing a psychiatrist, you were thought of as being a wacko. But because of good ol' Dr. Phil, people know we need to talk to someone who just sits there and is nonjudgmental and says, "Do you think it's a good idea not to have a bowel movement for three months?" Because a lot of stuff gets clogged up there, and you gotta get some of it out. And getting it out is painful, and you can bleed.

IF I HADN'T BEEN an actor, I would have been a coach, and I would have been a good one. All teaching is communicating.

I ONCE WENT to group therapy. Everyone there blamed someone else—their mother, their father, their agent. When it got to me, I said, "You're all full of shit. You're gonna be here forever. Look in the mirror. You are responsible for every mistake you made."

THE STUPIDEST THING I ever did was turn down *Terms of Endearment* to do *Cannonball Run II*. Jim Brooks wrote the part of the astronaut for me. Taking that role would have been a way to get all the things I wanted.

I'VE MADE FUN OF MYSELF the person, but I don't take roles where I make fun of the actor. I've worked too hard and too long with too many good people, and I respect myself as an actor.

I HATE PREJUDICE of any kind, whether it be color or sexual preference. I don't give a shit if you had a goat. If it's a happy goat and you're happy, I'm happy for you. However, I may not want to have dinner with the both of you.

MY AUTOBIOGRAPHY is a good book, considering it was written in three days.

I LIVE IN JUPITER, FLORIDA, which is Perry Como's hometown. I get second billing.

Interviewed by Ross Johnson | Photograph by Bryce Duffy

BORN WAYCROSS, GEORGIA—02.11.36

> HE WAS DRAFTED BY THE BALTIMORE COLTS IN 1955 AFTER A STANDOUT CAREER AT FLORIDA STATE UNIVERSITY, BUT NEVER PLAYED PROFESSIONAL FOOTBALL.

> HE RECEIVED HIS SOLE OSCAR NOMINATION FOR HIS PORTRAYAL OF JACK HORNER IN *BOOGIE NIGHTS* (1997). HIS BIGGEST BOX OFFICE SUCCESS CAME IN THE 1970S AND EARLY 80S WITH A STRING OF HITS: *DELIVERANCE* (1972), *THE LONGEST YARD* (1974), *SMOKEY AND THE BANDIT* (1977), AND *THE CANNONBALL RUN* (1981).

Fame

> **FAME IS** an intrinsic negative. People respond to you based on their preconceived notion of you, and that puts you at a continual disadvantage.
> —J. CRAIG VENTER

> **CELEBRITY** has its uses: I can always get a seat in any restaurant. —JULIA CHILD

> **FAME MAKES YOU** a target, but it also allows you to put your ethics into play. —ROSEANNE

> **THERE'S A REAL HYPOCRISY** about people who pursue fame for the first half of their lives and then pretend to resent it afterward. —HUGH HEFNER

> **FAME** can take interesting men and thrust mediocrity upon them. —DAVID BOWIE

Happiness

> **WHETHER IT'S** alcohol or drugs or other activities, a great percentage of the population of this planet is looking for diversions from its daily misery.
> —J. CRAIG VENTER

> **FOR SUPREME HAPPINESS**, a man has to reach one of his grand goals. —GERALD FORD

> **MODERATION**. Small helpings. Sample a little bit of everything. These are the secrets of happiness and good health. You need to enjoy the good things in life, but you need not overindulge. —JULIA CHILD

Money

> **A WISE MAN**, Ray Price, told me recently that there's one thing he's learned in life. In fact, he called me on the phone to tell me this, and I said, "What is it?" He said, "Money makes women horny."
> —WILLIE NELSON

> **YOU CAN'T BORROW** money without collateral. You have to have something to get started with. That's the problem: you got to have that taw. You shoot marbles? You shoot that taw marble because you can knock the other marbles out easier with it. Each man has his own taw, and if he gets good with that taw, he can knock the hell out of some marbles. And he can win, but he has to have strong fingers and the right aim. It's like anything else: You got to work at it. —J.R. SIMPLOT

> **IT'S A GREAT ASSET** to a company to have people who like each other. I can remember giving a talk to the MTV people at a management meeting in the Keys. It was a party atmosphere. Everyone insisted I drink tequila. So I threw one back. That's what binds you.
> —SUMNER REDSTONE

> **MONEY?** The more you have, the easier it is to get more. —BUZZ ALDRIN (PICTURED, ABOVE LEFT)

> **THE ONLY WAY** you can make a deal is if you're ready to blow it. —ROBERT EVANS

> **THE PERSON** to negotiate with is the person who can deliver. —RUDOLPH GIULIANI

> **THE FIRST THING** that came into my mind when I signed the grill contract for $137.5 million was "I'm going to make my sisters millionaires. After all these years, they're finally going to be millionaires." And they did become millionaires—with the same old troubles as everybody else. —GEORGE FOREMAN (PICTURED, ABOVE CENTER)

> **NOBODY** was ever surprised he was let go.
> —JACK WELCH

Fear

> **FEAR** is an impossible thing to avoid. —ROD STEIGER

> **FEAR IS SUCH** an elemental emotion, it's hard to break down into a definition. But I can tell you what it can do. If it paralyzes you, it can kill you. If it makes you more aware of what's happening around you, it can keep you alive. —JAMES NACHTWEY, WAR PHOTOGRAPHER

> **THE MOST IMPORTANT** lesson my dad taught me was how to manage fear. Early on, he taught me that in a time of emergency, you've got to become deliberately calm. He used to say, "The more people are yelling and screaming around you, the calmer you should become. Become unnaturally calm. Somebody's got to be able to figure a way out of the jam. And you'll be able to do that." —RUDOLPH GIULIANI

Death

> **I STARTED WRITING** cheating songs when I was too young to have any idea what I was writing about—broken hearts and things like that. I just think it was something I already knew, something I had experienced in another lifetime. —WILLIE NELSON

> **WHEN YOU'RE DEAD**, you're dead. —LARRY FLYNT

> **HEAVEN IS** a place you can go and drink a lot of draft beer and it don't make you fat. You can cheat on your wife and she don't get mad. You get a beautiful female chauffeur with nice, hard tits—real ones. There are motorcycle jumps you never miss. You don't need a tee time. —EVEL KNIEVEL

> **I'LL NEVER ADJUST** to the loss of Nellie. We were married for fifty-three years. No man ever had a finer wife. Prior to her loss, I had some fear of death. Now I have no fear. I look forward to seeing her again. —JOHN WOODEN

> **ROY:** Shirley MacLaine said I was a tiger in a previous life. She ought to know best, right? SIEGFRIED: I don't know what I was before I was me. I enjoy what I am today. I'm sure it's all preparation for the life after.

> **MAYBE WHEN YOU DIE,** you come before a big, bearded man on a big throne, and you say, "Is this heaven?" And he says, "Heaven? You just came from there." —KIRK DOUGLAS

> **I HAVEN'T** decided yet how I feel about reincarnation. But as my dad always used to remind me, I was born the same month and year Hank Williams died: January '53. —LUCINDA WILLIAMS

> **I DON'T KNOW** about reincarnation, but I've been places where I've never been before and I know what to expect. —SUGE KNIGHT

> **IT'S UNEQUIVOCALLY CLEAR** that life begins at birth and ends at death. And if most of the people on this planet understood that, they would lead their lives very differently. We always try to find religious or mysterious forces to fill in for our inadequacies, but heaven and hell are both here on earth every day, and we make our lives around them. —J. CRAIG VENTER

> **WHAT I KNOW** about heaven is that it's not here. —HEATHER LOCKLEAR (PICTURED, ABOVE RIGHT)

And now, a little perspective

> **NO MATTER HOW BAD** things are, they can always be worse. So what if my stroke left me with a speech impediment? Moses had one, and he did all right. —KIRK DOUGLAS

> **QUADRIPLEGICS** envy paraplegics. You think, "Man, they've got it made." —CHUCK CLOSE

> **PEOPLE WERE EXCITED** when we landed on the moon. You go to the moon a couple more times, and they're not so excited. —BUZZ ALDRIN

> **I AM** the spokesperson for Bombay Sapphire. But the truth is, by the time you get halfway through the bottle, you really don't know what you're drinking anymore. —OSCAR GOODMAN, MAYOR, LAS VEGAS

> **I REMEMBER** John Lennon saying, "Sid Vicious died for what? So that we might rock?" You've got to keep that in perspective. At the end of the day, they're just phonograph records. —TOM PETTY

> **IF THE COMPANY** is pleasant, the wine gets better. —SUMNER REDSTONE

Keith Richards { GUITARIST—WESTON, CONNECTICUT }

> **SO FAR,** so good.

THERE'S A CANVAS, it's called silence. Where do you want to make your mark? A little dab here? And don't forget, don't cover the whole canvas—we don't want a Rubens here!

I DON'T wave a flag for anything. I'm a musician.

TO LEARN THE BLUES, it takes a while, and you never stop. What did I learn? I learned how to learn the blues, but I ain't stopped.

AS YOU GET OLDER, younger people think you know where it's at. But it's a forlorn hope, because everybody's growing up at the same time, you know? Somebody who's fifty, by the time he's fifty-five, he's done a whole lot more shit. That's what I've realized—Jesus Christ, these people think I know what I'm doing. OK, I'll fool them! But at the same time, you know it's a bluff. The important thing is what comes next, and are you ready for it?

SOME OF IT, you really want to *un*learn.

CHUCK BERRY is food—the man who brought you "Sweet Little Sixteen," "Too Much Monkey Business," "Roll Over Beethoven." Unfortunately, his biggest-selling record was "My Ding-a-Ling." But that's his own preoccupation; I don't want to go there.

ROCK 'N' ROLL'S great weapon is humor.

I LOVE to play lead, too, but I like to sneak in, which is why I love to play with Ronnie [Wood]. With a quick nod and a wink, we can switch over in what we call the ancient form of weaving. It's a druidic sort of thing, we like to think, very mystical—ha!

I'M AN UNPURE PURIST, something like that.

ELECTRIC is another instrument. Yeah, it looks the same, and you've got to make the same moves, but you have to learn how to tame the beast—because it is a monster.

DRUGS, I think people make far too much of it.

WHEN I WAS DOING drugs, it would be the finest stuff you can get. If I was doing opium, it would be good Thai opium. When I did smack, it would be pure, pure heroin—no street shit. I wasn't undiscerning, except when I got desperate.

I LEARNED HOW TO PUKE properly. First, find a receptacle if you can—that's rule number one. You eject it in a stream—a Technicolor yawn, parking a tiger. At the same time, you're taking a crap—which is kind of difficult to do. If you can do that, I'll put you in Cirque du Soleil.

THERE'S THIS perennial thing that people have: How do you do it? Why do you do it? Like it's—what do *you* do? How do you go to an office every day? Compared to that, my job is *easy*.

UNLESS YOU REALLY WANT TO do this all the time, don't jump in the pond. There's piranhas in there, for chrissakes.

WOMEN are a beautiful complication, and I look forward to far more beauties and far more complications.

I'VE DONE A LOT of dadding. Whoo, I tell you what: it grows you up pretty quick when that little bugger starts waking up. Suddenly there's this little cute ball of stuff yelling its head off. *Boom!* Snap to! Oh, man, I better take *care* of this.

DAUGHTERS ARE far easier to bring up. My first was Marlon, my son, and he gave me a good fight, man. He would drag my ass sometimes, before I could talk to him and instill the wisdom of not doing that.

I OCCASIONALLY borrow pot from my kids. They do a little weed occasionally. "Here, Dad"—or more likely, "Dad, have you got any?"

POISON'S NOT BAD. It's a matter of how much.

TO ME, smack is the big deal. That is such a cheeky, cheeky, cheeky little drug. That one can get you right by the tail before you know it, man. It's a real leveler. I'm a fucking superstar, but when I want the stuff, baby, I'm down on the ground with the rest of them. Your whole lifestyle becomes just waiting for the man and talking to junkies about whether the shit's good or not: "It's not as good as the last lot, is it? I'm not going to pay him then." And guys pulling shooters on you: "Give me your stuff!" and all that. You just become a wreck. Which is kind of disgusting in a way, but at the same time, I can't say I regret going there.

QUITE HONESTLY, you're probably in a den of madmen. For some weird reason, we've been given extra leash.

YOU CAN'T BELIEVE how great this job is. I'll do it as long as people want to listen to it.

SOME GUYS have a hard way of saying I love you.

BEEN THERE, done that.

Interviewed by John H. Richardson | Photograph by Kevin Mazur

BORN DARTFORD, KENT, ENGLAND—12.18.43

> RICHARDS BEFRIENDED MICK JAGGER WHEN BOTH WERE SCHOOLBOYS AT WENTWORTH PRIMARY SCHOOL.
> HE HAS SUNG LEAD VOCALS ON AT LEAST ONE SONG IN NEARLY EVERY ROLLING STONES STUDIO ALBUM AND CONCERT SINCE 1967.
> HE HAS BEEN ARRESTED ON DRUG-RELATED CHARGES SEVERAL TIMES AND WAS BRIEFLY IMPRISONED, ALONG WITH JAGGER, IN 1967.

Joan Rivers { COMEDIAN — NEW YORK CITY }

> **DON'T EXPECT PRAISE** without envy—until you're dead.

COMEDY is an angry white man's game. Even if you're Chris Rock or Joan Rivers, you're really an angry white man.

GOD DOESN'T CARE that I have a sandwich on Yom Kippur. He cares that I helped a blind man across the street.

TRUTH IS what I miss in a companion. Someone you can get into the car with after the party and say, "That fucking cunt, did you hear what she said?"

MY SECOND HUSBAND committed suicide, and I did suicide jokes. You laugh to get through it. I started thinking about jokes while I was walking uptown on 9/11.

ADMIRATION should keep you at a distance.

I ADORE SACHA COHEN. I was one of the first to say, "You've gotta see him" when he was starting on HBO. I've been asking everybody, "What's he like? What's he like?" But I don't want to meet him and find out that he's a shit like Will Ferrell. And you can certainly put that in. It's disappointing to meet someone whose ego is bigger than his talent.

MEN LOOK GREAT when they're a little used. They've done it, and they know about it. That's William Holden to me. Robert Mitchum. George Clooney is getting that look. That wonderful, wonderful lived-in look.

MEN, you know what it's all about. It's all about continuing a race. You have to look good so he fucks you, so the next generation can come along. And once you've spawned, you can die.

LOOK, if Cleopatra hadn't had a great makeup man, she'd have gone down in history as a pig.

DID YOU SEE the Golden Globes? Ugly Betty wins a Golden Globe. Whatever her name is. The woman who plays Ugly Betty. And she gets up there and says, "This is for all the ugly women all over the world, 'cause it's not about beauty. It's about inner beauty." And the camera shows the audience, and there are all these women Botoxed to death—hair extensions, fake breasts—and they're all nodding, "That's right, that's right."

THEY ALWAYS SAY how mean I am. But let me tell you, the smart ones get it. When I took out the jokes about Cher, she said, "Why am I not in your act anymore?"

OLIVIER ONCE SAID to me, "I walk out onstage, spread my arms, and I tell myself, 'This is my circle. No one may enter it without my permission.'" How great is that? Only now, at this point in my life, do I walk on a stage and say, "This is my space. And if you don't like it, fuck you." Took me thirty-five years to get to this space.

I'M IN A BUSINESS where it's not about race. It's about talent. And hard work. Period. You got it, you make it. You don't got it, you don't make it. Over and out.

TELL A JOKE to a comedian, and he won't laugh. He'll point at you and say, "That's funny."

BUSINESSMEN—with a capital *B*—when they go into a meeting, they don't find anything funny.

YEAH, IT'S TRUE. I was $37 million in debt. I'm not a businesswoman. My husband was a businessman. I never had to worry about business. Afterward, some son of a bitch took me public and absconded with the funds. And all these horrible bottom-feeders came in and bought up my name and my likeness.

WHAT IT DOES TO YOU? When you're in debt for the rest of your life? When you cannot work? When you're sitting there at fifty-eight years old, and they're telling you you cannot use your name or your likeness? You cannot sell a piece of jewelry, you cannot go on television? Try that one on for size. That's when you wish you were a dyke. You can handle it then.

AT ONE POINT, we were in a meeting with the bottom-feeders, and I had these beautiful gold earrings. They were given to me as a gift from Vincent Price, who was like a father to me. They were very heavy, and I took one off and said, "Why don't you just take my fucking earrings!" And I threw it at one of the men, and it hit his face and cut him. And my lawyer said, "Joan, can you please step outside?" When I did, he said, "That's gonna cost another million. Next time, don't wear any jewelry."

THE GUY WHO ABSCONDED with the money, by the way, the SEC got him. He went to jail. A couple of butt-fucks later, and he's out. Meanwhile, I'm still paying off my company. I will until the day I die.

A LOT OF DOWNS. A lot of ups. I'm still standing. A little osteoporosis, but I'm still standing.

MY LAST WORDS? They might be, "But it was a joke. Put down the gun! It was a joke! *Arrgh!*"

Interviewed by Cal Fussman | Photograph by Michael Edwards

Salman Rushdie { NOVELIST—NEW YORK CITY }

> **PEOPLE HAVE ASKED ME** about those years, and I've said, "They were very difficult." And they've followed with, "Yeah, but now you're really famous!" As if that balanced the scale. Nine years of your life / really famous. Fine. It's like the pound of flesh. Imagine, along comes the devil, who says to you, "I'm in a position to tell you that you're going to die when you're seventy-two years, four months, and fifteen days old. And you're going to be a nobody. However, if you're prepared to die when you're sixty-three years, four months, and fifteen days old, I could arrange for you to be a celebrity." There are people who would take the deal. That's the insanity of the world we live in.

HOME is the place where you feel happy.

I GIVE IT THE FIRST ENERGY of the day. When I get up, I go to my office and start writing. I'm still in my pajamas. I haven't even brushed my teeth. I just go straight to it. I feel that there's a little package of creative energy that's somehow been nourished by sleep, and I don't want to waste that.

EVERY SO OFTEN, a day comes along that seems to be a breeze. It just seems to come. Who knows what forces are inside you at that moment?

YOU CAN SMELL a slimeball.

IF YOU had to pick one book from the last sixty or seventy years, you'd probably pick *One Hundred Years of Solitude*.

I'LL TELL YOU what divorce hasn't taught me: it didn't teach me not to get married again.

MUSLIM WOMEN know very well the problems of Muslim culture. They're at the sharp end of it. And I've often believed that when the change comes, it will come from there.

I STUDIED HISTORY at Cambridge—not literature. One of the great lessons I was taught there was that the question, what if? is uninteresting. What matters is the answer to, what is? Ask, what is the case? What is so? Believe me, those questions are not so easily answered—because people disagree on even the simplest description of an event in an age when one man's hero is another man's terrorist.

A WORLD where medical advances allow us to live forever is a terrifying thought. Imagine the crowd.

THE EXPERIENCE taught me a lot about the human capacity for hatred. But it also taught me the opposite: the capacity for solidarity and friendship. You were asking before about courage. Well, how's this? A woman working at a bookstore gets phoned by an anonymous voice that says, "We know where your children go to school," and she doesn't stop selling the book. Bookstores were firebombed—and they did not stop selling the book. My Norwegian publisher was shot three times in the back and survived by the skin of his teeth because he's a very fit man—he used to be on the Norwegian ski team. And his first reaction upon recovering was to reprint the book.

THE WORST DAMAGE DONE to me was that somehow the characteristics of the attacks against me were transferred to me. Because it was not funny, how could I be funny? Because it was kind of abstruse and theological and far away and incomprehensible, then I must be all those things. I'm not like that. I'm like this.

THE MUSIC of your youth is always the music that sticks with you. If I could go back in time to see any rock concert? Well, I'm old enough to have gone to Woodstock, but I didn't. I guess I wouldn't have minded that—even though it was muddy, I hear. On second thought, maybe the movie's better.

EVERY SO OFTEN, I go to a party and everybody says, "Look at him! He's a socialite!" As if writers who occasionally enjoy themselves are suspect! I guess Scott Fitzgerald had this much worse than I do. And yet, when the millennium came round and people were asked about the best thing ever written, every list of the best American books had *The Great Gatsby* as number one. So here was this person who was accused of being a lightweight, flibbity-jibbity playboy who wrote the greatest American novel. How did he do that? He didn't do that by getting drunk at parties. He did that by being a genius. And by knowing how to husband his genius and knowing what to do with it—and that requires work.

I WOULD LOVE to have J. K. Rowling's book sales. Yes, it would change my life. I'd buy a plane. Then I wouldn't have to take my shoes off at airports.

IF I COULD MEET anyone over lunch? Shakespeare. "How do you do it?" For a long time my question was, but was Shakespeare good in bed? And I'm afraid the terrible answer is that he probably was.

Interviewed by Cal Fussman | Photograph by Bruce Davidson

BORN BOMBAY, INDIA—06.19.47

> RUSHDIE'S SECOND NOVEL, *MIDNIGHT'S CHILDREN* (1981), WAS AWARDED THE BEST OF THE BOOKER PRIZE IN 2008—THE BEST BOOK TO WIN THE COVETED BOOKER PRIZE IN THE FORTY YEARS OF ITS EXISTENCE.

> HIS BOOK *THE SATANIC VERSES* (1988) WAS MET WITH INTERNATIONAL PROTESTS BY MUSLIMS AND A FATWA ISSUED BY THE SPIRITUAL LEADER OF IRAN.

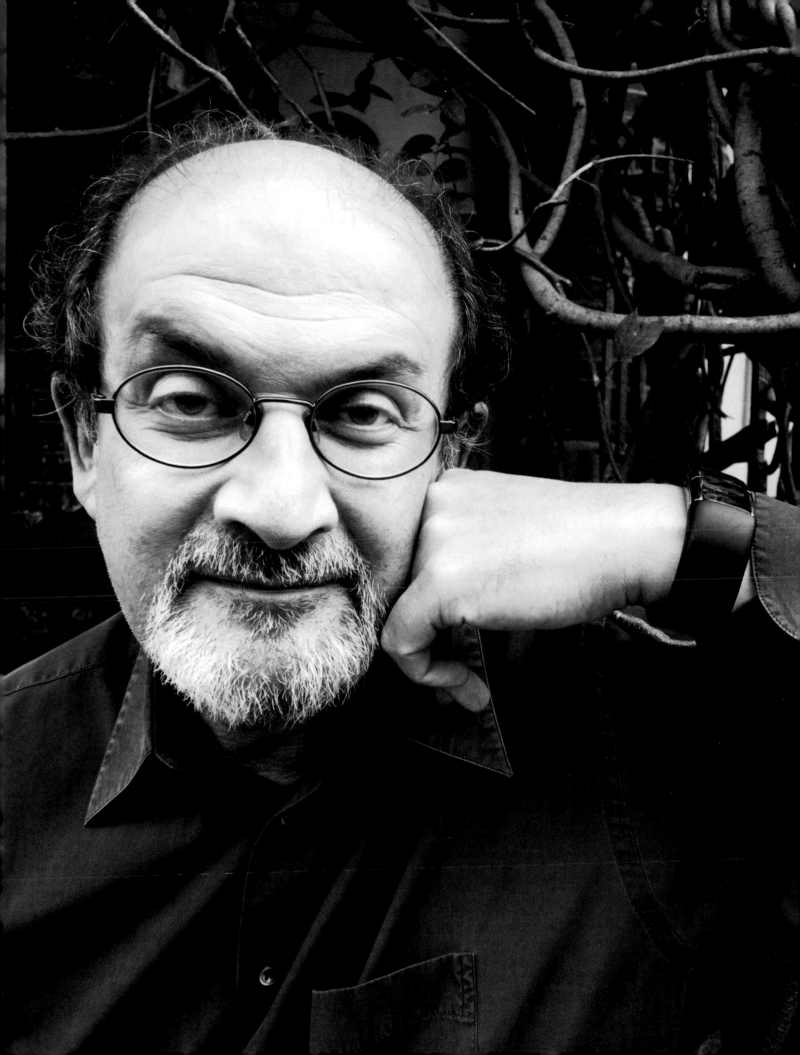

Al Sharpton { REVEREND—NEW YORK CITY }

> **PEOPLE** feel you more than they hear you.

YOU'VE GOTTA TALK to the audience in front of you. In a church, I use biblical references. When I'm talking to a business crowd, I talk about bottom line, profit motive. I spoke at Dillard University in New Orleans just yesterday, and those were youngsters about eighteen, so I told them to get involved in politics and not get caught up in thinking they're a ho or a bitch. And they were all shocked. "Al Sharpton said that?" But I had their attention.

FAITH UNTESTED is just a hunch.

ONCE, I WAS GOING to meet John Kerry, and I called Bill Clinton for advice. He talked to me all the way from the airport to a restaurant and all the way through lunch and back in the car, a good fifty minutes. Just before I went in to see Kerry, I said goodbye—and when I got inside, Kerry was on the phone with Clinton.

PEOPLE REMEMBER what you repeat. Jesse Jackson's chants seemed elementary to a lot of the media—"I am somebody," "Keep hope alive"—but people remembered them. I learned that from Jesse.

WHEN BUSH SPOKE at the National Urban League, Jesse and I both ended up in the front row. Bush looked at me and said, "It's not easy to run for president, Al. You did a good job." Which was very disarming. And at the end of his speech, he comes down to the front row and gets to Jackson first, and Jackson—out of respect, not because he agreed with Bush's policies—gave a faint smile and shook his hand, and the cameras went off. I thought, "I better not do that because they'll use that photo." So when they got to me, I purposely kept punching him on his lapel, telling him, "You got to change your policies." I knew damn well Karl Rove wasn't going to use that picture. Actually, I was hoping the Secret Service would throw me to the ground—I could have used that picture! And sure enough, the next day the papers used the shot of Bush shaking hands with Jesse. The headlines read, "BUSH APPEALS TO BLACK AMERICA." And I went, "They got you, Jesse!"

IN SOME WAYS, it was easier when you had the barking dogs and the fire hoses. Now it's not getting the promotion or not being elected. So it's more difficult to dramatize—and easier for people to ignore.

THE HARDER THE STRUGGLE, the greater the reward.

MANY BLACKS didn't sympathize with O. J. the person; they related to O. J. my cousin, my nephew, my father, who entered a criminal justice system that was stacked against him. So many times, we go to jail on flimsy evidence.

DENNIS KUCINICH is very serious. He reminds me of the guy in high school who, if you tell a joke, he'll find a way to say it's politically incorrect. During the campaign, we did an appearance with the Dalai Lama. I talked about peace and Martin Luther King, and then Kucinich starts giving a multipoint peace program, like we were debating. I said, "Dennis, this is not *real*."

I ALWAYS GO BY instinct and then wrestle with where my instinct brought me.

I'VE SAID I WAS WRONG about a lot of things. I said I was wrong getting into a public fight with Jesse Jackson. But I've never said I was wrong about Brawley 'cause I don't feel I was wrong about Brawley. Suppose I had said I was sorry for supporting the guys in Central Park? Thirteen years later, when the DNA came out showing that these kids were innocent, what kind of fool would I have looked like?

YOU'RE NOT JUST THERE for a season, you're there for a reason.

WHEN YOU GROW UP GLIB, you know what to say to get you in the papers. You know what's gonna get you quoted. But I gave that up. I stopped doing a lot of name-calling; I stopped just saying things that were quotable and started really weighing my actions, weighing my words, weighing my deeds.

YOU GOTTA GIVE the media drama. A kid shot in the Bronx forty-one times—that's a one-day, two day story. Getting people to go protest in front of police headquarters for fifteen days and go to jail—former mayors, congressmen, and all—that'll keep the media on it, and if the media stays on it, somebody's got to be indicted and somebody's got to pay for the crime.

AT THE END OF THE DAY, most people are decent.

I DON'T TAKE attacks personally. Ed Koch and I used to condemn each other from morning to night, and now we work together on the Second Chance program. And I went and spoke at his birthday dinner—'cause it's not personal. We represent points of view. The minute you start thinking everything is personal, you need to get into another business.

WHEN I USED TO TALK about voter registration and voter fraud, a lot of people thought I was just fabricating things. After Florida 2000, some of those same people said to me, "I can't believe this, but you were right."

SOMETIMES you just have to live long enough for your message to catch up.

Interviewed by John H. Richardson | Photograph by Danielle Levitt

BORN BROOKLYN, NEW YORK—10.03.54

> SHARPTON RAN FOR MAYOR OF NEW YORK CITY IN 1997 AND FOR PRESIDENT IN 2004. FORMER NEW YORK CITY MAYOR ED KOCH ONCE SAID OF SHARPTON AND HIS PURSUIT OF JUSTICE ON BEHALF OF AFRICAN-AMERICANS, "HE IS WILLING TO GO TO JAIL FOR THEM, AND HE IS THERE WHEN THEY NEED HIM."

> HE ONCE WORKED AS A TOURING MANAGER FOR JAMES BROWN.

William Shatner { ACTOR, RECORDING ARTIST, AUTHOR—LOS ANGELES }

> **SEX** should be a template for your day. You need to start slow and end completely.

THERE'S SOMETHING to be said for the niceness and politeness of Canadians, saying thank you and being concerned with a stranger, being helpful and all that. By the same token, I would wish for Canada and my fellow Canadians to include in that politeness a kind of drive that occasionally results in a little ass kicking.

THE ESSENCE of paint ball is the fact that when you get hit by a ball full of paint, it hurts just enough to say, "Ow, I gotta get out of the way," but not enough to say, "I quit."

THE LINE between making a total ass of yourself and being fundamentally funny is very narrow.

I WAS ALWAYS working. Maybe you weren't aware of the movies I was making or the television I was doing or the shows I was creating or the books I was writing; there have been thirty. But I have always been solidly at work, running as fast as I can. You just haven't been conscious of it. Suddenly I'm above the radar.

IN THE NEXT SIX MONTHS, two shows will be coming out. One is vaguely called *Shatner in Concert*, which is a concert reality show based on my album. The other one is based on a book I wrote called *I'm Working on That*. It's a scientific look at how the science of today, and scientists themselves, were affected by *Star Trek*—though the *Star Trek* theme is very oblique. It's mostly about how I don't understand the science of today.

MARRIAGE is a reflection of your life in general: how you treat people, how you argue, how secure you are in your own thoughts. How vehemently do you argue your point of view? With what disdain do you view the other's point of view?

WE MEET ALIENS every day who have something to give us. They come in the form of people with different opinions.

THE CONUNDRUM of free will and destiny has always kept me dangling. Everything in the universe follows concrete rules: The galaxies move in predictable ways. Stars are formed within definitive parameters. Viruses mutate. From the highest to the lowest, physics shows us that everything works according to rules we can observe. The only fly in the ointment is man's free will. I could go down those stairs and leave right now, right in the middle of this interview, and I could do so by my own free will, alienating *Esquire* magazine. But I choose not to alienate *Esquire* magazine, and I stay. I think I'm operating under free will. But am I? That's the dilemma. God is either in the destiny or in the free will. Unfortunately, I don't have the answer this morning.

WHETHER IT'S DRUGS or artistry or athletics, all life seeks to re-create that ultimate sexual moment.

YOU HAVE TO CREATE your life. You have to carve it, like a sculpture.

WHAT I'VE LEARNED about acting is that I'm constantly learning, I'm constantly challenged. Playing the role of Denny Crane on *Boston Legal*—that's on Tuesday nights at ten o'clock on ABC, folks—I'm constantly looking for color, for variants, for shade and nuance. The difference between a laugh and no laugh is refinement. I'm constantly seeking that refinement.

BEING AN ICON is overblown. Remember, an icon is moved by a mouse.

SEVENTY-FOUR IS A FOREIGN LAND. I'm an old man, but I'm still pumping weight. I'm lifting fifty pounds, thirty reps, three sets. And then squats, all the rest. I'm athletic, I ride show horses in competitions, I hunger—my passions are every bit as unbanked as they were when I was thirty-five. So I don't know what seventy-four means. I'm seventy-four. This is what it looks like. I'm ready to slug it out with the next guy.

EMPATHY is a learned characteristic. Some people take longer to learn it than others.

WHEN I PLAYED the death of Captain Kirk, the night before, out in the desert, I forced myself to think of what my own coming death would be like. There is a moment, I feel, in that marginal area between consciousness and death, just at the last moment, when you say to yourself, "Oh, my God, I'm really dying . . ." and then you're out, you're dead. For me, Kirk had always lived a life of awe and wonder; those were his feelings about the universe and everything he encountered. And that's why I played those scenes the way I did. The meeting of every new alien was never marked by fear or apprehension. Rather, the emotion was always one of awe, the magnificence of creation. I felt like he would greet death in this same spirit. When it came time to film, I ad-libbed a bit in the scene. Just as he was about to die, I had him say, "*Oh my*," as though he'd seen something, and then, before he could express it, he was dead. And that came out of my own hope that, when my time comes, I will look at my death with the same kind of awe and wonder. Maybe, in that instant, the secrets of the universe will be revealed.

Interviewed by Mike Sager | Photograph by Chris Buck

BORN MONTREAL, QUEBEC, CANADA—
03.22.31

> SHATNER PLAYED CAPTAIN JAMES T. KIRK ON *STAR TREK* FROM 1966 TO 1969 AND THE TITLE CHARACTER ON *T. J. HOOKER* FROM 1982 TO 1986.
> HE HAS RECORDED TWO SPOKEN-WORD ALBUMS, THE FIRST OF WHICH WAS RELEASED IN 1968.
> IN 1999, HE FOUND THE BODY OF HIS THIRD WIFE AT THE BOTTOM OF THEIR SWIMMING POOL, AN EVENT HE REVISITS ON HIS SECOND ALBUM IN THE SONG "WHAT HAVE YOU DONE."
> HIS CHILDHOOD NICKNAME WAS TOUGHIE.

Homer Simpson { NUCLEAR POWER PLANT

SAFETY INSPECTOR }

 WHEN SOMEONE TELLS YOU your butt is on fire, you should take them at their word.

THERE IS no such thing as a bad doughnut.

KIDS are like monkeys, only louder.

IF YOU WANT RESULTS, press the red button. The rest are useless.

THERE ARE MANY different religions in this world, but if you look at them carefully, you'll see that they all have one thing in common: they were invented by a giant, superintelligent slug named Dennis.

YOU SHOULD JUST NAME your third kid Baby. Trust me—it'll save you a lot of hassle.

YOU CAN HAVE many different jobs and still be lazy.

I ENJOY the great taste of Duff. Yes, Duff is the only beer for me. Smooth, creamy Duff . . . zzzzzzzzzzzzz.

YOU CAN GET FREE STUFF if you mention a product in a magazine interview. Like Chips Ahoy! cookies.

YOU MAY THINK it's easier to de-ice your windshield with a flamethrower, but there are repercussions. Serious repercussions.

THERE ARE SOME THINGS that just aren't meant to be eaten.

THE INTELLIGENT MAN wins his battles with pointed words. I'm sorry—I meant *sticks*. Pointed sticks.

THERE ARE way too many numbers. The world would be a better place if we lost half of them—starting with eight. I've always hated eight.

IF I HAD A DOLLAR for every time I heard "My God! He's covered in some sort of goo," I'd be a rich man.

BE GENEROUS in the bedroom—share your sandwich.

I'VE CLIMBED the highest mountains . . . fallen down the deepest valleys . . . I've been to Japan and Africa . . . and I've even gone into space. But I'd trade it all for a piece of candy right now.

EVERY CREATURE on God's earth has a right to exist. Except for that damn ruby-throated South American warbler.

I DON'T NEED A SURGEON telling me how to operate on myself.

SOMETIMES I think there's no reason to get out of bed . . . then I feel wet, and I realize there is.

LET ME JUST SAY, Winnie the Pooh getting his head caught in a honey pot? It's not funny. It can really happen.

EVEN THOUGH it is awesome and powerful, I don't take no guff from the ocean.

I NEVER ATE an animal I didn't like.

A FOOL AND HIS MONEY are soon parted. I would pay anyone a lot of money to explain that to me.

GIVE A MAN A FISH and he'll eat for a day. Teach a man to fish and he'll get a hook caught on his eyelid or something.

I MADE A DEAL with myself ten years ago—and got ripped off.

NEVER leave your car keys in a reactor core.

ALWAYS TRUST your first instinct—unless it tells you to use your life savings to develop a Destructo Ray.

WHEN YOU BORROW something from your neighbor, always do it under the cover of darkness.

IF A SPACESHIP LANDED and aliens took me back to their planet and made me their leader, and I got to spend the rest of my life eating doughnuts and watching alien dancing girls and ruling with a swift and merciless hand? That would be sweet.

I MAY NOT BE the richest man on earth. Or the smartest. Or the handsomest.

NEVER throw a butcher knife in anger.

THE OFFICE is no place for off-color remarks or offensive jokes. That's why I never go there.

MY FAVORITE COLOR is chocolate.

ALWAYS FEEL WITH YOUR HEART, although it's better with your hands.

THE HARDEST THING I've had to face as a father was burying my own child. He climbed back out, but it still hurts.

IF DOCTORS are so right, why am I still alive?

I'M NOT AFRAID to say the word "racism," or the words "doormat" and "bee stinger."

ALWAYS HAVE PLENTY of clean white shirts and blue pants.

WHEN THAT GUY turned water into wine, he obviously wasn't thinking of us Duff drinkers.

I LOVE NATURAL DISASTERS because we're allowed to get out of work.

WHEN I'M DEAD, I'm going to sleep. Oh, man, am I going to sleep.

WHAT KIND OF FOOL would leave a pie on a windowsill, anyway?

Interviewed by John Frink and Don Payne

> SIMPSON MADE HIS TELEVISION DEBUT IN 1987 ON *THE TRACY ULLMAN SHOW*, IN A SERIES OF SHORT FILMS.

> WITH HIS FAMILY, HE WAS AWARDED HIS OWN HALF-HOUR SHOW, *THE SIMPSONS*, WHICH PREMIERED ON FOX IN 1989. IN 2008, THE SHOW BEGAN ITS TWENTIETH SEASON, TYING *GUNSMOKE*.

Jerry Stiller { ACTOR—NEW YORK CITY }

> **NEVER GO FOR** the punch line. There might be something funnier on the way.

IT CAN MAKE YOU SAD to look at pictures from your youth. So there's a trick to it. The trick is not to look at the later pictures.

MONEY IS SENSUAL. Every time I see Les Moonves, I get an erection. What can I tell you?

BEING on a sitcom stops me from getting Alzheimer's.

YOU'D BE SURPRISED what people will do. I was going in for a hip replacement—I'm on the gurney, and they're rolling me in— and all of a sudden this young hospital worker says, "Mr. Stiller, I do voice-overs. Can you get this to your agent?" And he gave me a tape, which I stuck between my legs as I went in for surgery. I thought to myself, "This can't be too serious an operation."

HOLLYWOOD never knew there was a Vietnam War until they made the movie.

WE DIDN'T HAVE THE MONEY for a Passover seder when I was a kid, so our family would show up at relatives' homes unannounced. We were seder crashers.

DURING THE DEPRESSION, my father took me to vaudeville. When we came home, we had no money. I remember my mother turning her pocketbook upside down. Not a penny. "Go out and hack!" she screamed at my father. "Nobody wants a cab," he said. "They can't afford it." My mother kept at him, saying that we didn't even have enough money to buy milk. As he headed for the door, he said to her, "You hate vaudeville." And she said, "Maybe if I wasn't with you, I'd like it." I remembered that all my life, and I would use it onstage with [my wife] Anne. The difference is our audience would laugh at it.

WHEN I TOLD my father I wanted to be an actor, he said, "Why not a stagehand? You'll work every night."

FRANÇOIS-JOSEPH TALMA SAID that superior intelligence makes for middling acting and middling intelligence makes for superior acting. I live by that.

WHEN THEY'RE LOOKING at your shoes, it means you're not doin' too good.

DON'T EVER ask anyone for an opinion of your performance. They're liable to tell you.

IT'S SILLY TO THINK that your entire existence depends upon other people's feelings about you.

YOU'LL ALWAYS KNOW if I'm in the audience when Ben or our daughter, Amy, is performing. I'm the one laughing loudest.

I'M STILL WAITING for the girls I loved as a teenager to call and say, "What a fool I was."

ANNE AND I have been married almost fifty-two years now. What do I love most about her? She can forgive very easily.

LIFE CAN TAKE YOU to funny places. I was doing Shakespeare not far from where I played softball as a kid. Here I was in a codpiece, playing Peter in *Romeo and Juliet* before an audience of Latinos. And a guy in the audience shouts out, "Give it to her, Pepito!"

IT'S BEST TO spend your money. You can't take it with you. And if you try to pass it on to close friends or relatives, you may not be helping them. You may be hindering them. You know the old saw: "Better to learn how to fish than to just eat the fish."

I WAS NOT THE FIRST FATHER on *Seinfeld*. There was another father, whom I replaced. I was out of work at the time. My manager had retired. I was close to seventy years old, and I had nowhere to go. I get this chance on *Seinfeld*. I hadn't even seen the show. The idea was for Estelle Harris, who was the screamer, to be the boss lady of the Costanza family. And I was supposed to be her Thurberesque husband. The part called for me to wear a bald wig to look like George and to act very meek. But after a couple of days, I realized that acting meek was going to get me fired just like the last guy. On the fourth day, I said to Larry David, "This ain't workin'. Can I do it my way?" The scene started, and Estelle began screaming at me, "You're the one who ruined his life! You're the one who wasn't a good role model! You're a lousy father!" Only this time I shot back, "You're the one who made him sandwiches in bed! You're the one who coddled him and treated him like a baby!" All the cameramen broke out laughing. Then Jason [Alexander] came over and said, "Don't be afraid to hit me." I said, "But you're my son. You're thirty-five years old! I can't do that." What the hell. The next time Jason said, "Dad, can I have the keys to the car?" *Bang!* I gave him this whack. Everybody screamed. Then Estelle went over to Larry and said, "Can I hit him, too?"

I DON'T KNOW if the people have changed or if Jewish humor has changed the people.

IT'S DIFFICULT to reach back to the people who gave you your first break, because most of them are dead. So I try to be helpful to the newcomers. But please, don't send me your screenplays.

WHEN ANXIETY is not attended to, it's time to start worrying.

MY WIFE SAYS, "Jerry loves to go through life suffering. Why should I take away his pleasure?"

Interviewed by Cal Fussman | Photograph by Chris Buck

BORN NEW YORK, NEW YORK—
06.08.27

> WITH HIS WIFE, ANNE MEARA, STILLER WAS HALF OF ONE OF THE MOST SUCCESSFUL COMEDY ACTS OF THE 1950S AND '60S, STILLER AND MEARA.
> HE HAS APPEARED IN FOUR MOVIES WITH HIS SON, BEN: *HOT PURSUIT* (1987), *HEAVY WEIGHTS* (1995), *ZOOLANDER* (2001), AND *THE HEARTBREAK KID* (2007).
> HE APPEARED IN A FILMED SKIT INTRODUCING THE CANADIAN ROCK BAND RUSH ON THE GROUP'S THIRTIETH ANNIVERSARY TOUR, IN 2004.

Oliver Stone { DIRECTOR—SANTA MONICA, CALIFORNIA }

> **I'M NOT A GREAT MAN.** I'm a fuckin' man like you, struggling through the goddamn day.

I BELIEVE in this country. But I don't think it belongs to a certain bunch of screwballs who think we ought to dominate the world.

ALI G is the greatest comedian since Groucho Marx.

I'VE LIKED different women at different times in my life. I've been attracted to white women. I've been attracted to black women. I've been attracted to Asian women. I've been attracted to various subspecies of women. I can say with gratitude that I've been able to experiment.

I'VE HAD A VERY STRANGE relationship with the feminine. All my life. Far beyond the musings of an interview. I could not describe it and feel comfortable.

CONTRARY to what some people may think, I'm a good listener.

I'VE BEEN out of the country for seven of the last fourteen years. When I add up all the films, that's what I get. It gives you an interesting perspective on America. I was in Morocco during the Iraq war and also in Cuba, Thailand, France, and England. I read the newspapers from back home, and I read the papers where I was. The difference was devastating. I was appalled and saddened by the coverage I saw in America, because the people were really being shielded and insulated from the truth. It was extreme. It was an absolute travesty.

WHAT'S THE MOTIVATION for the war in Iraq? Oil and geopolitics. That's it.

THE MARCH OF TIME is stunning. It's been one surprise after another. No one could ever have predicted President Reagan and his success. Never. We knew him as a General Electric actor. No one could have predicted the Bush dynasty, either. Such a strange story. In a sense, it's totally *Manchurian Candidate*. There's George Bush Sr., pushed around by his strong and stunning wife, a perfect match for the Angela Lansbury character. Barbara Bush is the brains and strength of that family, a true matriarch. Young Bush is like the Laurence Harvey figure. Very scary. Very spooky. Brainwashed. He has a vacancy in his eyes. We've all seen it. I don't know why more people didn't see it in the first place.

I TAKE MYSELF SERIOUSLY. I respect myself because, frankly, some people invest a lot of energy in disrespecting me.

YOU DON'T want to be a director at seven in the morning with an actress who is not a great morning person.

WATCHING DE PALMA film *Scarface* taught me a lot about how to get past the ego, past the self. A director has to be like a baseball catcher. He's got to catch every pitch. He has to call the signals correctly. And he's got to hit. A good catcher has got to hit the ball.

THERE'S SO MUCH NEGATIVITY in the establishment press about what's happened to the young people of the sixties. I can't believe the revisionism: the spoiled American monsters. It's almost like if you were in any way a freethinker at that time, if you behaved freely, you are automatically dismissed today as if you're damaged goods. "Todd So-and-so, who was demonstrating in Berkeley in '68, is now a happily married real estate broker in Putztown, Pennsylvania." It's like, look what he did: he sold out.

I HAD HOUSES, ranches, women, children—a lot of things. Everything went out in the divorce. It was a typical California divorce, very punitive, which destroys the ability of the income earner to really recoup a life. I got divorced at the peak of my earnings, and I've never again matched that peak.

IT'S VERY HARD to make money, harder still to hold on to it. I've let a lot of money slip through my hands.

I DON'T KNOW if you've ever read an economics book. They call it the dismal science for a good reason.

THE KOREAN WOMAN I was lucky enough to meet brings me a sense of proportion and grace. It's a tea ceremony, a grace under pressure; it's effortless. For me, it's one of the greatest pleasures in life. What a pleasure to watch this woman move.

I HAVE THREE CHILDREN: two boys, one girl. And they've all been raised under different circumstances. I divorced the mother of the boys, and now I'm with the mother of my youngest child, an eight-year-old girl who's very bright and fiery. She is imbued with a sort of independence, a sense of the Korean-Japanese Asiatic order of things. There is an understanding of a hierarchy in life. There is an inner respect for the higher idea, which I find lacking in American children. In American children, there is no spirituality.

ALL OF MEN'S PROBLEMS stem from their mothers. The mother is so important.

PEOPLE HAVE such high expectations. There's no way I can live up to them.

I'M SITTING HERE talking about myself. I'm saying good and bad stuff about me, but it's all self-cherishing. It comes down to this: I'm proud of how I am. I'm proud of having achieved something. I'm proud of being asked to do this. How could I not be?

Interviewed by Mike Sager | Photograph by Jake Chessum

BORN NEW YORK, NEW YORK—09.15.46

> STONE RECEIVED HIS FIRST OSCAR NOT FOR DIRECTING BUT FOR WRITING THE SCREENPLAY FOR *MIDNIGHT EXPRESS* (1978). HE LATER WON FOR DIRECTING *PLATOON* (1986) AND *BORN ON THE FOURTH OF JULY* (1989).

> STONE ALSO DIRECTED A DOCUMENTARY ABOUT FIDEL CASTRO, *COMANDANTE* (2003), AND HAS ASKED TO FILM IRANIAN PRESIDENT MAHMOUD AHMADINEJAD FOR A SIMILAR PROJECT.

Billy Bob Thornton { ACTOR, WRITER, MUSICIAN—LOS ANGELES }

 IT'S NOT that I don't like being interviewed. I don't mind it at all. It's just that my answers aren't always what people want to hear.

I WAS THIS POOR KID from Arkansas who loved music and baseball. I'm raised in a household with a hotheaded little Irish basketball coach and a mom who's a psychic. If you want to be schizophrenic, there's your recipe.

EVERYBODY thinks I'm a weirdo. I have all these reputations: I'm a blood-sucking vampire. I live in a dungeon. I eat orange food. I'm like, "No, I don't. Or, wait a minute, yeah, I do." I have a recording studio in my basement. I stay down there a lot. I guess that's the dungeon. I eat papaya every morning—it's orange. It's not all I have all day, but it is orange. And Angie [Jolie] and I had this notorious "blood vial." Leave it to the press to call it a vial. It was a little clear locket that big around, and we poked our fingers and put a drop of blood on it. We've been vampires ever since.

PRETTY MUCH every movie I've done, for some creepy reason, has been parallel to my life in some way. When Angie and I split up—and she's like my best friend forever and still is one of my best friends—but when we split up, what'd I go away and do? *Bad Santa* and then *The Alamo*—you know, my last stand. You don't have to analyze that too closely.

I NEVER GO ANYWHERE. I'm either at home or working—because I don't think I fit in. I can fit in, but it's like an acting job. Most of my acting is done in public, you know?

SEX doesn't have to be with a model to be good. As a matter of fact, sometimes with the model, the actress, the "sexiest person in the world," it may be literally like fucking the couch. Don't count out the average-looking woman or even maybe the slightly unattractive woman or the really unattractive woman. There may be this swarthy little five-foot-two stocky woman who just has sex all over her.

IF I WANT TO TALK a problem over with someone, I always call a woman.

NEVER GET A TATTOO with somebody's name on it unless you're ready to get another one put over it.

IF A COP STOPS YOU and asks, "Do you have any pot in there?" I've always found it's best to say, "You know what, officer? I'm just going to level with you. I smoked a joint with a friend a few hours ago, and he left a roach in the floorboard here." Because if you don't tell him, he's going to find it. He may still take you to jail. But maybe not.

I'VE BEEN CLEAN of drugs for twenty-seven years now.

I'VE EATEN wheat- and dairy-free for years. I eat only raw food. I exercise. I do everything right in my life in order to be able to drink Bud and have a smoke.

UNTIL THEY OUTLAW drinking, I'm not going to quit smoking.

YOU WANT a beer?

YOU'LL NEVER CATCH ME writing *Star Wars*. A) I'm not interested. B) I wouldn't know how. All I can write about is stuff I've either done or seen. That's my process, right there, if I had to boil it down. I've never said that to anybody. I usually say I don't have a process. But yeah, I do have a process. It started when I was born.

SEX ON-SCREEN can be awkward. I would never consider it fun. The *Monster's Ball* scene is a whole movie in itself. I get a little turned off when people say, "Hey man, how about that Halle Berry! You're a lucky son of a bitch!" It's like, man, see it for what it was: two desperate people who had a desperate need for each other in that moment because they both hated themselves.

I WAS A MUSICIAN before I even knew acting existed. There are critics who will give you a bad review or dismiss you just because you're an actor. But there's plenty of bands out there that suck on their own merits without ever having been actors.

WHEN I WAS GROWING UP in the sixties and early seventies, the idea behind being a band or being an actor was to be different. So as a result, you had all these different types. You had Jethro Tull and you had Don McLean. And they were on the same radio station. Now the point is to be the same.

THE FACT that I'm not friends with Tom Waits is a tragedy. I don't even know him, but I love him.

THEY SAY BROWN is the new black and your fifties are the new thirties. I turn fifty August 4. I don't worry about it, frankly. My girlfriend likes me fine. I have a baby I can take care of. I'm not on a walker or anything. I'm an athlete. I still play ball. I feel so lucky to be alive that I never bitch about my age.

YOU EVER WONDER why pubic hair doesn't turn gray? Why is that?

Interviewed by Amy Wallace | Photograph by Susanna Howe

BORN HOT SPRINGS, ARKANSAS—08.04.55

> THORNTON'S GIVEN NAME IS IN FACT BILLY BOB.
> THORNTON'S 1993 SHORT FILM *SOME FOLKS CALL IT A SLING BLADE* WAS THE BASIS FOR HIS CAREER-CHANGING FILM, *SLING BLADE* (1996). HE WON AN OSCAR FOR THE SCREENPLAY AND A BEST ACTOR NOMINATION.
> THORNTON HAS BEEN MARRIED FIVE TIMES, ONCE TO ANGELINA JOLIE.

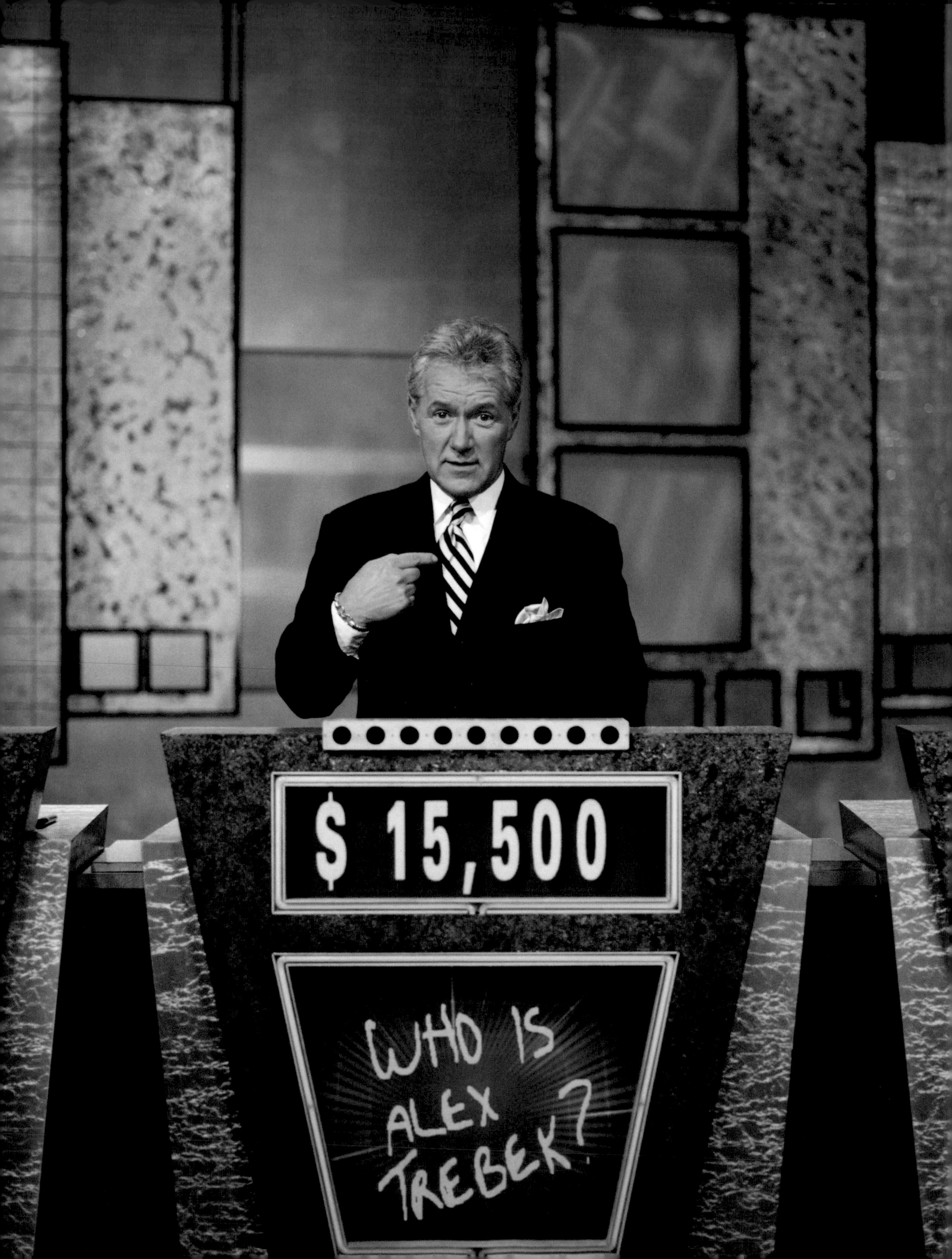
$ 15,500
WHO IS ALEX TREBEK?

Alex Trebek { *Jeopardy!* HOST—LOS ANGELES }

> **OURS IS A QUIZ SHOW,** not a game show.

I'M CURIOUS about everything. Even subjects that don't interest me.

TAKE YOUR JOB seriously, but don't take yourself too seriously.

PEOPLE ASK ME, "How would you do as a contestant on the show?" And I tell them I would do fairly well among senior citizens, but against a good thirty-year-old, I would have trouble because I cannot recall information as quickly as I used to. You used to say something, and I would go, *boom*, right away, very sharp. Now it's like, "Oh, yes, but wait a minute, uh, uh . . ."

DON'T MINIMIZE the importance of luck in determining life's course.

YOU GO to the Rockies, and you stand there, and you're looking up, saying, "Yep, that's impressive." And then you go to the Himalayas, and you're like, "Oh, *shit!*"

IF YOU CAN'T BE in awe of Mother Nature, there's something wrong with you.

WE ARE ALL experts in our own little niches.

WHEN WE DID the college tournament in Ohio recently, I was telling the audience about our trip to Africa—and I've been to Africa now, I don't know, a half dozen times—and I got teary eyed. I started to cry. This is kinda dumb. I'm in front of three thousand people, and I'm getting weepy talking about Africa. What the hell's Africa to me? Well, I go to Africa, and I stand there, and I am overwhelmed by the thought that this is where I'm from. I *came* from here. And I feel comfortable. It's like, Hey, I'm home.

CANADA? Marvelous country.

MY MUSICAL DEVELOPMENT stopped when Frank Sinatra died.

DON'T TELL ME what you believe in. I'll observe how you behave, and I will make my own determination.

A GOOD EDUCATION and a kind heart will get you through life in pretty good shape.

GIVE ME A GUN and put me near somebody who is just mean, and I'll blow him away. No second thoughts about it.

SEX? Unfortunately, as you get older—and I shouldn't admit this—there are other things that become more important in your daily life.

PAY YOUR DUES. For God's sake, pay your dues. Jesus. I see all these people who want to be overnight stars, and that is so bad. It'll just screw you up so badly.

EVIL EXISTS. I believe that.

FATHERHOOD? I love it. It introduced an element of fear into my life. When you're a bachelor, you don't give a shit. You can do anything. But when you become a father, you get scared about everything.

MY DAD didn't throw out too many things. His basic philosophy was, "Don't throw out something because someday it'll come in handy." And it's true. I mean, I have weather stripping in there that's older than you. Workmen come over and do stuff, and invariably they don't have the right tools or the right part. I walk into my garage and come back with the part they need.

IT'S JUST AS EASY to be nice as it is to be unpleasant, and the rewards are far greater.

MY DAD drank pretty heavily, and he never missed a day of work in his life. So I never looked at drinking as a serious problem, but drugs to me are a serious problem. I think it's a generational thing. I think older people don't feel as uncomfortable around drinkers as they do around dopers.

I DON'T GAMBLE, because winning a hundred dollars doesn't give me great pleasure. But losing a hundred dollars pisses me off.

IN MILITARY COLLEGE, they teach you how to make your bed so you can bounce a silver dollar off it. I made my bed perfectly, and the guy came in and said, "Oh, this is really good. Who did this?" "I did this, sir!" "That's really good. What's your name?" "Trebek, sir!" "Has anybody torn up your bed yet?" "No, sir!" So he tore up my bed. Jesus, what the hell's going on here? What kinda crap is this? In the military they say, "We're gonna break down your spirit in order to rebuild it." Don't give me that bullshit. I can take an order without you behaving like a jerk.

IT'S VERY IMPORTANT to have a good sense of who you are and not be jerked around by other people and their opinions of you. Merv Griffin, who developed *Jeopardy!* and *Wheel of Fortune*, had a great line once. I used to personally answer all the mail that came in to *Jeopardy!* whether it was favorable or unfavorable, and Merv said, "You know how I handle the nasty mail?" I said no. He just grabbed it and folded it up and crunched it up and threw it in the wastebasket. He said, "I don't bother with it."

IF YOU DON'T HIT your categories, you're gonna be standing there with your thumb in your ear.

YOU ASKED ME about my pet peeves. One is TV commercials that seem to place an emphasis on stupid and illegal behavior.

IT'S VERY IMPORTANT in life to know when to shut up. You should not be afraid of silence.

Interviewed by A.J. Jacobs | Photograph by Bryce Duffy

BORN SUDBURY, ONTARIO, CANADA—
07.22.40

> TREBEK HAS HOSTED *JEOPARDY!* SINCE 1984.
> AFTER STARTING AS A NEWS REPORTER FOR THE CANADIAN BROADCASTING COMPANY, HE CAME INTO HIS OWN AS A QUIZ SHOW HOST, ON SHOWS INCLUDING *PITFALL, THE $128,000 QUESTION,* AND *DOUBLE DARE.*

Donald Trump { TITAN—NEW YORK CITY }

> **THE BEST THING** I've ever done? Well, I've created four beautiful children. You mean, other than that?

MY FATHER WAS A BUILDER in Brooklyn and Queens, a very smart businessperson who understood life. He taught me to keep my guard up. The world is a pretty vicious place.

MY MOM was a wonderful woman who was, in many ways, the opposite of my father. Very relationship oriented, very warm and open and generous to people. So I got different qualities from both. It was a great combination.

MY LIFE essentially is one big, fat phone call.

HOLD ON. Gotta take this one . . . *Reeeeegis,* my man! How you doing? . . . The best pitcher in baseball going against us tonight. And Roger was great last time, but he's forty-one. Yeah, I'm going. Definitely. Are you? . . . *Ohhh!* . . . And you can't get out of it? . . . *Reeeeg!* You *can't* go see that! You can see that any night. This is a once-in-a-lifetime game. *Once in a lifetime!* You can't sit through a Broadway show with the Yankees playing the Red Sox in game seven! Go tomorrow night! Look, *I'll* get you a ticket. *Reeeeg! Reeeeeeeeeg!* Look, even if you sit home and watch it on television, you're *not* gonna go to a Broadway show . . . If you change your mind, let me know. I love you, darling. Take care. Be good.

THAT was Regis.

THE MOST IMPORTANT THINGS in life are your relationships and your health.

FOR ME, business comes easier than relationships.

WORK HARD to take the gamble out of the gamble.

THE WORLD TRADE CENTER was never appreciated until its death. Now people realize how great it was. There are very mixed views on what to do. If you try to build something bigger, it might become a target. Who's gonna occupy that space? In another sense, it certainly seems the fitting thing to do—to build something bigger and better than what was there before. Unfortunately, I don't think what they're building is going to be as good as what was there.

GOING THROUGH tough times is a wonderful thing, and everybody should try it. Once.

I WAS WALKING down Fifth Avenue with Marla Maples in 1991. This was at the peak of the bad market. Across the street, I saw a man in front of Tiffany with a tin cup. I looked at Marla and said, "You know, right now that man is worth $900 million more than I am." When I told Marla this, she didn't run away. Of course, I would have saved a little money if she had.

I HAD A LOT of friends who went bankrupt, and you never hear from them again. I worked harder than I'd ever worked getting myself out of it. Now my company is much bigger than it was in the eighties—many times. *The Guinness Book of Records* gave me first place for the greatest financial comeback of all time.

FIGHTING for the last penny is a very good philosophy to have.

MY CHILDREN have shown me that they are willing to work hard to become successful. That's very important—because when children grow up in wealth, you always have doubts.

I LEARNED A LOT from my brother Fred's death. He was a great-looking guy. He had the best personality. He had everything. But he had a problem with alcohol and cigarettes. He knew he had the problem, and it's a tough problem to have. He was ten years older than me, and he would always tell me not to drink or smoke. And, to this day, I've never had a cigarette. I've never had a glass of alcohol. I won't even drink a cup of coffee. I just stay away from those things because he had such a tremendous problem. Fred did me a great favor. It's one of the greatest favors anyone's ever done for me.

IF YOU DON'T HAVE an understanding of your opponent, things aren't going to work out very well for you.

CEO COMPENSATION has gotten outrageous. Some of these guys come into these big, monster, powerful companies, and all of a sudden they're making forty, fifty, sixty million dollars a year. It's one thing if you create a company and you start from scratch. But some of these companies have been around for a hundred years. You increase the price of a bottle of ketchup by one penny, and you look like a genius. It seems ridiculous. The solution? Have the people who own the stock vote on it.

A BUS coming from a church in Louisiana gets wiped out. It's a difficult thing to figure. You would think that a bus coming from a church would be absolutely protected. But it wasn't. You look at what's going on in the world and you say, "Boy, God has to be pretty tough."

HAS SEX CHANGED over time? Not that I've noticed. I hope I can say that in fifteen years.

I NOD, and it is done.

Interviewed by Cal Fussman | Photograph by Michael Edwards

BORN NEW YORK, NEW YORK—06.14.46

> TRUMP EMERGED AS ONE OF THE MOST POWERFUL REAL ESTATE MOGULS OF THE '80S.

> FORCED TO DECLARE BANKRUPTCY IN 1990, HE BOUNCED BACK BY THE END OF THE DECADE.

> HE IS COPRODUCER OF NBC'S REALITY SHOW *THE APPRENTICE.*

Jack Valenti { HEAD OF THE MOTION PICTURE ASSOCIATION

OF AMERICA, AIDE TO PRESIDENT JOHNSON, ADMAN,

FIGHTER PILOT—WASHINGTON, D.C. }

 TEXANS have a special seeing of history and some molecular connection to deeds far away done. I wouldn't be born in any other state.

I FLEW FIFTY-ONE combat missions during World War II, and we got shot at every time. Churchill wrote, "Nothing in life is so exhilarating as to be shot at without result." Yeah, I know that.

ANYBODY who has seen a child being born has to believe in God.

WHAT AMERICANS KNOW BEST is how to make films that will be hospitably received by every creed, country, and culture. We make films for the world. People who hate the American government love American films. People who burn the American flag are greatly affectionate toward American films. I don't believe any other American enterprise can make that statement.

A FRIEND is someone who, when you're wounded and brought to your knees, is the first one on the spot. And he doesn't leave until you're ambulatory again.

I ONLY stay in hotels that have gyms.

YES, I was in the motorcade when JFK was shot. Do I still have images of that day? It's not just images. Every minute of that day, literally, is scarred in my memory. It was a nightmare that was real.

AFTER THE MOTORCADE broke up, I went to Parkland Hospital, where the president had been taken. One of Johnson's aides came up to me and took me to a room where the vice president had been sequestered. It was empty except for a lone Secret Service man, a man named Lem Johns. He said, "Mr. Valenti, I'm to take you to Air Force One. The vice president wants you now." I had no idea why. We got in a police car and went careening out to Love Field. The plane had been moved to a remote corner of the field. Very menacing-looking guys with Uzi-type weapons were guarding it. I had a tough time getting on, even with the Secret Service men. But I got on. And I went midships—Air Force One in those days was a 707, and the office was in the middle of the airplane. I got there, and it was thickly crowded, and then suddenly from the rear of the plane came this six-foot-four-and-a-half figure of Johnson, a huge man. And he sat down and he beckoned to me and I came over and he said, "Jack, I want you on my staff, and I want you to fly back to Washington with me." He didn't say, "Would you like to be on my staff?" I said, "Yes, sir, Mr. President." I had no idea what being a staff member to a president was. I had not even visited the White House. I did ask him one dumb question. I said, "Well, Mr. President, I don't have a place to live." He looked at me and seemed to be thinking, "Who is this dumbass I'm bringing on my staff?" But he said, "Until your family gets up here, you can live with me." And I did. I lived on the third floor of the White House for almost two months.

HAVING WORKED for a president, I'm very reluctant to criticize a president. I know what they go through.

THE POSSIBILITY OF FAILURE is like a vagrant ghost that wanders around with you and causes you to be a little bit anxious. But it's hard to do anything that will have some measure of impact unless you take risks. If you take the easy way or the comfortable way or the safe way, you're not going to leave a big legacy.

I INVENTED the movie ratings system thirty-six years ago. I wanted to free the screen from any fragments of censorship: make any film you want, and you don't have to cut a millimeter of it. But with that freedom comes responsibility.

MY FAVORITE MOVIE is *A Man for All Seasons*, written by Robert Bolt, directed by Fred Zinnemann, and starring the finest living English-speaking actor, Paul Scofield. It's an impeccable movie. It's like a fine jewel in a case, and you don't want to change anything about it.

PEOPLE VOTE viscerally, not intellectually.

YOU WOULDN'T HAVE a country if you didn't have the First Amendment. But the price you pay is that you have to allow into the marketplace that which you consider to be tawdry, meretricious, vulgar, unwholesome, false, and just plain stupid.

IF YOU'RE NOT persuasive, you don't exist.

SEX is about appetite. Love is about endurance.

I ALWAYS WANTED to run for public office, but I never tested myself to see. I always wanted to be in the Congress or the Senate. I thought about running for mayor of Houston at one time, but I never did, and I really don't know why.

EVERYBODY ought to be wearing cowboy boots. Go to Lucchese in San Antonio and get the best.

Interviewed by Cal Fussman | Photograph by Rainer Hosch

BORN HOUSTON, TEXAS—09.05.21
DIED WASHINGTON, D.C.—04.26.07

> VALENTI PIONEERED THE VOLUNTARY MOTION PICTURE RATINGS SYSTEM AS A WAY TO PROTECT FREEDOM OF EXPRESSION FROM CENSORSHIP.
> HE CAN BE SEEN CROUCHING TO LYNDON JOHNSON'S RIGHT IN THE FAMOUS PHOTOGRAPH OF JOHNSON BEING SWORN IN AS PRESIDENT OF THE UNITED STATES ABOARD AIR FORCE ONE ON NOVEMBER 22, 1963.

Steven Van Zandt { MUSICIAN, ACTOR, DEEJAY—NEW YORK CITY }

> **YOU GOTTA** have cinnamon in your coffee. Pour it on.

HERE'S the wonderful thing that Bruce Springsteen and David Chase are capable of: those two guys have the remarkable talent of transporting you to their own time zone, to their own rhythm, and slowing things down. That's an extraordinarily important talent these days, when everything is temporary and disposable and going by at a hundred miles an hour. In the old days, they would have been called wizards, because they control time.

SCANDINAVIA is another planet. They get health care, education; there's no homeless; they barely have a prison system. We joke about how they're overtaxed, but it's the same fucking 50 percent I'm paying.

ART IS NOT a luxury.

I REMEMBER when flying was fun. When did we become a Third World country? What day was that?

FEBRUARY 8, 1964, there was not one single rock 'n' roll band in the country. February 9, the Beatles played *The Ed Sullivan Show*. February 10, everyone had one. In the garage. Garage rock is traditional rock 'n' roll. If you think of it as the early Stones, you're fine.

MY LIFE BEGAN on February 9, 1964.

TO HAVE IMPACT in two minutes and thirty seconds—that's very hard to do. It's much easier to write Pink Floyd's *The Wall* than it is to write "Louie Louie."

THE HISTORY OF ROCK 'N' ROLL is the history of America in the twentieth century.

BRUCE WASN'T gonna get a third shot. His first record did like ten thousand, second one did like twenty thousand, and they were just done with him. And somehow, by sheer willpower, that song got done—four or five months recording one song. Turned out to be worth it. They sent it out without the record company even knowing, and a couple of big rock stations picked up the song, the "Born to Run" song.

PEOPLE GOT UPSET when we'd start playing bigger places. But you can either play sixty nights in the club, or you can play the arena. *Hmm*, let me think.

I MODELED the role on *The Sopranos* after my real role in life with Bruce. You'd see Silvio have to deliver bad news, Tony Soprano would get totally angry, and guess what? That's part of the job of being the consigliere or being the best friend in real life. The main job of a producer is telling the artist the song's not good enough yet. You try to be as truthful as you can be without being insulting. And then you get past it. I enjoy doing that.

EVERY SUCCESSFUL PERSON needs to have at least one person in their life who's not afraid of them. That you gotta give Bruce credit for, because it's easy to surround yourself with people who don't know your character flaws, and you can pretend to be God.

NEBRASKA was written and recorded as a demo. He played it for me, and I said to him, "I think you should put it out as is." He said, "What are you talking about? It's just demos." I said, "Because you didn't intend to put it out makes it extraordinarily intimate." Eventually, he agreed, and they put it out.

WE HAVE NO PLACE for greatness in our society anymore. Is there no talent, or is there no infrastructure to support talent?

I LEARNED EVERYTHING I know from leaving the E Street Band. And of course, one of the things I learned is I never should have left.

THE BEATLES were a *band*, which we had never seen before. Four guys working together. Brothers. I had no interest in being Elvis Presley. We thought the Beatles were best friends. We thought the Stones were best friends. We bought the illusion, and it's the illusion that matters sometimes. That's what makes art work; that's what makes religion work.

I BELIEVE that hundreds of years from now, history will be divided into pre-1960s and post-1960s. Questioning things as a regular part of normal life—that didn't exist for my father's generation.

LITTLE RICHARD opens his mouth, and out comes liberation.

IN EUROPE, everybody in the audience has the new record before they come to the show. Why? Because that's the script of the stage production they're about to see and participate in. They come, and they all sing every word of every song. They don't move; they don't go to the bathroom; they don't order hot dogs.

I'VE HAD OFFERS through the years to write a book, but I don't feel that I've quite done enough yet. I got some big ideas left.

Interviewed by Ryan D'Agostino | Photograph by Danny Clinch

BORN BOSTON, MASSACHUSETTS—
11.22.50

> VAN ZANDT, AN ORIGINAL MEMBER OF BRUCE SPRINGSTEEN'S E STREET BAND, LEFT TO RELEASE FOUR SOLO ALBUMS IN THE 1980S. HE JOINED THE BAND WHEN IT WAS RECONVENED IN 1995.
> HE APPEARED AS SILVIO DANTE ON HBO'S *THE SOPRANOS*.
> VAN ZANDT HOSTS A SYNDICATED RADIO SHOW CALLED *LITTLE STEVEN'S UNDERGROUND GARAGE*.
> HIS ROCK AND ROLL HIGH SCHOOL PROJECT AIMS TO ESTABISH A HISTORY CURRICULUM BASED ON ROCK MUSIC.

Gore Vidal ⟨ PROVOCATEUR—HOLLYWOOD ⟩

> **SOMEBODY WAS HERE** the other day from BBC Radio. It's odd to meet a rather elderly man who says, "I've been reading you all my life." It makes you feel a slight chill.

GOD has been expelled. I think he knows when he's on a losing wicket.

I WENT INTO A LINE OF WORK in which jealousy is the principle emotion between practitioners. I don't think I ever suffered from it, because there was no need. But I was aware of it in others, and I found it a regrettable fault.

THERE WAS MORE of a flow to my output of writing in the past, certainly. Having no contemporaries left means you cannot say, "Well, so-and-so will like this," which you do when you're younger. You realize there is no so-and-so anymore. You are your own so-and-so. There is a bleak side to it.

YOU HEAR all this whining going on: "Where are our great writers?" The thing I might feel doleful about is, where are the readers?

EVERYTHING'S WRONG on Wikipedia.

MY GENERAL RESPONSE to boarding school was "Anything to get away from that fucking mother of mine." She was a monster.

SOME OF MY father's fellow West Pointers once asked him why I turned out so well, his secret in raising me. And he said, "I never gave him any advice, and he never asked for any." We agreed on nothing, but we never quarreled once.

EVERY FOOL I knew had gone to university. I didn't think it necessary. I'd seen some of the results, you know?

WHEN I WAS YOUNG, I was bored shitless with being desired by others. I don't look in the mirror anymore.

I LIVED with Howard for fifty years, but what we had was certainly not romantic love, not passionate love. And it certainly was nonsexual. Try and explain *that* to the fags.

NONPROFIT STATUS is what created the Bible Belt. The tax code brought religion back to this country.

AT A CERTAIN AGE, you have to live near good medical care—if, that is, you're going to continue. You always have the option of not continuing, which, I fear, is sometimes nobler.

THERE ARE SOME joys in the higher hypochondria.

WHEN YOU get a hereditary disease, you realize you're part of the main. No matter how much you may have tried to be your own man, you're going to be like your parents.

I'VE DEVELOPED a total loathing for McCain, conceited little asshole. And he thinks he's wonderful. I mean, you can just tell, this little simper of self-love that he does all the time. You just want to kick him.

PATRIOTISM IS as sickening today as it has ever been. I was watching the news before you came, and there was a lot of coverage of Kosovo and the problems there. They showed footage of people burning an American flag. And the newscaster got all broken up and teary eyed. He says, "I guess [*sob*] I just feel something here, folks, when I see the American flag being burned." And I said, "You fucking *asshole*." Whatever happened to the news?

WHEN SHE was running for the Senate, Hillary's psephologists discovered that the one group that really hated her was white, middle-aged men of property. She got the whole thing immediately—I heard she said, "I remind them of their first wife."

"YOU GOT TO MEET everyone—Jackie Kennedy, William Burroughs." People always put that sentence the wrong way around. I mean, why not put it the true way, that these people got to meet me, and wanted to? Otherwise it sounds like I spent my life hustling around trying to meet people: "Oh, look, there's the *governor.*"

I MET A LOT of people, but I didn't get to know them.

PEOPLE IN MY SITUATION get to read about themselves whether they want to or not. It's generally wrong. Or oversimplified—which is sometimes useful.

FOR A WRITER, memory is everything. But then you have to test it; how good is it, really? Whether it's wrong or not, I'm beyond caring. It is what it is. As Norman Mailer would say, "It's existential." He went to his grave without knowing what that word meant.

I WAS the meanest kid on the block.

WE'RE THE MOST CAPTIVE nation of slaves that ever came along. The moral timidity of the average American is quite noticeable. Everybody's afraid to be thought in any way different from everyone else.

GET RID of religion. It'll do you no good.

AS THE GREEKS sensibly believed, should you get to know yourself, you will have penetrated as much of the human mystery as anyone need ever know.

I WASN'T LIKE EVERYONE, you know. What everyone did, I was sure *not* to do.

Interviewed by Mike Sager | Photograph by Chris McPherson

BORN WEST POINT, NEW YORK—10.03.25

> VIDAL IS THE AUTHOR OF TWENTY-NINE NOVELS, A SHORT-STORY COLLECTION, SIX PLAYS, AND EIGHT SCREENPLAYS.

> HE RAN FOR CONGRESS IN NEW YORK'S TRADITIONALLY REPUBLICAN 29TH DISTRICT IN 1960 AS A DEMOCRAT-LIBERAL. HE LOST, BUT HE RECEIVED MORE VOTES IN THE DISTRICT THAN JOHN F. KENNEDY DID.

James Watson { SCIENTIST—COLD SPRING HARBOR,

NEW YORK }

> **NEVER FIGHT** bigger boys or dogs.

THE COST OF DNA sequencing is going to change the world much faster than I would have thought. We can resequence someone now for $150,000. Can you reach the $1,000 genome? I'm skeptical of that. But just $15,000 would change the world. You'd do a thousand Greeks and a thousand Swedes and find out what's different about them. Anytime a child has problems at school or something where you worry something is wrong, you'll do a DNA diagnosis.

I'VE GIVEN MY DNA to two of these companies. I've told them they can publish everything except the structure of the gene that will tell me if I'm predisposed to Alzheimer's. I don't want to know.

NEW IDEAS require new facts.

YOU EXPLAIN THINGS by way of ideas. Why do we have a government that is run by rich trash? Because they've used their money to buy the presidency. Bush is a tool for the people who don't want an inheritance tax. And Frist isn't an innocent bystander, with his own family fortune—hundreds of millions. The piece of shit, I hate him.

FOR ALL MY LIFE, America was the place to be. And we somehow continue to be the place where there are real opportunities to change the world for the better.

I'M BASICALLY a libertarian. I don't want to restrict anyone from doing anything unless it's going to harm me. I don't want to pass a law stopping someone from smoking. It's just too dangerous. You lose the concept of a free society. Since we are genetically so diverse and our brains are so different, we're going to have different aspirations. The things that will satisfy me won't satisfy you. On the other hand, if global warming is in any way preventable and it's likely to come, not doing something would be irresponsible to the future of our society.

SHOULD YOU BE ALLOWED to make an anti-Semitic remark? Yes, because some anti-Semitism is justified. Just like some anti-Irish feeling is justified. If you can't be criticized, that's very dangerous. The whole Larry Summers thing, to say that men are a bit strange and their strangest quality is their ability to understand mathematics—you're not supposed to even think it.

I TURNED against the left wing because they don't like genetics, because genetics implies that sometimes in life we fail because we have bad genes. They want all failure in life to be due to the evil system.

I'VE WONDERED WHY people aren't more intelligent. Why isn't everyone as intelligent as Ashkenazi Jews? And it may be that societies work best when there's a mixture of abilities—the bright people would never be an army. Or has our intelligence been limited by leaders killing off any potential competitors? I suspect time is not a factor. The Ashkenazi Jews have done it in a thousand years. So these are the sorts of things we'll find out—how many mutations would you need to be more intelligent?

I WENT TO A MEETING on genetic enhancement in New York City, and a few of us were for it. The rest were appalled. To me, that's just a defensive reaction of people on the top—they're afraid someone else might be on the top. But what if you were really dumb? Wouldn't it be nice to have a child who would let you get out of the slums? If you could make people with ten-point-higher IQs, we'd probably have fewer wars.

FRANCIS CRICK said we should pay poor people not to have children. I think now we're in a terrible situation where we should pay the rich people to have children. If there is any correlation between success and genes, IQ will fall if the successful people don't have children. These are self-obvious facts.

I'VE SEEN NO EVIDENCE of a god, so I'm not going to think about one.

BEING RAISED NONRELIGIOUS made you free. You could look at the evidence. Whether being nonreligious or a Democrat was more important, I can't tell you.

IF I HAD BEEN married earlier in life, I wouldn't have seen the double helix. I would have been taking care of the kids on Saturday. On the other hand, I was lonely a lot of the time.

I LIKE WRITING good sentences. In the minimum amount of space, you get the maximum amount of information. So when people ask me what I can still do, I say I finished this essay and I wrote every word of it and I'm seventy-eight. I haven't lost my ability to know what a crappy sentence is.

DO THINGS as soon as you can. If a decision needs to be made, make it. It gives you more time to change your mind.

Interviewed by John H. Richardson | Photograph by Danielle Levitt

BORN CHICAGO, ILLINOIS—04.06.28

> WATSON WON THE NOBEL PRIZE IN 1962 FOR DISCOVERING, ALONG WITH FRANCIS CRICK, THE DOUBLE-HELIX STRUCTURE OF DNA IN 1953. HE SPEARHEADED AND LED THE GOVERNMENT'S HUMAN GENOME PROJECT FROM 1988 TO 1992.

> IN 2007, WATSON BECAME THE SECOND PERSON TO HAVE HIS ENTIRE GENOME PUBLISHED.

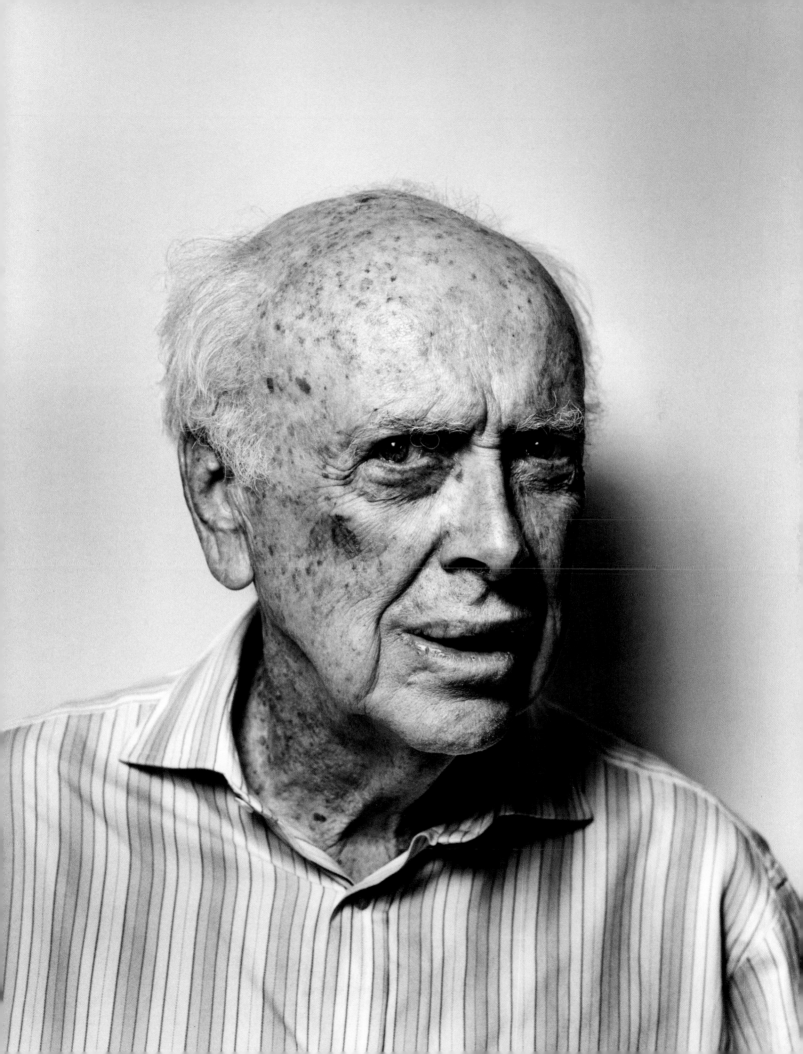

Ted Williams { BALLPLAYER—HERNANDO, FLORIDA }

> **THE BIGGER** people are in life, the more big-league they are. That's been my experience. You meet less shits the higher up you go.

SOME GUYS are just a little more inherently tough than the next guy. I think that's God-given genetics.

I WANTED TO PLAY baseball. I don't know why, but I wanted to play. I had the opportunity, and I had desire. And talent. I heard some guy sayin', "Boy, that kid really looks good. He's quick. He's got good wrists." I said, "If that guy thinks I've got quick wrists now, wait'll the next time he sees me."

I DON'T ENVY Bill Clinton, but I am appreciative of him. He's done a lot of good things. And his wife—to me, she's the Joan of Arc of this country. Boy, I'll tell you, she's terrific. She has stuck with the guy. She's the greatest strength he's got.

DEMOCRATS are a strange breed—although the greatest American we'll ever know in our lifetime is Roosevelt, no question about it. He wasn't my particular hero, but I give him tons of credit as president. But he could have been a little "under the table" too, you know.

YA GOTTA BE READY for the fastball.

I DECIDED I'd have a Cadillac. What the hell. I was kind of successful, and certainly it's a prestigious car. I got more tickets in that car. I figured, "Shit, they're just lookin' for Cadillacs so they can grab 'em for speeding."

I COULD HAVE STARTED smoking in the late twenties, but I didn't. I knew then that nicotine could attack every weakness in a person's body.

DiMAGGIO'S the greatest player I ever saw.

THE MOST FUN I ever had in my life was hittin' a baseball. And the best sound I ever heard in my life was a ball hit with a bat. Powww!

I TAKE TWO THINGS into consideration if you're a guest: the city you're from and your exposure to baseball.

PITCHERS ARE DUMB. They don't play but once every four days. They're scratchin' their ass or pickin' their nose or somethin' the rest of the time. They're pitchin', most of 'em, because they can't do anything else.

IN ORDER TO BE CALLED great, ya gotta have the circumstances surrounding ya.

I WAS A UNITED STATES MARINE pilot. It was the greatest experience of my life, and the greatest people in the world that I ever met were in the Marine Corps. The two things that I'm proudest of in my life, one is that I was a marine. The other thing is that I was lucky enough to play the game I loved.

BOB FELLER'S the greatest pitcher I ever saw.

THE BEST? I don't really believe that. In my heart, I can't say and believe that I was any better than Lou Gehrig or Babe Ruth or Ty Cobb.

I'M NOT SURE in my own mind that there's a supreme being. I don't have that much faith.

ROGERS HORNSBY was some kind of guy. Everybody thinks, "Oh, Hornsby—what a mean bastard." He treated me like a son, couldn't have been nicer. And he gave me the greatest single piece of advice on hitting that I ever got: wait for a good pitch to hit.

SIXTY FEET SIX INCHES. If it had been two feet either way, it would have changed the whole thing.

I'M A REAL SMART son of a bitch. I'm an old, dumb ballplayer and a real smart son of a bitch.

Interviewed by Scott Raab | Photograph by Ted Valenchenko

BORN SAN DIEGO, CALIFORNIA—08.03.1918
DIED INVERNESS, FLORIDA—07.05.2002

> IN NINETEEN SEASONS WITH THE BOSTON RED SOX (1939 TO 1942, 1946 TO 1952, 1953 TO 1960—HE TWICE LEFT THE GAME TO SERVE AS A MARINE CORPS PILOT), WILLIAMS GARNERED 2 MVPS, 6 AMERICAN LEAGUE BATTING CHAMPIONSHIPS, 521 HOME RUNS, A LIFETIME AVERAGE OF .344, AND 17 ALL-STAR GAME APPEARANCES.

> UPON HIS DEATH, HE WAS CRYOGENICALLY FROZEN.

E.O. Wilson { BIOLOGIST—CAMBRIDGE, MASSACHUSETTS }

> **WELL,** it's definitely the egg.

NOW, IF I WERE a good philosopher, I'd say that's an unanswerable question. But I'm a biologist, and I say it's answerable. It's the egg. The egg that first obtained the mutation that's manifested in the proto-chicken. That produces the next mutated egg that produces the next stage of the proto-chicken.

AN ANT COLONY is far more intelligent than an ant.

ANTS ARE the dominant insects. There are fourteen thousand known kinds. Each one is unique in its anatomy, its social behavior, its history. No matter where I go—except possibly Antarctica or the high Arctic, and I don't go there because there are no ants there—no matter how different the human culture, no matter how different the natural environment, there are the ants.

YOU HAVE AN ANT PROBLEM? Then we start with a modest but nonetheless telling example of the importance of scientific information. If the ants are the small black species that appear in people's kitchens in later winter and early spring, sometimes in great numbers, you have no problem, because these are most likely European pavement ants that nest outdoors and are attracted to the interior of your house in searches for food. The best way to handle European pavement ants is to find out how they're getting in the house. It's usually one crack, or one inconspicuous hole. And then just put a little boric acid on top of it. It repels them.

ONE BY ONE, the great questions of philosophy, including, Who are we? and Where did we come from? are being answered to different degrees of solidity. So gradually, science is simply taking over the big questions created by philosophy. Philosophy consists largely of the history of failed models of the brain.

YOU ARE NOT a real scientist until you make a discovery. And if you make a great discovery, you're a great scientist. You can be a complete jerk and go the rest of your life just saying dumb things and never finding anything again, but you're still a great scientist.

IF SOMEONE could actually prove scientifically that there is such a thing as a supernatural force, it would be one of the greatest discoveries in the history of science. So the notion that somehow scientists are resisting it is ludicrous.

THE INTELLIGENT DESIGN FOLKS say, "You haven't explained everything." What they don't appreciate is that that's what biologists do for a living. And, one by one, the things that can't be explained are explained.

BETWEEN SCIENTISTS, you can have high competitiveness and jealousy and petty nitpicking, because we are human. But once something is nailed, the person who did it usually gets the credit, and we move on.

FREUD'S PLACE in history was to simply point out that a lot goes on in the brain that is not conscious thought. But then he should have gone back to the laboratory, because what he did then was to dream up a whole series of scenarios about the subconscious, most of which turned out to be wrong.

WHAT MAKES HUMANITY is not reason. Our emotions are what make us human.

RELIGION is a manifestation of deep emotion that will out, one way or the other—either in an atheistic political ideology or an excessive fierceness in being secular. Or the Red Sox. In other words, we constantly seek a tribe that we feel is innately superior and has the great truths, and we want to identify with them. We shouldn't deny that.

I'M A VERY PATRIOTIC American. Pure reason would say, "Well, America is your tribe, and there are certain things you grew up with, were encultured with, and that's why you're behaving the way you are." And then I say, "That's right." I repeat, I'm a very patriotic American. I want America to be the best. I want America to prevail—not conquer, but prevail. I want this country to be foremost in its qualities and its virtues and its accomplishments. And also, to stay together as a closely united country. And I know why I think that way. It's five million years of evolution. My brain is programmed to think that way. But that doesn't lessen my patriotism.

LET'S BE SENSIBLE, guys. We're not gonna tear off on Mars, and we're not gonna send off colonists to the nearest star system. We're gonna live here. This is what our bodies and our minds are adapted to.

WE HAVE TO GET an entirely new mentality. Getting set for a long haul into the future. In which we grow. Not in numbers—we'll probably shrink in numbers—but we grow. In our understanding, in our happiness, in our harmony—because we realize that there's no other way to survive as a species.

I THINK we're in the early stages of it now. Don't you?

I THINK WE WILL make it, because one quality people have—certainly Americans have it—is that they can adapt when they see necessity staring them in the face. What to avoid is what someone once called the definition of hell: truth realized too late.

IF YOU HAVE ANTS in your house, be kind to them.

Interviewed by Tom Junod | Photograph by Henry Leutwyler

BORN BIRMINGHAM, ALABAMA—06.10.29

> ALWAYS A LOVER OF ANTS, WILSON DISCOVERED THE FIRST KNOWN U.S. COLONIES OF FIRE ANTS WHEN HE WAS THIRTEEN.
> TWO OF HIS BOOKS, *ON HUMAN NATURE* (1978) AND *THE ANTS* (1990), WON THE PULITZER PRIZE.
> HE IS A PROFESSOR EMERITUS AT HARVARD UNIVERSITY.

Cal Fussman

The best thing about the wisdom that comes from these interviews is that I actually use it.

Take Robert De Niro. The man does not like to be interviewed. I knew that going in. So I asked him to break bread with me. Not to have lunch. I asked him to *break bread*. Something about the way I asked made him laugh with a snort through his nose like a wise guy, and so we sat at the restaurant he owns, the Tribeca Grill. The cover of the menu was painted by his father.

He was guarded, but at some point the tearing of bread, the lifting of wine, and the clatter of silverware made the interview feel more like a meal, and I asked him if he had any regrets.

"When a parent dies," he said, "it's the end." He told me he'd always wanted to chronicle his family history through his mother. He sensed a part of her wanted to do it, too, and he offered to send over some people to record it. But she was a little antsy, so he backed off. Not long afterward, she died. And what he wanted to preserve for his children was gone.

When I walked away from that lunch I knew exactly what I had to do. My own parents were about to celebrate their fiftieth anniversary, and my brother and I were throwing a party for them. We'd booked a banquet room in a hotel and invited family and friends. We figured we'd have good food, dancing, and some speeches. But now there was something else.

I got a tripod, mounted an ordinary video camera on it, and set it before my parents. I asked them about their marriage, their lives, and what they'd learned along the way.

I went out and filmed family talking about them. I filmed their friends. Then I got a college student to weave the best footage together and insert old photos. My brother jumped in to help edit.

We made a movie.

We broke this forty-five minute film into seven segments and showed it on a big screen at the party. It brought forth laughs. It brought forth tears. My parents called it the best night of their lives. I don't know if their great-grandchildren will ever meet them. But they will have that film.

At the end of the credits there was a thank you to Robert De Niro. It never would have happened without him.

A.J. Jacobs

I was writing a book called *The Know-It-All*, and I heard *Esquire* was interested in interviewing Alex Trebek. So I pleaded for the assignment.

I drove a rental car to his Beverly Hills mansion and rang the doorbell. His son answered and told me his dad was out back. I walked to the yard and asked a Mexican gardener if he'd seen Trebek. He waved me back. Another gardener waved me further. I asked the third Mexican gardener where Trebek was. "You found him," said the gardener. Some reporter I am. I didn't even recognize Alex Trebek in his own yard.

He took me into his office, which was lined with Russian textbooks and Civil War tomes. As we talked, I was confronted by a Trebek I never expected. No prissy milque-toast, he goes out of his way to swear like Uncle Junior on *The Sopranos* ("bullshit" and "asshole" are two favorites). No cold-blooded Spock, either, he tells me he's an impulsive romantic—he left military college after four days to chase a girl.

I won't say that Trebek was entirely without pretension. Occasionally, the pompous side of him peeks through—he tells me that he speaks English, French, some Spanish, and that he can "fool around in other languages," which struck me as very annoying for some reason. He also used the word "escarpment" in casual conversation. And he related to me an elaborate pun he once made on the names of Edith Cavell and Enos Cabell, a semi-noted British nurse and first baseman, respectively. But overall, he's a decent guy.

Tom Junod

What I remember from my interview with Katie Couric was the sexual tension. It was overwhelming—distracting, really. I mean, I had a job to do, and it wasn't *that*. You know? But there wasn't a lot I could do. It had all started at an *Esquire* party several months earlier, where I was at the same table as Katie. I kept trying to engage her in witty repartee, and every time I did so, David Granger kept standing up to make a speech. Barry Sonnenfeld, who was sitting next to me, kept chortling that I was going down in flames. Later, I found out that as she was leaving, Katie had asked the coat-check girl who I was, and opined that, after Sonnenfeld, I was the cutest guy in the room. And so the stage was set. I went to visit her at her rather small, rather cramped, rather intimate office at 9:30 on an October morning. She closed the door. She was wearing no makeup, and her blue eyes were beaming. Being the professional that I am, though, as well as a married man, I kept talking about my father, whom I had buried the day before. An hour of talking about nothing but death and dying, and the metaphysical implications of such, calmed her down a little and permitted me to finish my interview. It depressed the hell out of both of us, to tell the truth. On the way out, though, she stopped me. "By the way," she said, "do you have Barry's number?"

Scott Raab

I heard Ted Williams before I saw him.

"*Raab!*" he was bellowing. "What in the *hell* kind of name is Raab?"

"It used to be *Rabinowitz*," I hollered back. "Russian. *Jew*."

I got up from my chair in his den and walked toward the voice and there he was, Teddy Fucking Ballgame, six feet four inches tall and eighty years old, wearing his bathrobe, pajamas, *and* slippers—and a wiseass smile—shambling down the hall from his bedroom with a walker. I stuck out my hand for a shake.

"Go ahead," he snarled. "I can't go if you're in the fuckin' road. C'mon, *Raab*. Whattaya want? Whattaya want me to do?"

If only he'd had a wet towel, he would've snapped my ass with it. That's how the cranky old bastard rolled—he was playing, probing, testing. He liked to shout, and he seemed to like somebody shouting back. He was just what he was—a jock, a marine, a kid with a fire inside that nothing in this world could ever quench.

"I don't want no fuckin' press," he said as we sat down. "Not around here."

Bullshit. We were scheduled to talk for an hour. Two hours later, his aide was still nagging at him to stop the interview. Baseball, cars, history, politics ("All you Democrats are the same," he told me. "I can tell by the head on you—it's one helluva lookin' head"): clear as a bell and smart as hell. Me, I would've sat and listened all day.

John H. Richardson

Of all the people I have interviewed in twenty years as a reporter, I wanted to keep talking with Roman Polanski the most. We met in his office in Paris, but he led me out to a charming little restaurant on a charming little square and we ate a leisurely lunch. Then we went back to his office and talked for the rest of the afternoon. When I left, he insisted on making me reservations at the hottest restaurant in Paris. Then we went downstairs to his apartment, and he introduced me to his beautiful thirty-three-year-old wife, Emmanuelle Seigner, who was visiting with Lee Radziwill, who insisted on sending me back to my hotel in her private car since the chauffeur was just waiting down there anyway. It was all of a piece with his conversation, which was so generous and sophisticated. He seemed to float in the blood of history the way only Europeans can, speaking with simple authority about his childhood in Poland and his mother's death in Auschwitz. He was very honest in the most offhand way. "After Sharon, I had no other interests and occupations. Of course, there was sex." He was full of wisdom and epigrams. "I think Americans love pleasure secretly." "Some people live in a straight line. Others have, what do you call it? A sinusoid?" And he became adorably animated when he was talking about art of any kind. "*Portnoy's Complaint* is great! It's so beautifully written!" "*Moby Dick* is so contemporary in style, you know? Books of that period did not start with 'Call me Ishmael.'"

Mike Sager

After interviewing Gore Vidal at his Los Angeles home, Mike Sager e-mailed to the Esquire *offices an account of his time with the eighty-two-year-old writer. Sager's note, which was not intended for publication, is below:*

He had bed head—his well-known forelock was sticking straight up. His replacement knee was bothering him. There are stairs everywhere in his house—two up here, three down there, and the second floor, too—and he has to be led around by his godson, a beautiful French boy with a long frizzy ponytail. (He also has a Filipino houseboy in a white coat, who looks to be about sixty-five himself.) He misses Howard, with whom he lived for fifty years but never had sex. (The death scene in *Point to Point Navigation* is one of the best I have ever read in certain ways.) He seemed depressed. He says he doesn't write anymore because everybody he used to write to impress is dead, other writers included. (To him, writing was a competition.)

He read David's letter* and asked if Harold Hayes was still alive. Then he asked if Clay Felker was still alive. Then, mumbling something about Buckley (I take it he was mentioned in the note—like a good messenger, I did not read it) he put the letter on the side table. During the course of our 11 a.m. interview, he used the letter as a coaster for his tumbler of scotch.

He really is quite the guy, pretty much a living embodiment of the last century: star-crossed American royalty, one of the first out fags, famous novelist when there was such a thing, when novelists were like movie stars, friend to everyone from Eleanor Roosevelt to JFK, to John Updike and Tennessee Williams, William Burroughs, Paul Bowles, the Beats, and then the whole career in Hollywood and in politics… he is really one of our leading intellectuals…and he never went to college!!

Here is some bonus dialogue from our conversation…don't know what to do with it, but it was there to be harvested:

Me: You had a calling: You knew what you wanted to do from an early age—you needed to write, you were determined. So many people today in the world suffer because they have no *calling*. They don't know where their place is, what they should be doing.

Gore: Who gives a fuck?

*Sager had presented Vidal with a letter from editor-in-chief David Granger, regarding a future writing assignment.

{ INDEX }

{ INDEX }

{ PHOTO CREDITS }

Design by Level, Calistoga, CA

Library of Congress Cataloging-in-Publication Data

Esquire the meaning of life : wisdom, humor, and damn good advice from 64 extraordinary lives / edited by Ryan D'Agostino.
   p. cm.
 ISBN 978-1-58816-646-3
 1. Success. 2. Celebrities--Interviews. I. D'Agostino, Ryan. II. Title: The Meaning of Life.
 BJ1611.2.E87 2009
 920.009'04--dc22
 [B]

                     2009000233

10 9 8 7 6 5 4 3 2

Published by Hearst Books
A division of Sterling Publishing Co., Inc.
387 Park Avenue South, New York, NY 10016

Esquire and Hearst Books are trademarks of Hearst Communications, Inc.

www.esquire.com

For information about custom editions, special sales, premium and
corporate purchases, please contact Sterling Special Sales Department
at 800-805-5489 or specialsales@sterlingpublishing.com.

Distributed in Canada by Sterling Publishing
c/o Canadian Manda Group, 165 Dufferin Street
Toronto, Ontario, Canada M6K 3H6

Distributed in Australia by Capricorn Link (Australia) Pty. Ltd.
P.O. Box 704, Windsor, NSW 2756 Australia

Manufactured in China

Sterling ISBN 978-1-58816-646-3